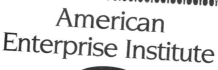

*The American Enterprise Institute for Public Policy Research*
*A Conference on Philosophy, Religion, and Public Policy*

# Democracy and Mediating Structures

# Democracy and Mediating Structures

## A Theological Inquiry

*Edited by Michael Novak*

*Politics begins in mysticism, and mysticism always ends in politics.*
CHARLES PEGUY

American Enterprise Institute for Public Policy Research
Washington, D.C.

Cover illustration by Karen Laub-Novak

**Library of Congress Cataloging in Publication Data**

Main entry under title:

Democracy and mediating structures.

    (AEI symposia ; 80-A)
    Bibliography: p.
    1.  Social policy—Congresses.  2.  Social
institutions—Congresses.  3.  Social structure—
Congresses.  4.  Religious ethics—Congresses.
I.  Novak, Michael.  II.  Series: American
Enterprise Institute for Public Policy Research.
AEI symposia ; 80 A.
HN18.D426        361.6'1        80-11633
ISBN 0-8447-2175-1
ISBN 0-8447-2176-X (pbk.)

AEI Symposia 80A

*Printed in the United States of America*

# Contents

# Foreword

There is more to our society than just government and individuals. There is a range of structures in between that are meaningful, legitimate, efficacious, dynamic, and—under the rubric of what we might call the old politics—generally ignored.

Long before the attempt to combat social problems fell under the control of government's massive bureaucracy, elements in the community addressed individual problems. Instead of supplementing this local initiative, government has all too often supplanted it.

With the publication of *Democracy and Mediating Structures*, the American Enterprise Institute takes another step in its effort to encourage more public policy debate on the vital role of these in-between institutions. This edited text from the 1979 Summer Institute on theology and economics stems from the second in a series of conferences co-sponsored by AEI and the Department of Religion at Syracuse University. The conference was held at Airlie House in Warrenton, Virginia, from June 24 to June 29, 1979. The first conference, held in July 1978, resulted in the publication of *Capitalism and Socialism: A Theological Inquiry*.

Special thanks are due to Dr. Ronald Cavanagh, chairman of the Religion Department at Syracuse, and to Michael Novak, resident scholar at AEI, for their work in organizing, shaping, and directing the conference.

Advancing the roles of mediating structures is not a panacea for the ills of our society. But it could represent a big step toward a "new politics" in which we recognize the needs of today's and tomorrow's society rather than the outmoded perceptions of the past.

WILLIAM J. BAROODY, JR.

*President*
*American Enterprise Institute*

# Preface

This lively volume is drawn from the proceedings of the 1979 Summer Institute on theology and economics. The Summer Institute is jointly sponsored by the Department of Religion at Syracuse University, under the leadership of Dr. Ronald Cavanagh, and the American Enterprise Institute. The much-praised earlier volume, *Capitalism and Socialism: A Theological Inquiry*, represents the papers and discussions from 1978.

The sponsors and participants of the institute elected to focus more narrowly in 1979 on those "mediating institutions" that fall between the two poles of most conventional socialist and capitalist analyses, the state and the individual. There are many such institutions. In order to focus on a representative range of such institutions, papers were sought on the church, the family, the labor union, and the corporation. These papers and short segments of the discussions that followed each of them are presented in this volume.

Departing from most conventional political and economic analysis, which tends to focus either on the state or on the individual, the 1979 seminar experienced many happy turns in the intellectual experience of an intensive week at Airlie House in Virginia. Arguments were lively, interchange was fruitful, and evaluations from those who participated were high. We hope the reader reaches a similar judgment.

The institute was able to draw upon the ongoing AEI project on mediating structures and particularly upon the pioneering proposal by Peter L. Berger and Richard John Neuhaus, *To Empower People: The Role of Mediating Structures in Public Policy* (Washington, D.C.: American Enterprise Institute, 1977). Berger and Neuhaus define mediating structures as "those institutions standing between the individual in his private life and the large institutions of public life" (p. 2). The authors specifically treat four such institutions (neighborhood, family, church, and voluntary association), and they explicitly define the "megastructures" as big government, big business, big labor, and the large bureaucracies of education and the professions.

In contrast to Berger and Neuhaus, the planners of the Summer Institute defined the concept of mediating structures more broadly to encompass all private, nongovernmental structures, including corporations, unions, and universities. Thus, for example, Tom Kahn and Richard B. Madden were invited to speak on the union and the corporation, respectively. In this way, it was hoped, we could best explore the Berger-Neuhaus thesis that democratic pluralism must be nurtured by public policy in order to avoid "totalitarianism . . . which overcomes the dichotomy of private and public existence by imposing on life one comprehensive order of meaning" (p. 3). The definitional differences between the Berger-Neuhaus thesis and the lectures and discussions presented here accentuate the complexity of a pluralistic society.

We hope this volume will help to make the continuing discussion of mediating structures more concrete and the argument swirling around it more vigorous. The concept opens up fresh horizons in the complementary fields of religious ethics and public policy.

Many participants of 1979 urged that extensive discussion should be given in 1980 to at least one of these institutions, the corporation. Accordingly, it is our hope that in 1980 the Summer Institute will continue this line of inquiry in "The Theology of the Corporation."

Gratitude is owed to all who helped to make the Summer Institute of 1979 a reality, and particularly to John W. Cooper for overseeing countless details both at the conference and in the publication of this volume.

MICHAEL NOVAK

# Editor's Note

Most of the texts that follow are based upon an oral delivery and derived from an edited transcript. In their published form, they have retained the flavor of their original immediacy, in a form quite different from that of essays written out in advance in the privacy of one's study.

# Mediating Structures and the Separation of Powers

*James Luther Adams*

Nothing makes one long for water more than to be without it in a desert. The loss of the mediating structures that exist between the individual and the state creates such a desert, one that was experienced by millions of people in Nazi Germany. One of the first things Adolf Hitler did after seizing power was to abolish, or attempt to abolish, all organizations that would not submit to control. The middle organizations—for example, the universities, the churches, and voluntary associations—were so lacking in political concern that they created a space into which a powerful charismatic leader could march with his Brown Shirts. Paradoxically, in taking the way left open to him, Hitler developed a mediating organization himself. By the use of mass persuasion, psychic violence, blackmail, and terror his organization practically wiped out the others as if they were tottering ninepins. He persuaded his followers to abandon freedom for absolute unity under a *Führer*. This toboggan slide into totalitarianism was accelerated by the compliance of governmental structures, provincial and local, including the secondary school system. Considering this broad range of compliance, we may define the totalitarian society as one lacking effective mediating structures that protect the self-determination of individuals and groups.

The suffering and death brought on by Nazism—in Germany as a nation, in the holocaust for the Jews, and throughout the world—staggers the imagination. The whole story, to be sure, is a complicated one that can easily be oversimplified, especially if we ignore the complicity by default of the Western allies after Hitler came to power. And when the allies did turn to resistance they surrounded us with the shades of Dresden and Hiroshima and Nagasaki. As Wilfred Owen said, our feet should be sore as we walk "in the alleys cobbled" with our fellows who died in the struggle.

I have mentioned the Nazi tyranny here at the outset not only because of its intrinsic significance. I have mentioned it also because of my months of witnessing at first hand the struggles and strategies

1

of the Protestant churches in the anti-Nazi underground. My oldest friend in Germany, a pastor and university instructor who after the collapse of Nazism became a professor of theology at Heidelberg, was a leader in this resistance. For several months he was a prisoner in Dachau concentration camp, having been taken forcibly from his parish. The network of the underground was so efficient that his associates outside knew in advance the very day on which he would be released. Immediately after his release he returned to his activity in the resistance movement, where I joined him and in turn myself came into the grasp of the Gestapo. It was my association with him and his fellow resisters that brought to me a vivid and enduring awareness of the significance and function of mediating structures in making the consent of the governed into an effective, and often dissenting, power. These mediating structures I came to see as the indispensable separation of powers in a democratic society.

The term "mediating structures" has been given currency in some circles today by a small book by Peter L. Berger and Richard John Neuhaus.[1] These authors define mediating structures as those existing between the individual and the state. In this book they center attention upon the neighborhood, the family, the church, and the voluntary association, structures rooted in the private sector. We should note that, in contrast to the usage adopted by these authors, the literature of political science has tended to identify the middle structures as those existing in both the governmental and the private sector. This usage can be traced at least as far back as the seventeenth century to the writings of Johannes Althusius, the "father" of modern systematic discussion of our subject. Althusius includes among the middle organizations the lower tiers of government, such as the provinces (or states) and the local governments, along with the family and other associations not under the direction of the central political order. Another distinction that must be taken into account is that between voluntary associations, which one may choose to join or not to join, and involuntary ones, in which such a choice is excluded. According to this conceptualization, the state and the family have been seen as involuntary, for one may not choose whether or not to belong to a political order or to a family. Membership is "given" and inescapable. In modern democratic society the church is viewed as a voluntary association. However, be-

---

[1] *To Empower People: The Role of Mediating Structures in Public Policy* (Washington, D.C.: American Enterprise Institute, 1977), 45 pp. This serves as an introduction to the basic ideas of an extensive project sponsored by the institute and partially funded by the National Endowment for the Humanities.

cause it is frequently tied closely to the family, it in some respects possesses involuntary elements.

In the context of these distinctions we see that Berger and Neuhaus have included under the rubric of mediating structures both voluntary and involuntary groupings. Moreover, they have given attention to the state (and its mediating structures) only insofar as its policies relate directly to the internal concerns of the neighborhood, the family, the church, and the voluntary association. They have not dealt with the state in other respects, especially in order to center attention upon the need for participation and self-determination in the mediating structures selected, a need of crucial significance in our kind of welfare state.[2] In the present essay, however, I have taken the broader definition of mediating structures as obtaining in the public as well as in the private sector.

The democratic society, then, is an association of associations. This web includes a plethora of groupings, commercial, industrial, educational, artistic, professional, recreational, and philanthropic. To be sure, the individual is not absorbed without remainder in these groupings. Members, at least in principle, retain their independence, their own rights and responsibilities. In this connection a perennial problem emerges, that of combining unity and liberty within and between the mediating structures. The criterion here is more an aesthetic than a moral one, the maintenance of unity in the midst of variety. As we have seen, Nazi Germany succumbed to suffocating unity.

In order to achieve their purposes, the various associations elicit commitments. The life-blood that flows through this pluralistic network of arteries and veins is an ever-renewing vitality in the face of reappearing enervations, impediments, and distortions. The vitality depends upon bondings and compacts engendered and nourished by mutual confidence in the midst of a diversity of interests, perspectives, and ideals. It is precisely in order to prevent self-enclosed, that is, idolatrous, commitments hostile to mutual confidence and uncoerced participation that a principle of separation of powers is required. This conception of the division of powers, it should be noted, is more embracing than the division of powers familiar to us in the American Constitution, the division in government between the executive, the legislative, and the judicial powers. It is more embracing because it allows for the continuous growth of new channels of participation and

---

[2] For a critical and extensive discussion of this and other related studies by Berger and Neuhaus, see the articles by Theodore M. Kerrine, Jay Mechling, and David Price (and rejoinders by Berger and Neuhaus) in *Soundings*, vol. 62, no. 4 (1979), pp. 331–416.

decision making. At the same time, it allows room for the relative independence of the associations while rendering them accessible to mutual criticism and influence.

Without participation in these spaces that function as wedges preventing overweening powers from presenting a united front against criticism—without participation in the separation of powers under law —the citizen can become impotent, thus opening the way to domination, even if he or she feels free. The individual can become a torso of a human being; or, as the poet Christoph Morgenstern would say, the person can become only "a knee that hobbles through the world." In changing historical situations freedom depends upon these associations for its redefinition as well as for its achievement or preservation. Considering the importance of people's participation or failure to participate in these groups, we may say, By their groups shall you know them.

Participation, however, requires power.

### The Nature of Power

Power is to be distinguished from force, although force must be viewed as a form of power. In its most general sense, power is the ability to exercise influence—active power. As Plato observed, however, it is also the passive capacity to be influenced by and the capacity to resist other powers. Power includes, then, the ability to make decisions affecting the values of others.

What, then, is social power of the sort required for the functioning of mediating structures? The answer to this question reveals a variety of ingredients. Social power depends upon the creation and maintenance (and also the recurrent transformation) of an efficacious social will in a more or less unified enterprise. I say "more or less unified," for if coercion is not to be resorted to, the sought-for unity must make a space for openness and variety through mutual interchange. It is within this ethos that the individual in freedom comes to identify with the enterprise and the organization.

This kind of social will, then, is a complex thing. It includes the capacity of the group to engender leadership, to elicit a supporting, consenting constituency that can tolerate a reasonable amount of dissent. Creative dissent is not only necessary for growth in the organization but also for the maintenance of the integrity of the individual. The leadership and the constituency require experience that produces the skills of organization, procedure, and strategy, a division of labor—in short, the skills that belong to governance by discussion. All of these skills and sensitivities are invaluable for the society as a whole; the

4

skills may be transferred to other enterprises. They presuppose the articulation of common goals undergirded by mutual trust, a quality that can persist in the face of changing situations. In moments of stress nothing less than seasoned friendship will suffice. These are not the moments for new-hatched, unfledged comrades.

Social will depends, then, upon latent as well as upon manifest functions. The manifest function of an organization may be the particular policies or goals promoted. The latent function will be the friendships, the growth of the individual in interpersonal competence and in the skills acquired, and also an improved capacity to communicate effectively with others. Social power is a complex exercise in communication, in the process of influencing and being influenced.

The incentives for participation in voluntary organizations, of course, vary greatly. One view is that the individual in working in an organization is merely seeking recognition, and that he is therefore only interested in personal psychic rewards. Max Weber in his essay on voluntary associations holds that the principal motive is the search for the opportunity "to put oneself over" or to gain prestige. He asserts that in belonging to a church the individual may aim in part to enhance his credit-rating.[3] One wonders whether Weber would be content to attribute only these motives to his membership in the community of scholarship.

These self-regarding motives appear commonly in human affairs. But, surely, one need not adopt the ascetic view that the only authentic motive for participation is complete self-denial— in earlier days this view took the form of the question, Would you be willing to be damned for the glory of God?

With respect to the claim that only subjective psychic rewards are sought for, we must recognize that the civic-minded citizen involved in a voluntary association concerned with public policy does not expect or hope for rewards accruing only to his own private benefit. Nor does he center attention on the psychic rewards. On the contrary, this citizen expects to spend time and money in a common cause that will issue in the general benefit. This fact becomes especially clear if one considers the citizen who in pursuing an unpopular cause may not only face controversy but may also earn obloquy—for example, in the promotion of the rights of blacks or of women or of gays or of the poor. Moreover, sociological studies amply demonstrate that avoidance of

---

[3] Max Weber, "Proposal for the Sociological Study of Voluntary Associations," *Journal of Voluntary Action Research*, vol. 1, no. 1 (Winter 1972), pp. 20–23. From "Geschäftsbericht," *Verhandlungen des ersten deutschen Soziologentages von 19–22 Oktober, 1910*, in Frankfurt a.M. (Tübingen, 1911), pp. 52–60.

participation in controversial voluntary associations is often motivated by the intention to allow nothing to get in the way of personal success in one's business or profession. The associations dealt with by Berger and Neuhaus are associations characteristically concerned with community values (where controversy is almost inevitable).

## Mediating Structures and the Religious Dimension

We have noted some of the social and psychological functions of the structures mediating between the individual and the state. I turn now to a brief and very broad theological interpretation.

The structures we have been considering exist on the horizontal level (if we may employ a spatial metaphor). The religious consciousness, however, is concerned also with structures that obtain in a vertical dimension and which in both positive and negative ways relate the whole human enterprise (and nature) to a deeper, or higher, reality that transcends and qualifies all activities on the horizontal level. This mediation is quite different from that which is ordinarily associated with the mediating organizations.

Strikingly enough, in the context of our discussion, those who have pointed in decisive ways to the vertical dimension have been called "intermediaries."[4] The important intermediaries referred to here include a founder of a new religious movement and his disciples, a prophet, a mystic, and a charismatic personality. Figures such as these speak *de profundis* in the name of the holy, they speak of both its distance from and its nearness to all human concerns, of the creative and fearful powers that work from the depth of being, bringing both fulfillment and judgment. These intermediaries point to the divine host that must be reckoned with.

Characteristic in Judaism and Christianity is a concern for history and also a communal concern that looks toward social salvation in community and not toward the escape of the individual from history into the suprahistorical. The intermediaries give rise to institutions that provide identity and direction to a community with a goal in and beyond history. They give rise to what we have called social will, the social power of the group formations that spell out history. The intermediaries disclose the divine reality as offering both a gift and a corresponding duty, a gift and a task, the task being to strive for justice and mercy in society, to engage in a struggle between justice and injustice. One may

---

[4] Robert R. Wilson, *Prophecy and Society in Ancient Israel* (Philadelphia: Fortress Press, 1980).

characterize this divine reality as a creative, sustaining, judging, transforming, community-forming power working within history.

In this connection we must observe more closely the ways in which the intermediaries render this orientation historically relevant, and observe also the types of authority entailed.

Within the religious community the intermediaries point to paradigmatic events such as the Exodus from oppression, the message and suffering of the social prophets, the proclamation by Jesus in word and deed of a coming kingdom of righteousness and peace, the calling of the disciples, the activity of the Holy Spirit at Pentecost. These and similar events are termed "acts of God," the working of divine grace calling for dedicated response. From a theological perspective these are mediating events, and they presuppose a covenant that gives to the community and its members a vocation. Here the ideas of covenant and vocation are mediating concepts. Hence, one can speak of the vocation of Israel or of the Christian community and its members. In the Christian community each of the members, according to St. Paul, is by grace endowed with special gifts (*charismata*). None of these gifts is in the possession of the believer, yet they impose the obligation of stewardship relating them to the unity or common good of the community.

We do not need to enter here into a discussion of the distinction between common grace and grace sufficient for salvation. But we must take into account the question of authority. Here the distinctions (suggested by Ernst Troeltsch and Paul Tillich) between heteronomous, autonomous, and theonomous authority are crucial for the interpretation of the ground of meaning. Heteronomous authority demands submission to a tangible, fixated "other" (*heteros*) that claims to be absolute and thus to be exempt from radical criticism. In contrast, autonomous authority validates meaning by appealing to the independent (or socialized) self (*autos*) that in principle renounces absolute claims. Autonomous authority, to be sure, can become empty and degenerate into what amounts to heteronomous submission. Theonomy rejects as idolatrous and demonic the identification of any finite authority with the infinite, of the relative with the absolute. It recognizes a divine reality beyond the self and beyond every fixation imposed by the "other." This orientation aims to fulfill (rather than abrogate) the intrinsic humanity of autonomy, and yet acknowledges dependence upon a transcending, creative, divine power that supports inclusive meaning and also holds everything finite under judgment. It aims to respect the divine command, "Thou shalt have no other gods before me."

This command is one that is all too seldom respected, as the history of culture and religion amply demonstrates. Human beings, especially in groups, search for (false) security and are driven to attach themselves in polytheistic fashion to particular "spaces"—a book, a social system, a church, a human faculty (reason or feeling), or a nation (blood and soil). For this reason nationalism has been called "modern man's other religion." Perhaps the natural religion of humanity is polytheism, as David Hume suggested—heteronomous polytheism. Yet, under prophetic challenge heteronomy may be drawn toward theonomy. Or a regnant heteronomy may give rise to the protests of autonomy. But autonomy may carry heteronomous elements within it or may seek its way toward theonomy. We see, then, that these distinctions obtain not only in the area of the explicitly religious; they may obtain in all spheres of meaningful existence.

In the face of these options and the demand for theonomous authority, we can now indicate the different levels or aspects of vocation. It is exercised not only in the immediate relationship of the soul to God and in the interpersonal relations with other human beings but also in the search for viable institutional structures. The prophet repeatedly points to contemporary heteronomous or autonomous violations of vocation and calls the community to "turn" to renewal of covenant and to faithfulness to it. In the spirit of the demand for timeliness religious leaders have spoken of the obligation to interpret the signs of the time in order to achieve new relevance and meaning in response to the judging and creative powers of the divine.

In this connection the Jewish and Christian communities provide mediating ceremonies manifesting the presence of the divine with its gift and its task. In Christian practice these are called sacraments— means of grace. Matrimony and the formation of the family is one of them; baptism and confirmation are others. Considering the broader social vocation, one might with boldness interpret responsible involvement in the continuing reformation of mediating structures to be a means of grace, sacramental in the sense of being a spiritual bond of sacred significance. Here we may see an aspect of the vocation of the lay apostolate.

A multitude of obstacles to the exercise of vocation is always present. The term "institutionalism" suggests the perennial danger of centering attention on the institution as an end in itself. That way lies idolatry, the distortion of the vertical dimension. Toward the correction of this ossification, pietistic movements emerge, but they can narrow the vocation by confining it to the interpersonal level and eliminating the concern for broader institutional analysis and obligation. Similarly, we should observe a possible narrowing of scope through exclusive attention to the internal concerns of organizations to the neglect of the macrocosmic sphere of the embracing political and economic order.

The danger is also always present that a mediating structure will be used as a means of increasing only the power to dominate or to restrict the authentic rights of others. As with the Ku Klux Klan, this can lead to a self-serving, demonic attempt to play God. We see again the indispensability of the dispersion, the separation, of powers.

This outline of a theology of history, of a "public theology," is, of course, highly selective, covering (and concealing) wide stretches of history. Its presupposition is that history is made by groups exercising power—the power of influence and the power of being influenced. Its presupposition is also that power must be both distributed and shared if tyranny or domination is to be held in check. The outline can provide some guidelines for interpreting a variety of examples of the dispersion of power brought about by social will rooted in religious impulse. The description of these examples must also be highly selective, each example serving as an ideal historical type similar to Max Weber's ideal type of the Protestant ethic.

## Some High Points in the Historical Development of the Separation of Powers

Probably the oldest example on record of a structured dispersion of power comes from the period of prehistory, the fourth millennium B.C. in Mesopotamia before the advent of autocratic rule. The historian Thorkild Jacobsen has found plausible evidence in that time for what he calls "primitive democracy." According to the mythology of that early period, the gods and goddesses assembled in a council that had established the rule of arriving at decision only after discussion—the gods "asking one another" in order to clarify the issues until agreement could be reached. One might say that here the sign of an authentic god or goddess was its willingness to hear what the others wished to say. Jacobsen infers that this heavenly assembly was a projection of earthly councils of the time when the ruler was obliged to secure the consent of representative citizens in assembly. This assembly possessed the authority to grant kingship, and it could even rescind this kingship. A *separation* of powers did not obtain in this "primitive democracy"; yet, there was at least a collegial dispersion of power throughout the assembly.[5]

---

[5] Thorkild Jacobsen, "Primitive Democracy in Ancient Mesopotamia," *Journal of Near Eastern Studies*, vol. 2, no. 3 (July 1943), pp. 159–72.

More nearly approaching a separation of powers is the independent status assumed by the Hebrew prophets. As charismatic intermediaries, they in the name of a covenant proclaimed, "Thus saith the Lord"—to (and against) the king and the people. The definition and exercise of this independent role of intervention is a remarkable and singular cultural creation, not achieved without dust and heat. From this came the classical definition of the prophet in our tradition.

The "prophets" in countries adjacent to Israel were not independent; they were attached to the court—on expense account, as it were. The Hebrew prophets condemned as false prophets those who simply served the king. The singularity of the Hebrew conception of the liberty of prophesying—a separation of powers—must be understood in terms of the historical context of the time.

There is a fundamental difference between Israel and the neighboring kingdoms. It may be characterized as the contrast between a historical and an ahistorical orientation. In Babylon and Egypt a static, stratified social order was sanctioned by a timeless, suprahistorical cosmic model: the established order of society had been defined once and for all in this model. Accordingly, an impregnable space of heteronomous authority dominated time. One might call this a spatialized religion. In Israel, on the other hand, an event in time, the emancipation of the people from slavery in Egypt, had liberated them from a cramped, oppressive space, drawing them into a time-orientation. As Hegel suggested, time and its promise would be viewed as superior to any fixated space of a regnant social order. The memory of this event and of a covenant from Yahweh, "acts of God," became the sanction for a continuing struggle for freedom against tyranny, and thus for independent prophetic criticism or intervention. In the light of these "acts of God" the meaning of existence was found in the struggle for a righteous community of the future, the promise and demand of the covenant. Here, then, we encounter an eschatological orientation, a historical religion, time overcoming space. The individual and the community were held responsible for the character of the society, and especially for the protection of the deprived and the poor at the gate. Before their liberation from Egypt, had not the children of Israel been strangers and deprived of freedom?

Since the covenant and its law were in this and other ways applied and broadened, we may speak of the authority here as theonomous in contrast with the heteronomous authority respected in Babylon and Egypt. To be sure, one can discern "the birth of conscience" in one short period in the history of Egypt. So much for the contrast between a historical and an ahistorical orientation as it relates to the separation or nonseparation of powers.

In Israel the bifurcation of powers, that between the prince and the prophet, began to appear as early as the time of Samuel. Increasingly, the prophet became the relentless proponent of freedom, equality, and justice.[6] In general, we may say that a tension obtained between law, order, and security, on the one side, and reform, on the other. The covenant was thereby interpreted as inimical to special privilege, whether for the dominant class or for the nation as a whole. The separation of powers opened the way for radical criticism in the name of the covenant. It opened the way for institutionalized dissent. Understandably, Max Weber spoke of Hebrew prophetism as an anticipation of the power of the free press in modern society.

## Early Christianity

The Hebrew prophets apparently acted singly. They did not form a continuing organization as a mediating structure, though there were "schools of the prophets" (about which little is known). The members of the primitive Christian churches, however, did form an enduring organization. Jesus, like the prophets, appeared as an intermediary between the God of the covenant and the people of Israel. The "world" in its actual state he viewed in radically pessimistic terms full of warning. In defiance of regnant demonic powers holding individuals and society in their grip, he announced the advent of the kingdom of God. This message engendered a new community imbued with acute eschatological urgency and tension. With theonomous appeal he came into conflict with rigid interpretations of the Jewish law, offering a new freedom. He came into conflict also with questionable practices such as those of the money-changers in the temple and of the rich grinding the poor.

The early community came into conflict also with the Roman state. Under St. Paul the community recognized Roman law as the protector of civil rights and as a punisher of evil-doing. Yet, by its very existence the community violated Roman law. The issue at stake was one that has aroused recurrent controversy in the West, the question of freedom of association. According to Roman law—the concession theory—associations required permission from the Emperor in order to become "licit." Otherwise, they were "illicit." One of the reasons

---

[6] For some of these formulations, I am indebted to conversations with my colleague Paul D. Hanson and to his article, "Prophets and Kings," *Humanitas*, vol. 15, no. 3 (November 1979), pp. 287–303.

for the persecution of the Christians was this legal ground. Another reason was the Christians' refusal to pour libations in worship of Caesar.

In defense of their status the churches could point to the saying attributed to Jesus when he was confronted with the question of paying the tribute money to Rome: "Render therefore unto Caesar the things which are Caesar's; and unto God the things which are God's." This division of responsibilities was again and again confirmed by the claim that one must obey God rather than man. It is clear, however, that the Christians believed the state to have an authentic role. Therefore they could complain that Pilate failed in his duty by permitting an innocent man to go to the cross. At the same time, by claiming the independence of the church as an association they demanded a separation of powers.

Alfred North Whitehead, commenting on the admonition of Jesus about rendering unto God that which is God's, was wont to say that "however limited may be the original intention of the saying, very quickly God was conceived as a principle of organization in complete disjunction from Caesar."[7] This principle of organization had shocking consequences, for it meant that not everything belonged to Caesar. Here we observe a claim analogous to that of the prophets: the church assumed the status of an intermediary between the transcendent and the individual, between the transcendent and the Israelite society, and between the transcendent and the Roman civil religion.

In this separation of powers the early Christians broke not only with Rome but also with the theocratic conception of the Jewish state. More than that, they broke the connection between religion and ethnic heritage; they also broke the bond between religion and family, in the sense that the individual might join the church in independence of the family. Yet, none of these institutions of the world was in their view consigned to outer darkness. In accord with their eschatological orientation, they held that with the fulfillment of the kingdom of God, when God will be all in all, social institutions as well as individuals (and even nature) will be redeemed. Hence, the message of the prophets was confirmed. According to Father George Tyrrell, the Christian eschatology moved from immediate pessimism to ultimate optimism. The divisions of power were to be overcome through the power of God. Hope became an evangelical virtue.

---

[7] *Adventures of Ideas* (New York: The Macmillan Co., 1933), p. 69. Whitehead here speaks of "complete disjunction from Caesar," because the Christians "had no responsibility for the maintenance of the complex system" of the Roman Empire (p. 20).

The theonomous character of the authority for the intermediary role was attested by the belief in the rule of the Holy Spirit. This emphasis led the jurist Rudolf Sohm to speak of the *ecclesia* as a *pneumato*cracy. In this view, the church had no legal constitution, nor was it a democracy. The members of the church under the inspiration of the Spirit sought for consensus in all important matters, including consensus regarding the authenticity of the charismatic leadership.[8]

The latent sociological function of the early churches is worthy of special note. As a consequence of the spread of the churches in the Mediterranean basin, hundreds of people were given vocations in the maintenance and expansion of the organization, vocations requiring a great variety of skills. But with the growth of the churches after the periods of persecution, Constantine altered their status by making Christianity the official religion.

For reasons of space we cannot trace the changes and conflicts of power which punctuated the developments of the ensuing millennium. Viewing these developments, the church historian Leopold von Ranke went so far as to assert that the meaning of history in the West is to be seen in the struggle between the church and the state. Since the time of Charlemagne, a great variety of middle structures have appeared, including monastic orders, guilds, universities, and also deviant heretical movements. A major struggle occurred between the monarchical and the conciliar principals, between absolutism and constitutionalism. The latter in the name of a division of powers attempted to impose limits on government (on the pontiff and the emperor). The conflict was again rooted in what Whitehead called opposing conceptions of "God . . . as a principle of organization."

Conciliarism shifted the center of authority from the papacy to the bishops and the priests, a dispersion of power. Insofar as this impulse appealed to lay support we may see here an anticipation of the principle of subsidiarity set forth by the nineteenth-century Jesuit Heinrich Pesch. This conception was to gain favor in Roman Catholic circles in the twentieth century.

---

[8] The later bureaucratization of the developing episcopacy tended to replace charismatic leadership with officials possessing essentially legal permanence of tenure. Under the influence of Rudolf Sohm, Max Weber spoke of this development as the "routinization of charisma." Moreover, going beyond Sohm's distinction between charismatic and legal-rational authority, Weber added traditional authority as a third type. On the basis of this threefold typology Weber developed a philosophy of history, describing charismatic authority as the dynamic element transcending the other types of authority and opening the way to radical criticism and innovation. See James L. Adams, *On Being Human Religiously* (Boston: Beacon Press, 1976), chap. 13 (on Rudolf Sohm).

In the late Middle Ages still another factor came into play in favor of the dispersion of power. The rise of the cities created a new space for a lay civilization to develop independently of the declining support for ecclesiastical power. This dispersion of power was to appear in at least two ways: first, through the mobility of the lay population and, second, through sectarian movements that could flourish in the new space.

## The Radical Reformation

The division of powers crucial for modern history came with the Reformation, and especially with the aggressive sects in its Puritan left wing (also called the Radical Reformation). This movement appeared in the sixteenth and seventeenth centuries. In England in the first half of the seventeenth century the conflict was connected with the struggle against king and parliament which led to the Civil War.

The aggressive sects are to be seen in contrast with the withdrawing sects (a Troeltschean distinction). The latter withdrew from the "fallen" church and society to form enclaves "unspotted from the world" of ceaseless compromise. Living apart from this world ruled by the principalities and powers of evil, they did not form mediating structures, except in the sense of mediating between God and the individual soul. The aggressive sects, on the other hand, remained "in the world" to serve as a leaven to transform it. In this respect they may be compared with the prophetic intermediaries and interveners of ancient Judaism, bringing about a division of powers *within* society—in this case, intervening with a social organization demanding freedom of association. In making this demand they rejected the prevailing view of "Christendom" that uniformity of faith is an absolute prerequisite for a stable society. Those who held to this traditional conviction found in it the religious sanction to harry the heretics out of the land.

The Baptists, the Independents, and the Quakers regarded their congregations as "gathered" churches, in contrast with a territorial church, where membership was tantamount to being born in a particular jurisdiction and was therefore involuntary. They were a gathered church of voluntary believers who had experienced regeneration and who strove for an explicit faith in place of the implicit faith found in the hierarchical territorial church, the church of the masses. These left-wing congregations considered themselves to be under the immediate headship of Christ and the guidance of the Holy Spirit, committed to a way of living set forth in the Bible. They aimed to be "free churches," liberated from bondage in "Egypt," that is, from a monolithic, standing order.[9]

Even before the Civil War this same opposition appeared in New England, where the seceders from the theocracy of the Massachusetts Bay Colony launched out to form independent commonwealths of freedom. In the Fundamental Orders of Connecticut (1639) both religious and property qualifications on the franchise were abolished. Here began the challenge to all restrictive covenants, a struggle that is still with us. Under Roger Williams in Rhode Island, a strictly civil "covenant" (called "democratical") was adopted, providing for majority rule, government by consent, "due process of law,"[10] and freedom of association. But the doctrine of the free church was central here, as in old England.

In the demand for freedom of association the left-wing congregations generally appealed to the independence and structure of the early Christian churches as the model. In doing this they aimed to recover the idea of the church as the covenanted people of God (and, as we have seen, Roger Williams extended the concept to that of a civil covenant). They set themselves in opposition to the coordination of the hierarchical political-ecclesiastical hierarchies, the church-state establishment. In short, they broke away from the Constantinian order: they called for a separation of church and state and for a church of congregational polity.

Under congregational polity these churches aimed to be self-governing, self-supporting groups in which every member had the right and responsibility to participate in the shaping of policy—a radical dispersion of power. They therefore rejected the coercive taxation that supported the established church. Believers alone were depended upon for the financial support. One might say that the passing of the collection plate became almost a sacrament, as did the reading of the Bible in public and private. It has often been observed that this latter practice brought about a high degree of literacy.

Accordingly, this whole movement is often referred to as "radical laicism." In this spirit one of my professors in theological school used to remind us "that Jesus was not a parson." In these congregational churches the covenant was "personalized" by placing responsibility upon

---

[9] For a discussion of the major motifs of this movement see Michael Novak, "The Meaning of 'Church' in Anabaptism and Roman Catholicism: Past and Present," in D. B. Robertson, ed., *Voluntary Associations: A Study of Groups in Free Societies* (Richmond, Va.: John Knox Press, 1966), pp. 91–108.

[10] See James Hastings Nichols, *Democracy and the Churches* (Philadelphia: The Westminster Press, 1951), chap. 1.

15

the individual conscience and by affirming the priesthood of all believers. In accord with this view, congregational polity incorporated the principle of separation of powers into the structure of the congregation. The clergy were ordained by the congregation and, of course, were not under the aegis of apostolic succession; they were given restricted powers, other powers being reserved for the laity (in the church meeting). Among the Quakers the congregation had the obligation to protect and listen to minorities within the congregation, an anticipation of the idea of loyal opposition in government.

This demand for respect for minorities was related to a general characteristic of these independent congregations, the rule of Scripture as known through the witness of the Holy Spirit. They held that Christ demanded of them a church in which the Spirit is "free to blow where it listeth and make all things new." Hence, the term "radical laicism" is scarcely adequate as a description. Here again we encounter an intermediary factor, a church in which the authority is pneumatocratic. In principle the authority was theonomous and charismatic, though one readily finds also a biblicist literalism. To be sure, some of the groups to the left of the independent congregations gave rise to wilding growths. John Dennis, a critic in the eighteenth century commenting on the "enthusiasts" in these groups, said, "Where one is inspired, ten thousand will be demented." The basic conviction in the independent congregations, however, was that the Holy Spirit, properly listened to, engenders consensus.

Another feature of congregational polity should be noted here. The dispersion of power was so radical and the authority of the local congregation was so much stressed that one may speak of the protest against the centralization of power as a drive toward localism, the geographical localism of scattered independent congregations. The question as to the relationship between congregations was soon raised, and gave rise to attempts at nonhierarchical "connectionalism," a search for a broad, if loose, unity in the midst of variety.

It is a striking fact that this move toward localism found a parallel in the concurrent protest of small businessmen against the concentration of power and against special privileges in the chartered monopolies granted by the crown. Indeed, it is likely that some members of the independent congregations were also small businessmen. Nonconformity was to become the haven of the emerging middle class.

A similar parallel can be found with the emergence of democratic political thought in these circles. Some historians have suggested that the idea of political democracy was born in part as a consequence of analogy drawn from congregational polity. This transfer becomes partly evident in the Leveller movement. John Lilburne, its leader, in his later years became a Quaker. But the Levellers were influenced also by legal theories and by a conception of natural rights which took root in some of the aggressive sects. The doctrine of separation of powers was spelled out in the Leveller *Agreements of the People*, among the first written democratic constitutions. In Lilburne's view, separation of and competition among the powers was not sufficient. The powers, including the king, had to be subject to the rule of law, to some concept of justice.

Of special importance was the development of voluntary associations. Among the left-wing Puritans, associations were initially formed to disseminate their ideas among the church-members of the establishment. Presently, independent associations flourished. In fact, the heady wine of freedom of association gave rise to such a goodly number of groups that members moved readily from one to another, or to the formation of a new one. John Lilburne in the context of these associations developed dramatic agitation as a technique for arousing public opinion. Because of "good olde John" public opinion began to play a new and crucial role, another dimension of the division of powers. Thomas Hobbes in *Leviathan* was so fearful of threatening chaos that he described these associations, including the sects, as "worms in the entrails of the natural sovereign."[11]

During the century after the 1640s we see the appearance of many associations concerned with influencing public opinion on public policy and also with social reform. In *Two Early Political Associations* Norman Hunt has shown that in the first quarter of the eighteenth century the Quakers developed the major techniques we associate with the modern pressure group: disseminating information, raising public consciousness, collecting signatures, and bringing influence upon various agencies of the government—including the legislature and members of the royal family. Here again we see the institutionalizing of dissent.

One of the most significant advances in the eighteenth century was the rise of the independent Nonconformist academies for education, the Dissenting Academies—another division of power. Some scholars in the field have argued that the creation of free academies that could promote higher education without submission to the ecclesiastical rules and the creedal demands of, say, Cambridge and Oxford, constituted a major revolution.

---

[11] See D. B. Robertson, "Hobbes's Theory of Associations in the Seventeenth-Century Milieu," in Robertson, *Voluntary Associations*, pp. 109–28. See also his book, *The Religious Foundations of Leveller Democracy* (New York: King's Crown Press, 1951).

The British political scientist and historian A. D. Lindsay, following Sidney and Beatrice Webb's suggestion in *Industrial Democracy*, has stressed the importance of Nonconformity in the development of trade unionism in the early nineteenth century. His characterization of this influence deserves quotation here at length.

> Where Nonconformity was strong trade unionism was strong, and where it was weak trade unionism was weak. It was the Nonconformist chapels which supplied democratic experience and the leadership of industrial democracy, whether in trade unionism or in cooperation. The British labour movement inherited from this source its intense democracy, its belief in government by persuasion and consent rather than by force, or, more exactly, its preference for negotiation and discussion and argument rather than compulsion, its idealism and its inclination to pacifism. It inherited also from Nonconformity its experience of the power for leadership inherent in the most apparently ordinary people, its concern with and care of what it calls the "rank and file."[12]

We are indebted to Max Weber for his contributions in this area of scholarship. I should mention in passing, however, a criticism of the characterization of the Protestant ethic presented in *The Protestant Ethic and the Spirit of Capitalism*. Weber asserted repeatedly in that work that he intended to confine his attention exclusively to economic behavior. Initially, he planned to produce a second volume on Protestant political behavior, but he later changed his mind. The result is that his conception of the Protestant ethic is lopsided. He gives no attention to the development of voluntary associations concerned with public policy or to the democratic internal structure of the small congregations. He presents none of the evidence of that aspect of the Protestant ethic. These Protestants were not peas in a pod, to use Emerson's phrase; they were vigorous, if not always consistent, proponents of the separation of powers and of a pluralistic society.

Likewise, Weber's treatment of Cotton Mather and Benjamin Franklin overlooks the fact that these two figures were prototypical in their formation of mediating structures. Franklin himself formed six or eight of the most important voluntary associations of that time, and he expressed indebtedness to Mather, who a century before had urged church members to form associations for philanthropic purposes.[13]

---

12 "The Philosophy of the British Labour Government," in F. S. C. Northrop, ed., *Ideological Differences and World Order* (New Haven: Yale University Press, 1949), pp. 250–68.

13 See James L. Adams, *Being Human*, chap. 12 (on Weber).

I am not aware of any attempt on Franklin's part to set forth a theoretical analysis of the nature and purposes of mediating structures. During the next two generations, however, that attempt was made by three eminent religious leaders: Lyman Beecher, a New Haven Congregationalist; Francis Wayland, a Baptist and the president of Brown University; and William Ellery Channing, a Unitarian in Boston.[14] Much of this writing preceded that of de Tocqueville on democracy in America.

It is a curious fact that relatively little attention has been given to the experience of the seventeenth-century independent congregations as a background for understanding the conceptions of the division of powers set forth by the founding fathers of the American Constitution. The attention has been given, rather, to the writings of, for example, Montesquieu and John Locke—who himself cannot properly be understood apart from that background.

I turn now to a consideration of a political view of the division of powers as set forth by James Madison in *The Federalist* and in his other writings. Here we shall inevitably encounter certain motifs that have come to the fore in our historical survey.

### James Madison's Views on Mediating Structures

For Madison the separation of powers is the touchstone of a democratic society. Only through this division can freedom be achieved or preserved. Separation should therefore appear at the different levels in society, from the federal government to the various mediating structures in the public as well as in the private sector. Madison favored a government powerful enough to preserve order, an order balanced by a society with liberty enough to prevent tyranny. The major "desideratum," he says, is order and freedom.[15]

Presupposed, however, is a separation qualifying all levels, the basic separation between the society and the government. In a fashion somewhat similar to that of John Locke, Madison adopted the theory of a double-compact. According to this view, the people first formed themselves into a community, and then as a society formed a government. The government is not the creator of the society. Rather, it is the creature and the servant of the society to which it is accountable. The authority of the government issues from the society and its public opin-

---

[14] See my article, "The Voluntary Principle in the Forming of American Religion," in Elwyn A. Smith, ed., *The Religion of the Republic* (Philadelphia: Fortress Press, 1971).

[15] *Writings of James Madison*, ed. Gaileard Hunt, 9 vols. (New York, 1900–1910), vol. 6, pp. 85, 96.

ion, which place limits on the government. This public opinion comes from the minorities as well as from the majority, for both the majority and the minorities constitute society as a whole.

The separation of powers belongs in turn to all agencies of governance. In the federal government, partitions obtain between the executive, the legislative, and the judicial powers, and the legislature is repartitioned into different houses. Madison also recognized the need for different levels of government. In this connection he spoke of "the intermediate existence of State government." The states and their subordinate levels represent a separation of powers supplementing the partitions in the federal government.[16] They are mediating structures between the federal government and the society. (He felt, however, that the abuse of rights was a greater danger in state governments than in the federal.)

The society, however, is not an abstract entity; it is composed of a large number of groups functioning independently of the government and serving as mediating structures in addition to those within the government. In identifying the mediating structures in the society, Madison used a variety of terms, often synonymously: parties, factions, interests, classes, sects, and institutions. In *Federalist*, No. 51, he gave special attention to noneconomic and religious groups. In *Federalist*, No. 10, he dealt with economic groups, stating that these groups are formed according to whether people do or do not enjoy wealth. An association might be created by either haves or have-nots: creditors or debtors, rich or poor, propertied or nonpropertied. Madison also listed occupational groups that cut across distinctions of wealth. He mentioned "regular branches of manufacturing and mechanical industry," as well as "civil professions of more elevated pretensions, the merchant, the lawyer, the physician, the philosopher and the divine."

Misconceptions have arisen regarding Madison's view of mediating structures because of his somewhat pejorative definition of factions in *Federalist*, No. 10. "By a faction," he says, "I understand a number of citizens, whether amounting to a majority or a minority of the whole, who are activated by some impulse of passion, of interest, adverse to the rights of other citizens, or to the permanent aggregate interests of the community." But Madison also saw in factions a salutary dispersion of power, "a protection for freedom in society against potentially tyrannical intentions of the majority." Viewing the mediating structures all together, he said in *Federalist*, No. 51, that by this means "the society itself will be broken into so many parts, interests and classes of

---

[16] Ibid., p. 91.

citizens, that the rights of individuals, or of the minority, will be in little danger from interested combinations of the majority." This view is not dissimilar to the outlook of the independent congregations of the previous century.

Madison's position regarding the separation of church and state is well known and fits into this pattern. Of great importance here is his insistence on freedom of conscience and on "the free exercise of religion"—his phrase in the First Amendment. (We have noted already that this separation of powers stems in part from primitive Christianity.) Madison did not, in this connection, however, refer to theological or ecclesiastical doctrines.[17] He did not consider himself to be a deist. He was a practicing Presbyterian, having all his life maintained connections with leaders in this denomination. Mrs. Madison had once been a Quaker and was known to continue to defend this group. In the main he appealed for justification of his religious ideas to the common experience of mankind. He was attracted to the common-sense philosophy of the Scottish Enlightenment—Ferguson, Hutchison, and others.

In this connection Roy Branson, in a recent article, reminds us that Madison's concept of factions rests on a doctrine of human nature which in his formulations indicates no theological orientation. By reason of its succinctness, I quote here a passage from Branson's article:

> [Factions] arise from liberty being granted to the diverse aspects of man's nature. In addition to deplorable self-love, factions reflect man's reason arriving at opinions. Man tries to make his views more pervasive and potent by creating groups to inculcate and propagate them. Man's nature includes certain "faculties" or talents which lead him to possess certain interests. Again, man creates groups to achieve these interests. Madison never applauded self-love, but expression of opinion and exercise of talents were considered by him to be legitimate aspects of man's activity. The right to hold and communicate opinions is a basic right, and in this same essay, Federalist #10, Madison indicated how important he considered the right to exercise one's talents when he said that "the protection of these faculties is the first object of government."[18]

---

[17] In a letter he expressed his conviction that "the belief in a God, all powerful, wise and good is essential to the moral order of the world and to the happiness of mankind." *Letters and Other Writings of James Madison*, 4 vols. (Philadelphia, Penn.: 1865), vol. 3, p. 503.

[18] *Journal of the History of Ideas*, vol. 40, no. 2 (April–June 1979), pp. 246–47. For many of the citations in the above paragraphs, I am indebted to Branson's Harvard doctoral dissertation, "Theories of Religious Pluralism and the American Founding Fathers" (1967).

Here we see ingredients of the classical humanist tradition. Reason has an interest in the realization of human capacities; *logos* can disclose a *telos* toward which human life strives, and which judges the quality of that life. In sum, then, Madison believed that the separation of powers is necessary for the achievement of popular sovereignty, enabling the appearance of innovation and of evolutionary social change and reform, in adherence to the law of the Constitution. If we view his system of the separation of powers as a whole, we see that he favored a pyramid of separated powers, reaching from the bottom to the top, rather than a hierarchical order, from the top to the bottom. For this system of "order and freedom of government and society," these lines from Shakespeare are pertinent:

> So we grew together,
> Like to a double cherry, seeming parted
> But yet an union in partition.

### The Separation of Powers Today

Madison's conception of the separation of powers was set forth in a small preindustrial society, when the federal and the state governments were in swaddling clothes and when these governments—the so-called "negative state"—aimed to serve as umpire in the face of mediating structures. Moreover, wide expanses of frontier remained to be explored and inhabited.

Today, however, we live in a welfare state, a social-service state, an industrial state, and a garrison state. The government is no longer merely a negative state serving as umpire. It has become a positive state with an enormous bureaucracy and regulatory agencies in the face of powerful corporations. The scope of the problems has enormously increased the functions of the federal government. The garrison state depends upon giant corporations, and its policies reach across the planet. Moreover, the welfare state and the social-service state give substantial support to the states for the maintenance of a bureaucracy. The corporations in turn require millions of workers and an extensive technology. In short, the separation of powers in our time takes on larger dimensions and a much broader scope than a century ago, especially in the garrison state. The world situation confronts us with a unique problem in connection with the separation of powers. The size of the world powers, the United States and Russia, renders them almost impervious to the influence of mediating structures in the society and, in the United States, beyond the control of Congress in crucial moments. One thing is clear: Whereas a century ago domestic policy could claim priority, it cannot today be divorced from foreign policy.

For this reason especially, the centering of attention in the Berger-Neuhaus book on the internal concerns of the local mediating structures must be recognized as a limited enterprise, as the authors would also affirm. On the other hand, this concentration of attention is highly pertinent, for these authors point to an imbalance that obtains in the welfare state, where the policies are controlled mainly from the top down, leaving little room for self-determination on the part of the ostensible beneficiaries. Consequently, people in the mediating structures in this area are placed in the position of exercising only the passive power of adjustment to authority in precisely those matters that concern them most. Here one encounters in many quarters a mass apathy. This condition shows the perennial relevance of the localism evident in the seventeenth-century independent congregations. In the end, however, the achievement of localism in these earlier groups moved towards affecting state policies and thereby their own lives also.

But the prevalence of passive power is not confined to those who are on welfare. Mass apathy is readily evident today in the area of political concerns. In the last century the proportion of eligible voters who have participated in presidential elections has diminished by over 30 percent. One reason for this, it is said, is what one might call a lamentable form of localism, the relatively exclusive devotion to the concerns of the family. This trend has been explained as an aspect of our "achievement society." The heads of the family, conscious of the fact that all members of the family share in the prestige accruing from economic success, give their energy to enhancing that prestige. Political and community responsibilities are therefore given little attention. One is reminded of Plato's view that the family is the enemy of justice in the state. A society in which so much energy is directed to personal success cannot be rightly thought of as inhibited by apathy.

The individual is reduced to passive power also in other areas. One of the most important of the middle structures in our society is the mass media. Here again the individual usually exercises the passive power of listening, which is not accompanied by talk-back or by active participation. Before the radio or the television set no division of powers exists, except in the sense that the consumer may refuse to listen and turn off the apparatus. It is true, however, that the participation of the consumer in other mediating structures can provide him with reference groups that may serve to engender his critical judgment and to provide criteria for exercising judgment.

The prevalence of passive power appears at the place of work perhaps more than anywhere else. This condition results from the hierarchical structure of the corporation. This structure is institutionalized in the bureaucracy necessary in any large undertaking. But institutionalized dissent is lacking. In some quarters corporations and labor organizations have made attempts at improvement. But always heteronomy tends to smother autonomy. Moreover, the heteronomy of passive power engendered by large organizations in industry cannot help spilling over into the political sphere, thereby becoming an impediment to political democracy.[19] In many ways society today finds itself in a situation comparable to that in which modern political democracy came to birth as a protest demanding the dispersion and separation of powers. We have noted this situation in the seventeenth century. The struggle was, of course, to continue. In the economic sphere Adam Smith, in the next century, aimed to diffuse power by resort to the market mechanism. It has been generally overlooked, however, that he extolled this mechanism as a countervailing power to the authority and the special privileges of the great landed estates. The market mechanism was to give freedom, with the opportunity for initiative and rewards to the businessman and to the corporation—that is, to the small corporation of the time. What actually happened was the unanticipated rise of the giant corporations. An analogous process is to be seen in a development appearing in Adam Smith's time. Somewhere in *The Wealth of Nations* he speaks of the evangelical movement that gave to the miner a new sense of dignity by convincing him that he has an eternal soul, but soon after he joined a sect he found himself in a tight vise of moral control. So it is that the modern corporation has helped to bring about a higher standard of living and, in a period of increasing population, has given the opportunity for employment, and yet has also promoted a division of labor without a corresponding division of powers. At the same time the modern corporate community has produced units of disproportionate power in the commonwealth. In this respect Madison's description of the separation of powers has become obsolete. The imbalance is evident in the well-organized lobbies with their affluent expense accounts, a power that has been spoken of as greater than that of the government.

For the correction of the internal hierarchical structure of the large corporation, Germany has contrived what is called "codetermination" (*Mitbestimmung*). It is now legally required that the large corporation shall have representatives of labor on the board of directors.

[19] See Robert A. Dahl, "On Removing Certain Impediments to Democracy in the United States," *Dissent* (Summer 1978), pp. 310–24.

The labor unions are even training their representatives for these positions. Premier Helmut Schmidt has asserted that this development represents contemporary Germany's major contribution to democracy. It is perhaps premature to assess the significance of this dispersion of power. In my conversations with German business executives, however, I have been told that they find the practice of codetermination tedious, yet worth the effort by reason of the change in spirit. Alternative ways of bringing about the dispersion of power in the American corporation are described in a publication by David Ewing of the Harvard Business School.[20] More fundamental is Douglas Sturm's penetrating analysis, "Corporations, Constitutions, and Covenants,"[21] beginning with the question regarding the corporation in its current forms and proceeding to the proposal that the corporation adopt the procedures of constitutionalism (with its broad consensus in the population) and the qualities of covenant.

In discussing the imbalance in the division of powers we have given attention to that resulting from the inordinate size and power of the great corporations. An adequate treatment of the subject would, of course, include a consideration of the imbalance due to those who live in poverty and unemployment. It would also include a consideration of the imbalance due to the size and structure of the trade unions, and also that due to the enormous bureaucracies in the executive branch of the federal government. Just as Adam Smith could not foresee the size of the corporations of the future, so Madison could not foresee the size and virtual intractability of these bureaucracies and their powers, especially evident in the State Department and the Pentagon, in the administration of the welfare state and in the regulatory agencies.[22]

What we have been discussing is the theory and development of modern federalism. The word "federal" is derived from the Latin *foedus*—treaty, compact, covenant. This term illustrates Robert Louis Stevenson's aphorism, "Man does not live by bread alone but also by metaphors." Indeed, one could survey Western history in terms of the root metaphors, beginning with the domestic metaphor of a patriarchal society—in the Bible one finds such metaphors as God the Father and

---

[20] *Freedom Inside the Organization* (New York: E. P. Dutton, 1977).

[21] Article of that title in *Journal of the American Academy of Religion*, vol. 41, no. 3 (September 1973), pp. 331–53.

[22] For a seasoned analysis of the expansion of the federal government, see the writings of Arthur Miller, especially his articles, "Private Governments and the Constitution" (Santa Barbara, Calif.: Center for the Study of Democratic Institutions, Fund for the Republic Occasional Paper, 1959), and "Separation of Powers—Does It Still Work?" *Political Quarterly*, vol. 48 (1977), pp. 54–64.

the church as the Bride of Christ. The organic metaphor has been perhaps the ruling one. For Plato the state is the individual organism writ large. For St. Paul the church is the Body of Christ; believers are members of this Body. These organic metaphors have served in the main as a sanction for a hierarchical structure of organization with authority emanating from the head down. (Contemporary exegesis, however, has shown that the Pauline model is a coarchy and not a hierarchy.) Otto von Gierke, a major historian in this matter, has traced the development of the organic metaphor in medieval thought until its transformation into federalism—the combination of unity *and* liberty. This transformation moved toward a structure in which corporate decision making depended upon the constituent groups from below. In the sixteenth and seventeenth centuries the metaphor of mechanism played a leading role. In this same period, as we have seen, the idea of covenant, which had been used in ancient times, was revived.

I have surveyed the history of the idea of covenant with special reference to the separation of powers and to the role of mediating structures in relation to this separation in a pluralistic society. In this survey we have observed some of the signs of the decline of pluralism as a consequence of an imbalance in the division of powers as conceived by James Madison. Without attempting here to spell out further remedies for this decline, I would like to conclude by considering some of the theological perspectives mentioned earlier, but in a different context.

The idea of covenant is a political metaphor, drawn initially from the sphere of international affairs in the ancient Near East. It seems to be modeled on the kind of treaty made between a superior power and subordinate powers, with promises made on both sides. Through the Hebrew prophets the concept was given a new vertical as well as a new horizontal dimension. The vertical dimension related the human enterprise to a cosmic power requiring commitment in freedom to work for a righteous society.

We should pause here, however, to observe that a wide spectrum of structures has been sanctioned by the idea of covenant. This spectrum reaches all the way from authoritarian theocracy to spiritual anarchism. In this spectrum two motifs appear—reliance upon a cosmically oriented institutional structure of unity and reliance upon the divinely given dignity and spontaneity of the individual. A variety of ways of combining the two motifs has appeared in history.

As a political metaphor the idea of covenant rejects the notion that faithfulness to it is possible for the individual alone; the jurisdiction of the covenant covers, as it were, the whole territory and entails collective responsibility. Responsibility attaches to institutional as well

26

as to individual behavior. This view of responsibility rejects, on the one hand, a tight collectivism and, on the other, a merely atomistic individualism. In short, this conception of covenant calls for mediating structures to protect and nourish the individual and to relate the individual in responsibility to embracing structures. From a theological perspective, both immediate and mediate relationships are defined in the context of a cosmic orientation. Covenant reaches from the immediate and intimate to the ultimate. Dr. Daniel Elazar has pointed out that the covenant relationship is to social and political life what Martin Buber's I-thou relationship is to personal life.

The intimate and the ultimate—indeed, all parts of the interrelated world—the individual, the middle structures, the government, the society, and the divine creative ground of meaning—are held together by covenant. The bonding and binding quality of covenant, the ordering principle, is promises. God is the promise-making, promise-keeping reality upon which we ultimately depend as the reliable, creative, sustaining, judging, community-forming, and community-transforming power. Wherever these powers are working, the divine is working. Accordingly, to be human is to be able to make a commitment in response to the divine promise. But human promises all too often turn out to be fickle. The human being is a promise-making, promise-keeping, but also a promise-breaking creature. The divine reality, however, makes new beginnings possible, and thus is the promise-renewing power in life. This power is manifest not only in interpersonal relations; it can appear also in institutional behavior, even if only ambiguously and incompletely. The separation of powers in society makes possible intervention in the name of the promises, intended to prevent bondage to any finite power. It is the necessary, if not a sufficient, condition for avoiding the idolatry of domination or tyranny. It may even serve to reduce the violation of the divine command, "Thou shalt have no other gods before me."

The secular-minded person who is alienated by the churches or the theologians, or who for some other reason is not (in Weber's phrase) "religiously musical," may find unacceptable any theological formulation. Yet, this promise-making, promise-renewing power is the flywheel of meaningful human existence.

Edmund Burke expressed this conviction in covenantal terms in his memorable statement:

> Society is indeed a contract. Subordinate contracts for objects of mere occasional interest may be dissolved at pleasure —but the state ought not to be considered as nothing better

than a partnership agreement in a trade of pepper and coffee, calico or tobacco, or some other such low concern, to be taken up for a little temporary interest, and to be dissolved by the fancy of the parties. It is to be looked on with other reverence; because it is not a partnership in things subservient only to the gross animal existence of a temporary and perishable nature. It is a partnership in all science; a partnership in all art; a partnership in every virtue, and in all perfection. As the ends of such a partnership cannot be obtained in many generations, it becomes a partnership not only between those who are living, but between those who are dead, and those who are to be born. Each contract of each particular state is but a clause in the great primeval contract of eternal society, linking the lower with the higher natures, connecting the visible and invisible world, according to a fixed compact sanctioned by the inviolable oath which holds all physical and all moral natures, each in their appointed place.[23]

Here is an awareness of vocation which appeals to the fundamentally human promise-making and promise-keeping obligations, vocation which calls for both humility and resoluteness.

---

[23] E. Burke, *Works* (1861), vol. 2, p. 368.

# Discussion

QUESTION: You made reference in passing to the civil disobedience practiced by the early Christians, and you mentioned the saying of Jesus, "Therefore render unto Caesar that which is Caesar's, and unto God that which is God's." I think it is possible to interpret this passage in quite a different way. The Christians can be interpreted as saying, "We will do whatever we must in order to render unto God that which is His, but we will not challenge the government." They did not intend civil disobedience.

PROFESSOR ADAMS: Thank you for this question. It gives me the opportunity to offer some clarification. Let me say at the outset that the variety of interpretations provided by scholars reminds one of what the Mad Hatter said to Alice in Wonderland: "Here, you see, everyone gets prizes."

Some scholars have stressed the idea that for Jesus his kingdom was not of this world and that he did not wish to clash with Rome; more important matters were on his agenda. Other scholars (quite recently again) have claimed that Jesus was a zealot bent on the overthrow of Rome. Others have argued that Jesus believed in passive resistance and that he was a pacifist—though he did not condemn military service.

In any event, it is clear that the Christians refused to pour libations in worship of Caesar. Moreover, from the perspective of Roman law, they formed an association without imperial license. As a consequence, the church was an "illicit" association.

Yet, I would not be inclined to attribute civil disobedience to the early Christians. It is true that, like St. Paul, many of them in loyalty to Christ were willing to suffer imprisonment or martyrdom at the hands of the state. But apparently they did not believe in civil disobedience as we understand it today. They were not engaged in a general struggle for freedom of association. They did not demand freedom such as their own for other groups.

I referred to the passage in question in order to say that although the early Christians favored the payment of tribute money to the emperor, they did not hold that everything belongs to him. For our discussion of the separation of powers, the crucial element is found in Whitehead's observation (which I have mentioned earlier) that here one sees that God has become a principle of organization. Christianity was rejecting the civil religion of Rome and its institutions, and it was affirming the need for a separate organization to promote the worship of God beyond Caesar. This separation of powers endured for several centuries, and the theory reappeared in later history.

QUESTION: You mentioned in passing that it is difficult to find institutionalized dissent in the executive branch of government, probably more difficult to find than in business. Herbert Simon's books on organization deal with this problem of decision making in both types of organization. He indicates that a vast number of decisions are involved in every decision. Now, that may be institutionalized dissent. Or is it?

You mentioned also that unions in Britain took a cue from the independent churches of the seventeenth century, becoming an arrow of dissent against both business and the government. But, unfortunately, there is a common characteristic of all human beings, including professors just as much as businessmen: as soon as they rise to the point where they see the trade union can capture the state or the party, and really become the dominant factor, they then forget others who do not have power. Consequently, you have the trade union movement that is now in Britain. I think we need to remember that power is what is at stake in most associations.

PROFESSOR ADAMS: In dealing with the development of the separation of powers I attempted to give a sketch of the historical background, showing that in the seventeenth century the independent churches were opposed to the church-state establishment, and that early in the nineteenth century the trade unions encountered an analogous opposition. At this point, according to A. D. Lindsay, motifs from the earlier church struggle reappeared. In the nineteenth century in the United States, Massachusetts, especially in the courts, was the most die-hard in its opposition to organizations seeking to disperse power protected by the establishment. Here the opposition to collective bargaining was severe. Much of the same sort of struggle seen in the seventeenth century had to be fought again.

As you say, the moment a group acquires new power it will tend to forget its own earlier claims in favor of freedom. One reason is that within the organization itself a power struggle ensues, certain groups angle for control. The Italian sociologist Robert Michels called this "the iron law of oligarchy," the tendency of the eager-beavers to take control. I once heard Arnold Toynbee say that the trade-union leaders divided their energies, devoting half of these energies to the goals of the organization and giving the other half to preventing other people from climbing the ladder to power in the organization.

The trend toward oligarchy in an organization is supported by the indifference of the average member. Everyone knows that in almost every organization it is extremely difficult to maintain the interest and working support of all the members. Some years ago a team of American sociologists studied the trade union in Britain that was supposed to be the most democratic. They found that roughly 13 percent were interested enough to participate in decision making. On this problem I once heard this aphorism: "Every member has his own contribution to make, the problem is to get him to make it." The democratization of any organization is a perennial problem.

When I speak of the need for institutionalized dissent, I have in mind the fact that if the individual must *de novo* organize dissent, the advantage rests almost entirely with the established powers in the organization or the society. If, on the other hand, a generally recognized (that is, legitimized) channel of dissent exists, the individual not only knows how to proceed, he can also be recognized as doing something that the organization has made room for in its constitution. The alternative is for the individual to be attacked as disloyal or subversive.

An early example of institutionalized dissent (and separation of powers) is to be seen in the appearance of political parties. Before the formation of parties, significant dissenters were beheaded; after the formation of parties, they occupied opposition benches—on expense account. It is worth noting here that one of the larger trade unions in the United States has a two-party system. I have already mentioned the practice of codetermination in large German corporations, where labor representatives are legally required to serve on the boards of directors—a dispersion of power. Premier Helmut Schmidt has said that this practice is contemporary Germany's best contribution to democracy. Business executives from Germany with whom I have talked say that they find the discussions with labor representatives on the board to be tedious, but they add that the change in spirit makes the venture worthwhile. The trade unions, for their part, are attempting to reduce the tedium by sending their representatives to training courses. They want to become vigorous participants in board discussions.

Curiously enough, one of the effective means of dissent today is the independent research group employed by the organization. Such a research group is frequently in the government, in business, and also in the churches.

QUESTION: I wonder if sometimes we do not see too much in the model of economic activity when we apply it to other fields, such as to religion. I am sure that Madison had no use for the idea that in politics one works for one's own self-interest. That is the reason he defined factions the way he did. He hoped that factions would be neutralized, so that the politician could seek the public interest. It seems to me to be dangerous to extrapolate from the economic model to other areas. For example, we do not need to make analogies between contracts and the religious commitment of covenant. Does this sort of analogy trouble you?

PROFESSOR ADAMS: I quite agree with your objection to this analogy. A contract is made between two parties for a specific, limited purpose, and an equitable contract is one that in principle is between equals. In a religious covenant such as one finds in the Old Testament, the goal is the fulfillment of the meaning of life, the aspiration for a society in which righteousness and peace will prevail—the eschatological dimension. In the second place, a covenant between God and the people is not between equals. Moreover, in a contract each party attempts to achieve an agreement that will serve his own interest. It is an enterprise in bargaining and an attempt to make it legally binding. The basis of covenant in the Old Testament, however, is not legality or mere self-interest. The basis, as I have said earlier, is gratitude and affection on the part of those receiving the covenant and its vocation. Violation of the covenant is violation of law, but it is more than that; it is a violation of abiding affection and abiding loyalty.

One of the most deplorable things in the history of the idea of covenant is its deterioration into an idea of contract. In this view, the believer has made a contract with God, who promises, "If you do my will, I shall give you the reward of success in all things." The Book of Job is a protest against this idea of covenant as contract. In the face of disaster Job nevertheless says, "I know that my Redeemer liveth." Thereby he affirms the mystery of covenant.

Another aspect of covenant should be emphasized here in connection with the view that the basis of covenant is affection and loyalty. Hosea stresses this idea when he presents Yahweh as going in pursuit of the faithless bride, Israel, and as saying, "I know you have been faithless, but I want you to come back to me. Don't you know, I *love* you?" In other words, a new beginning is possible. Here the ethos is utterly different from that of contract. One can also see here a contrast with the Greek idea of Nemesis, where new beginnings are futile, for the vengeance of the gods is ceaseless and relentless.

Still another aspect of covenant should be mentioned. A contract, I have said, is between two parties for a specific, limited purpose, and a covenant is holistic. The Old Testament covenant (and also that of the New Testament) impinges upon institutional existence as well as upon the individual. In his essay fifty years ago on the Old Testament prophets, Ernst Troeltsch noted that if you examine the sins identified by them, you will find that they are not primarily sins of individual but of institutional behavior (to be sure, involving individual responsibility and participation). In this connection Troeltsch reminds us that some of the prophets were protesting against the impersonality of the life developing in the cities and in the money economy. In protesting against urbanism they were radically conservative in their idealizing of the previous, simpler life of the quasinomadic society. For example, in the adjudication of conflict the elder transcended the mere legalism of contract. He knew everybody in the families on both sides, and he knew their situation. Therefore, he could view the conflict in its multidimensional character.

Troeltsch goes on to say that in this respect the prophetic message was irrelevant for urban existence. The city is here to stay, and this aspect of the message is permanently irrelevant. Instead of this, one should say that the personalism of the prophetic message is permanently relevant.

Let me add something here about the difference we have been discussing, the difference between a contract and a covenant. Something of the ethos of covenant, it seems to me, lies behind the Burkean conception of social covenant, to which I referred at the end of my paper. Moreover, since our major theme here is the relation between the separation of powers and mediating structures, we should recall that Edmund Burke held that "platoons" of civic-minded citizens are the means whereby they can introduce criticism and innovation for the public good. They represent a separation of powers.

# The Promise of Democratic Socialism

*Robert Lekachman*

It takes a certain leap of imagination for an American to talk seriously about socialism. In the 1976 presidential election, six socialist parties got one-quarter of one percent of the popular vote. Nevertheless, I am going to suggest that my version of democratic socialism, which I will shortly try to explain, is not only desirable but possible, and that there are developments in the United States that are favorable to this outcome. Let me start first with the usual libertarian case, not for socialism but for capitalism, and then suggest why I find it unpersuasive in current American circumstances.

## The Case for Capitalism

Those like Friedrich von Hayek and Milton Friedman, who make a case for more than coincidence between political democracy and the institutions of market capitalism, argue more or less as follows: first, that private ownership of productive resources confers independence of income and wealth on owners and their employees, simply because they do not have to depend on the state for personal protection and economic livelihood; that associated with this separation between private and public enterprise is a limitation of the state's coercive power; and that, third, and more positively, these conditions mean freedom of economic choice for the individual in his or her role as a consumer, a worker, an entrepreneur, an investor, a bequeather of property. All these freedoms tend to encourage a habit of mind that is friendly toward freedom of opinion, political choice, and the voluntary activities we are here to consider. On this last score, the very fact that resources are largely private and considerably dispersed provides both the money and the ideological sanction for the proliferation of small journals of opinion and interest groups—to use the distinction Dr. Adams employed last evening—both expressive and instrumental organizations. This is an untidy arrangement, but the untidiness is desirable—it is an expression of the diversity of resources, the independence of those who wield them, and the friendship, therefore, between capitalism and freedom of a political, social, and individual kind.

That is a quick summary of the way economists, in particular, have tended to look at the connections between the institutions of capitalism and the institutions of political and social freedom.

At the threshold, this case is somewhat flawed by the uncomfortable fact that political democracy seems to be consistent only with some versions of capitalism. Capitalism, embarrassingly, flourishes in places like Chile, Brazil, South Korea, Taiwan, the Philippines, Indonesia, and other bastions of repression. In the past, it has been comfortable in fascist Italy, Spain, Portugal, Greece, and elsewhere. In short, capitalism has certainly existed without political democracy and without free play for intermediate organizations. In fairness, of course, one must say that it is difficult to find examples of democratic socialism without some significant degree of capitalism.

But dismiss these situations for the moment, and focus on the American case. The United States provides, I suppose, the strongest case for an association between capitalism and democracy, and the strongest example of healthy intermediate organizations, which have flourished and have been noticed by foreign observers almost since this country's independence. Why question—as I do—the benign character of capitalism's influence on the conduct of democracy in America?

## The Case against Capitalism

An incomplete list of my reservations about capitalism would include at least the following items. For one, capitalism badly skews and distorts the diversity of opinion, which is claimed as one of its great merits. Let us look at the electronic media for a bit—at television, in particular. The real message of commercial television is not the content of the programs; it is the commercials that surround the programs. The real message of television is the set of commercial values that leads the viewer to buy, and to buy a specific collection of commodities.

Television is a commercial medium, including public television. I have recently become a member of the board of advisers of Channel 13 in New York, a public television station, and it has been an interesting and educational experience. That station is nearly as aware as NBC is of its ratings, and it is subject, in some ways, to the same advertising pressure. One illustrative story: "Upstairs, Downstairs" is one of the great successes, of course, of public television. According to the tale I heard at Channel 13, here is how "Upstairs, Downstairs" got to occupy its space on public television. Mobil made a substantial grant to Channel 13 contingent on Channel 13's acquisition of the BBC rights to "Upstairs, Downstairs." Channel 13, perhaps wrongly, but by its own criteria, decided it did not want to show the program. Mobil said, "That is your right, as it is our right to withhold the grant that we are prepared to make if you do show it." In this conflict between principle and principal, principal won, as it frequently does when you consider the constant efforts of public television to beg money, which it has done with some success, largely from the corporate sector.

This is not to say that the people who run public television are showing things that directly represent the interest of corporate sponsors. What you get, instead, is an absence—an absence of sharp public discussion, of alternative news programs, of programs dealing with working-class history or the history of trade unions, for example. Consider "The MacNeil/Lehrer Report," which I am sure many of you have seen. This is a fair discussion program with the extremes excluded. Watch a discussion, and it will range from the responsible moderate left to the responsible moderate right, with the minority left—and the minority right, for that matter—excluded from the discussion.

I do not want to linger on television, but let me suggest a second limitation of pluralism. Increasingly, if you are going to run for public office, it is advisable either to be very rich or to have rich friends or sponsors. Public office is not yet limited to such individuals, but the proportion of millionaires in Congress steadily increases, and the same is true for political candidates. The cost of political campaigns, the expense of television advertising, the necessity of pleasing those who are in a position to assist in the funding of these operations, all constrict candidates' independence in formulating their political opinions.

A third limitation on the pluralistic operation of capitalism involves multinational corporations. Increasingly, as the scale of these corporations and the scope of their operations widen, they escape effective constraint by law. I am not suggesting that the multinational corporation deliberately breaks the laws of the United States. But by its capacity to shift operations and capital out of the United States into more hospitable economic climates—which frequently translate into authoritarian societies, with limitations on trade union activity and First Amendment freedoms—the multinational corporation often is able to escape many of the constraints of American law.

What else? Large enterprises, and small, have wasted natural resources prodigally. They have used the natural environment as a dump; and they have used human beings, on occasion, as consumers of unsafe products—also of useless products, many of which substitute for more useful products—junk food for real food, for example. I don't mean to say that businessmen are more wicked than the rest of us. I think wickedness is fairly evenly dispersed in the human race. But we all, to a great degree, act according to the role we are playing and the character in which we are cast. It is not that the businessman seeks to poison his customers, or prefers to dump poisonous wastes into the Love Canal and other installations. It is that if you are trying to minimize cost and maximize profits, there is a steady asymmetric pressure on you. You may be well meaning, a pillar of the community, entirely respectable, sensitive in personal relations, a good father, husband, and so on. Nevertheless, the constraints of your role push you toward underestimating the damage you may be doing to customers, neighbors, and the air and water that surround you because your own performance gets judged by how well you do in your particular product or division. This is inevitable. It is no judgment on the particular executives cast in these positions, but a judgment on the sort of organization that stimulates behavior that is objectively harmful.

I would like to summarize these miscellaneous objections to the way capitalism operates in this way. In reflecting on the way American society has evolved, it has often seemed to me useful to look at a tension in our history, a tension between a promise of equality and an encouragement of inequality. The promise of equality in our society is Constitutional. It is in the Bill of Rights; it is in the equal protection clause of the Fourteenth Amendment. Our basic documents express a commitment to the dignity of individual human beings, to the idea that all of us are civically equal—equal before the law, equal as voters, equal as participants in governing the society. That commitment is strongly entrenched in our institutions. Trial by jury, to take just one example, premises the individual good sense of citizens taken at random in judging the cases and crimes that are brought before them.

There is a tension between this idea of equality and the institutions of capitalism. The institutions of capitalism naturally, inevitably, promote a large set of inequalities. In the contest for profit, for personal status, for professional achievement, there are big winners, small winners, and losers. The distribution of income and, still more, the distribution of wealth, become extremely unequal. Because the constitutional market for freedom is not totally independent of the economic market for services, commodities, and professional services, those with large resources have a disproportionate say in how it operates. They are able to influence the conduct of the legal system, the operation of the political system, and the distribution of the benefits of political institutions in ways that are uncomfortable to those more attached to the political and legal guarantees of freedom than to the economic inducements of capitalism.

I have put it this way deliberately: there are markets for human and civil rights. If you are unfortunate enough to be accused of a crime, you will clearly do better if you can hire Edward Bennett Williams to represent you than if you are represented by an assigned lawyer from Legal Aid. If you have a cause to plead as a member of an organized group, you will do better if you can hire Clark Clifford to represent your group rather than some well-intentioned attorney from your home town. Pluralism, which political scientists used to think was a contest of many organized groups with no permanent winners, is less and less susceptible to that comfortable interpretation as time goes on.

To put it as Charles Lindblom does in his recent book *Politics and Markets*,[1] the large corporation has a certain natural advantage in pluralistic contests. That is, it has the same opportunities to influence the political process as organized farmers, labor unions, groups of professionals, the American Medical Association, the American Bar Association, and the National Education Association. It has the same freedom to lobby, to advertise, to petition, and to use all the miscellaneous devices of pluralistic pressure and persuasion. In fact, it has better than the usual opportunity, simply because its financial resources are larger.

The large corporation also has another, almost conclusive, advantage in its contests with its critics, with opposing interests, with other groups, and with the politicians: it is the provider of jobs and livelihoods. The corporation is in a position to expand or contract in a given political jurisdiction—in a position, for that matter, to leave. In our increasingly ominous economic environment, there is a growing contest among states, regions, and even cities to keep the enterprises that are already there and to attract new ones. When a question arises, then, over environmental regulations or tax policy or zoning exemptions, the corporate employer's argument often is simple and conclusive: if the politicians do not behave properly, the corporation will, with all due reluctance, pull up stakes and move somewhere else.

This tremendous natural advantage the large employer has over other contenders in our pluralistic system explains many things. It explains, for example, why tax reform has become a faded passion in our society. Practically every president comes in bravely promising to turn the tax code into a simple, equitable document. And then somehow the effort falls into the hands of Senator Long in the Finance Committee and his opposite number, Mr. Ullman, in the House Ways and Means Com-

---

[1] New York: Basic Books, 1977.

mittee. Two loopholes are closed, seven are opened, and the new tax bill becomes still more benign as far as the interests of corporations and affluent individuals are concerned.

A second example: we all recall, I daresay, that after October 1973, when OPEC imposed its embargo and the world changed, it was very popular in Congress to threaten all sorts of horrible things against the oil companies. Senator Stevenson proposed a federal oil and gas company, which, unfortunately, quickly got pronounced "FOGCO." FOGCO was an effort to set up something like a TVA to produce oil on federal oil lands. It vanished without a trace.

Senator Abourezk, now out of office, advocated nationalization of the energy industry. The late Senator Hart advocated divestiture, breaking up the oil companies by stage of production. Various other proposals floated about. It was only a lazy politician who did not make some sort of a gesture toward substantial limitation of the operations of the oil companies. Gone, gone, gone with the snows of winter, alas, are all these proposals.

Now, when I have talked to business audiences, I have generally encountered a sense not that business runs the country, but that business is under tremendous pressure from all kinds of radical professors, of whom I hope I am one; from environmentalists, consumerists, rabid politicians, even television—all kinds of interests beat up on the poor corporation. And, indeed, public opinion research suggests that large corporations are not terribly popular. Neither, however, are politicians, trade unions, universities, the medical profession, lawyers, or used-car dealers. The difference is that the large corporation is able, nevertheless, to get its way in an uncomfortable proportion of its contests. The political process works so as to defuse serious efforts to limit the scope and the profitability of corporate interests. This, of course, is the point.

### The Case for Socialism

I have been lingering too long on the limitations of capitalism, but partly because I wish to suggest to you why I am a socialist.

There is no effective socialist party in the United States; I suppose there are nearly as many versions of socialism as there are socialists. Therefore, each individual must do his or her own preliminary work of definition. Presumably this is less necessary in Europe, where organized parties of the left have explicit platforms. Let me suggest very quickly the kind of democratic socialism I have in mind before proceeding to why socialism is more friendly to pluralism, to the health of the intermediate organizations that we are here to talk about, than capitalism is.

In common with people like Michael Harrington and Irving Howe, I think of democratic socialism as having certain minimum characteristics. The first of these is considerably diminished financial inequality. If you asked how much equality I want, my answer would be Samuel Gompers's "more": not complete equality, obviously, but less inequality than now characterizes financial distribution. I would approach this substantially via the limitation of inheritance. It is interesting that John Stuart Mill, when he was arguing against progressive income taxes on the grounds that they dampen incentives, argued at the same time in favor of heavy inheritance taxes. Presumably, this was on the ground that the incentives of the deceased need not be stimulated, at least not by government policy, and, furthermore, that it is good for the character of the heirs not to inherit large fortunes. Mill supported heavy inheritance taxes in 1848, and this is still the approach I consider most suitable.

A second characteristic I would seek from socialism is a reduction in the scale of the corporation in our country. Now, this is not "small is beautiful." I do not think you are going to build large aircraft with E. F. Schumacher's intermediate technology—nor, for that matter, large computers in local workshops. Nevertheless, by every account, the scale of the large corporation is much less related to technological economies of scale than to various advertising, marketing, financial, and legal benefits—including the opportunity to control markets.

Now, free enterprise economists, of course, would be alarmed by the idea of limiting the size of corporations. I would argue that competition only works where it exists; and the scale of the large organization frequently limits the amount of effective competition that can occur. Diminishing the average size of the productive units would increase their number, and thereby the potential for competition.

Third, and closer to our topic of intermediate organizations, one can imagine a much wider variety of methods of ownership and control under a democratic-socialist form of organization than we have now. Individual proprietorships, shared public and private ownership, cooperatives, some explicit state enterprises, some worker-operated enterprises, —all would be conceivable.

There was an interesting effort in Youngstown, Ohio, to form a community union group to operate the steel works there, which since have been closed down. Unfortunately, the plan required a larger commitment of federal funds than the government was willing to make, or perhaps was legally able to make. But there is no reason, in principle, why you should not have extended variations of the German codetermination arrangement—enterprises partly owned (as they are now, in fact, through employee pension funds) but also partly managed by employees. It would be quite possible to achieve a diversity of forms of economic activity considerably greater than the present diversity— and, therefore, a diversity of political forms of life within the economic enterprise that would be greater than we have now.

Another argument for different forms of control is the tendency toward hierarchy and authoritarianism in the large corporation. Any large organization—public, private, mixed, profit, nonprofit—is going to behave bureaucratically. The larger the organization, the more intricate the bureaucratic structure. Bureaucracies may be less or more open, but they are inevitably hierarchical to a considerable extent. This is also an argument, of course, for smallness of scale. But I suspect that there would be more genuine diversity of internal organizational structure in a society in which the forms of ownership were varied. This is a leap of imagination, because we are so far politically from this sort of design that it is impossible to know how these structures would evolve. Certainly, given the constraints of market capitalism, the opportunities for them to evolve are not very wide at present.

A fourth advantage of socialism has to do with the media. The great problem of the media now is not censorship, is not blatant propaganda; it is commercialism and the exclusion of disquieting alternative views. Herbert Gans has written an interesting book called *Deciding What's News*.[2] He studied the operations of NBC and CBS news, almost as an anthropologist, spending months there observing what was going on. His conclusion was that nobody censors Walter Cronkite or John Chancellor. The sponsors did not direct the executive producers to distribute news time so as to promote their commercial interests. What the news operations do is promote a consensus view of American life. The journalists who make it up through the ranks to become anchor persons have come to believe in a standard package of the American creed, and this is what the news promulgates. It is the only point of view, in effect, that you get on television.

The best thing that could happen, under my vision of democratic socialism, would be much more diversity in the media, much more genuine variety of all kinds, than we have now. How do you achieve this? Again, we have to leap from the present to the future with no noticeable bridges between the two. But I assume you would have to have listener- and viewer-sponsored media. The technology of cable access is evolving to the point where it should be possible to have a whole series of programming that is union-sponsored, bank-sponsored, corporate-sponsored, church-sponsored, interest-group-sponsored, expressive-

[2] New York: Pantheon, 1979.

group-sponsored—all points of view. The deadly hand of the commercial advertiser is what now distorts our politics, as well as our cultural expression.

## A Look at the Future

What does all this come down to? Let me continue with an exercise in political prophecy. I think the next decade or more is going to be a time of trouble for the United States, for a specific economic reason, as well as for a number of cultural and political reasons. We have, I think, entered a new economic era, one that is totally unfamiliar to us.

Until October 1973, which is likely to be a watershed date in modern history, the great comfort in American politics has been our 3 percent annual growth in per capita output. Three percent does not sound like much, but if you go to work on an assembly line at age eighteen, and you never get promoted, and you retire in the fullness of years, your income will have more than doubled in real terms, simply because of the translation of those annual 3 percent productivity gains into higher paychecks. This growth has softened the normal disputes of politics over distributive issues. Growth has made it possible for politicians to say "something for you and something for you and something for practically everybody else"—maybe more for some than for others, but a division of wealth, rather than a taking from some and a giving to others.

The politics of growth are comparatively benign. Consider the last episode of mild social progress in our history, those three miraculous years 1964, 1965, and part of 1966, before the escalation of the Vietnam war blighted further social progress. Lyndon Johnson not only started a war on poverty and a whole array of social programs, he also cut taxes in 1964, so that altruism came cheap for the prosperous. Besides the fact that the programs for the poor were never as expensive as popular legend now tends to imagine, they coincided with an improvement in the real situation of prosperous and even affluent taxpayers, who were getting a tax cut at the same time. This temporary miracle, which was repealed by the middle of 1966, happened simply because the economy was growing quite rapidly. It was possible for a while to do something not really for everybody, but for more people at once than is usually feasible.

For a variety of reasons, we are extremely unlikely to resume economic growth at anything close to the rate of most of our history. The next decade's politics are going to be the nasty politics of distribution.

This, to my mind, explains a good deal of President Carter's unpopularity, and his apparent inability—which he shares with Congress—

to take action on almost any pressing national problem. The odd stasis that surrounds issues like energy and inflation is, I think, the early pain and social division that have begun to arise from the necessity, as yet dimly perceived, of facing such dilemmas as how to distribute national burdens and national resources. This necessity will ultimately lead, I believe, to some form of national economic planning. The form that is most likely to evolve in the next five to ten years is a highly conservative, corporate-dominated form of planning.

Since I am speculating with you this morning, let me speculate a little bit more about the politics of corporatism in our time. One of the more interesting arguments within the business community at present involves business people who, whatever the practices of their own corporations, are attached nostalgically to notions of free markets. I have heard Thomas Murphy of General Motors and Walter Wriston of Citicorp in New York speak with true passion of the wonders of the free market. General Motors, of course, has rather more than 50 percent of the domestic automobile market. Mr. Wriston's Citicorp is not in as strong a position among banks, but neither is it your average country bank, by any means. This is not to say that I dispute these gentlemen's sincerity. Theirs is an archaic point of view, however, in interesting opposition to the position taken by a small, but increasingly influential, group within the business community who favor some version of coherent national policy planning. These are people like Henry Ford II, Felix Rohatyn, and Michael Blumenthal, before he became secretary of the treasury. They have made a diagnosis of the economic climate not terribly different from the one I have just made; that is, their view emphasizes the new constraints upon growth, the necessity of more coherent national policy, and the impending transition to a politics of distribution from a politics of growth.

I suspect that we are going to shift toward a very conservative form of national economic planning, dominated by corporate interests and their agents. People like Mr. Rohatyn feel, properly, self-confident about their ability to influence and operate a national economic plan, one that is consonant with the interests of the corporate sector. It is the more archaic businessmen, I think, who frighten themselves with visions of John Kenneth Galbraith at the controls and other dangerous characters recalled to administer the economy. That is not the way it is going to happen, at least for some time. We are more likely to see conservative economists affiliated with the American Enterprise Institute or the Hoover Institution or other business-supported and -funded organizations directing our economic planning than a collection of radical social scientists.

## Prospects for Socialism

This is gloomy, but it is not the end of the tale, as I perceive it. I think we are going to go through an unpleasant corporate-dominated interlude; however, for a variety of reasons, I do not think that the corporate style of national economic planning is going to be successful. I do not think it is going to be able simultaneously to increase property income, maintain some kind of minimum structure of welfare services, and keep assorted interest groups, if not happy, at least unrebellious. Gradually the perception will spread, I believe, that the American egalitarian tradition, with its variety of intermediate groups, is far more consistent with a different type of arrangement. It is consistent with public control of major industries; with varied private, public, and mixed worker-cooperative arrangements in much of the economy; with a dispersion of wealth, income, and power—in other words, with democratic socialism.

In conclusion, all I would say is this: Capitalism, in its present form in the United States, is clearly faltering. It is unlikely to recover its vigor; it is, rather, likely to be succeeded by a more explicitly corporate-dominated form of planning, in which all the voluntary institutions will be much weaker and under much greater pressure than they are even now. If we are lucky, it is at least possible—I will not say probable—that we will subsequently move to a form of economic organization that is much more nearly consistent with our best political and constitutional traditions than either the capitalism under which we now live or the form of corporatism we are likely to experience very soon.

# Discussion

QUESTION: Because there are many democratic-socialist states in the world today, in eastern Europe, Russia, Africa, and so on, I wonder whether you would tell us how they are sure that in their media all ranges of opinions, including radical expressions at both ends, are fully expressed; how they are sure of fair elections in which anybody has a reasonable right to run. Could you fill us in on how socialism solves these problems?

DR. LEKACHMAN: That is a highly relevant question. The world is full of communities, of states, that call themselves socialist, none of them satisfactory to me. Of course, some of the states to which you alluded are the so-called people's democracies of eastern Europe, which are not democracies and are not popularly supported. Many others are new creations, such as the African socialist states, with histories of tribal government or imperial subordination to French or English hegemony. I would not call Russia a socialist state, nor would a good many Marxists. Very few of the states that call themselves socialist have a democratic tradition.

In Czechoslovakia, during the few months when Dubcek was trying to introduce "socialism with a human face," there was an effort, among other things, to encourage diversity, intermediate structures. It was, of course, too brief and too brutally interrupted by Soviet repression for us to know how far it would have gone. Nor would I advance Yugoslavia as a model socialist state; but there have been some interesting experiments there, too, in diversity of economic form, including worker management, which suggest that even within a one-party state you find some encouraging strivings for economic diversity.

Now, the unanswered question is, What would socialism be like in a country with a very strong democratic tradition? We have no answer to that. I would not call the Swedish form of organization socialism. It is a form of social democracy. It goes further in state influence than we do, and it certainly does not seem to have damaged Swedish democratic institutions. We have no example of a community with as powerful an attachment, historically and currently, to democratic institutions as the United States, England, or Canada have, where explicit socialism has been introduced.

QUESTION: It is rather current among economists today to challenge our capability of continuing high rates of growth into or through the next ten years or so. However, I wonder if this is not overly pessimistic. I think that economists, by and large, have in mind the value of marketable goods and services when they talk about the growth rate decreasing or maintaining its recent low level. If we were to include nonmarket goods—things that enhance the so-called quality of life, such as cleaner environment, more meaningful work, et cetera—would we still have a slowdown in growth?

Second, there seems to be an assumption that if the pie stops growing so rapidly, the contenders for pieces of the pie are going to become more angry and assertive in their claims. Some analysis has suggested that we normally have social strife when the pie is increasing—that is, when expectations are increasing in consequence of actual increases of standards of living—but that people are quieter in their claims for pieces of the pie when we are in a stagnant phase.

DR. LEKACHMAN: On the first point, I am in considerable sympathy with you. The way statisticians measure national income is almost idiotic. If the sale of cigarettes goes up, so will gross national product. If the medical costs of treating lung cancer, emphysema, stroke, and coronary occlusions also go up, the gross national product will increase for that reason, as well.

It may be that the public is learning to value improved air quality, improved water quality, safer products, diminished hazards in the workplace, and the like—more reliable product quality, in general—and that this is an element in perceived standards of life that does not get measured. I hope that is true. If there is such a translation of public attitudes, growth is going to be redefined in the way you are suggesting, and it is a sensible way. I think there is a great deal of market pressure against so redefining it, however, because the natural impetus of merchandisers is not to sell things on which they do not make a profit, and air quality is not yet patentable by a major corporation.

As to your second point, the history is mixed. It is true that during the eight-year reign of Eisenhower the Good, there was less social turmoil and less general commotion in a time of rather slow growth than there was between 1961 and 1968, when expectations were rising. It is conceivable, as you suggest, that if real income falls in the next decade, we will all adjust to smaller and fewer cars, shorter and cheaper vacations, a smaller supply of hardware and consumer goods—in general, a thriftier use of energy and resources. I don't know. There is more adaptability among human beings and institutions than people like me sometimes credit them with. But I think it is unlikely.

QUESTION: I wonder whether you aren't a bit too optimistic about the future role of the state and the political maturation that will take place in the democratic process. I am very sympathetic to your wanting to encourage diversity, plurality of viewpoints; but could not that be done, or ought not that to be done, with the government becoming somewhat stronger and more assertive in drawing the lines of what the public good is, without necessarily taking over? Could we not get government funding for a plurality of school systems, for instance, without the government having to own education? This would mean, in one sense, less socialism or less state control than we now have, but a greater promotion of public diversity. It would require a different concept of the state, it seems to me, and of government; and I wonder if that can come out of our American tradition, which is rather individualistic.

DR. LEKACHMAN: Let me start in reverse order. What you have just described is, I think, exemplified by the voucher movement. The notion of school vouchers started on the right with Milton Friedman, but it was picked up by people like Christopher Jencks on the democratic left in a somewhat different form. The school voucher would, in effect, give a parent a claim on education for a child of school age in any approved school—public, private, religiously oriented, whatever. Presumably, there would be some minimum state licensing, so that the state would not be supporting a program oriented around snake charming or something of the sort.

Interestingly, the latest version of Senator Kennedy's health program incorporates, as a central feature, what amounts to a medical voucher. Each client would be given a health card, which could then be turned in for comprehensive treatment at one of four varieties of medical installation: one, an independent group of physicians and other health suppliers; another administered by the health insurers; and two other forms of administration—a diversity of health services. There is something to be said for that.

I would find what you have said not necessarily an alternative to what I have described as a desirable diversity of forms of ownership and operation in the private economy, but a supplement to it, for this

47

reason: at the very best, a great deal of economic activity, given the state of technology, is going to take place in large units. Those are the units that must be either explicitly owned by government and social interests or regulated in the public interest by government.

For example, take the current argument about a windfall profits tax on the oil companies. There is a simple way to handle that, with a little social imagination. The oil companies' argument against the windfall tax is essentially this: Exploring for new energy sources is expensive and risky, requiring large capital sums; tax them away, and you will get less new energy than without the tax. For various reasons, I am unpersuaded by that argument. But suppose one were persuaded, and nevertheless were disturbed by the fact that the profits the oil companies stand to earn are going to be a series of windfalls not related to their own efficiency, but simply to the fact that OPEC is, for the present, able to set the world price of energy. Why not allow the oil companies the extra resources these windfalls will generate, but make them issue new voting stock in the name of the public, held by the Treasury, in the amount of the extra profits? They would be permitted to keep this stock in the absence of a windfall tax; in the presence of a windfall tax, it would be removed from their discretion. Adequate resources thus would be available to the oil companies, but they would not get the capital free, as the absence of a windfall tax would enable them to do. The public would share in the gains from the use of the capital, related to the size of the capital provided—capital essentially generated by OPEC.

Once we open our minds to this sort of thing, once the political possibilities become more real, there is going to be an endless array of possible modes of operation, ownership, sharing of streams of revenue and the like that we cannot even imagine now.

# Is There a Moral Basis for Capitalism?

*Paul Johnson*

It takes nerve these days to suggest there can be a moral basis for capitalism, let alone to argue that capitalism provides, on the whole, the best economic structure for man's moral fulfillment. No day passes without a prominent clergyman's denouncing the gross immorality of some large capitalist concern; and in most schools children are encouraged to hold their noses when such notions as "profit" and "private enterprise" are discussed.

Such attitudes, it seems to me, are confused. They are based on a lack of understanding of the relationship between man's moral development and the way he organizes his society. We can and do achieve moral maturity under any kind of economic and social system, including those we find morally repugnant. Indeed, history suggests that societies specifically contrived to promote morality rarely succeed. Such utopias tend to become theocracies, and theocracies—whether the temple-states of antiquity, Calvin's Geneva, or the Ayatollah's Iran—traffic in a spiritual intolerance that does violence to mind and to body. The core of man's moral condition is the free will he is bidden to exercise. Hence the question we should begin by asking is: What social system is most conducive to developing the informed conscience that enables man's free will to make the right choices?

## The Emergence of Individuality

The first thing to note is that the articulated concept of the individual conscience, though always present in our nature, took a very long time to evolve. The earliest recorded societies did not recognize that every human being has a unique personality, endowed with self-consciousness and a free will. In the ancient Egypt of the Old Kingdom, in the first half of the third millennium B.C., religious and political doctrine revolved around the assumption that only the pharaoh was a complete personality. His life and fate embraced those of all his subjects. They engaged in the infinite labor of building his tomb pyramid not from com-

49

pulsion but almost certainly with enthusiasm, because they believed that their salvation was subsumed in his: if his funeral and tomb arrangements were satisfactory, they would be carried into eternal life along with him.

Only very gradually did the ancient Egyptians "democratize" their idea of a Last Judgment, in which each human being was weighed separately in the scales of eternal justice. The great American Egyptologist, Professor James Breasted, has called this discovery "the dawn of conscience." It was an important human discovery as well as a religious one, for it implied that every individual was responsible for his or her actions and therefore, in a moral sense, free. This implication was first properly understood by the Jews, who probably derived the idea from the Egyptians. As the earliest parts of the Bible indicate, the Jews, like other primitive societies, had a strong belief in collective virtue and crime, and in collective rewards and punishments. These beliefs were very persistent, and the Jews were still trying to shake them off long after they became rigorous monotheists. Only in the two or three centuries before the birth of Christ were they really beginning to work out their theory of the immortal soul and the Last Judgment. At roughly the same time, the Stoic philosophers in the Greek world were developing the idea of the individual conscience, a necessary adjunct to the concept of free will. Jesus Christ and his great interpreter St. Paul were the inheritors of this new collection of thoughts about the human individual. The New Testament, which outlines their philosophy, is essentially libertarian and individualistic, since it asserts that the unique personality of each individual, as reflected in his moral choices, is infinitely more important than anything else about him—class, color, status, sex, or nationality.

The essence of Judaeo-Christian teaching—leaving out its conflicting notions of the actual mechanism of salvation—is that every man or woman, by the mere fact of his or her humanity, is a party to what I call the Divine Contract. The Divine Contract comes into operation at the age of understanding and terminates with earthly death, at which point judgment is given as to whether its terms have been fulfilled—and the inevitable consequences follow. The essence of the Divine Contract is that it is an individual bargain between God and man. There is nothing collective about it. Each man and woman determines the fate of his or her soul, and the terms of each contract are identical. Judaeo-Christianity, therefore, is based on absolute individuality and on total spiritual equality. In the Divine Contract, all are equal before the law, and each is wholly responsible for his or her actions.

In Christianity in particular, this ascendancy of the individual was reinforced by the Greek concepts that underlay Pauline theology. The tragedy, however, is that Christianity became the official religion of the Roman empire only after the classical spirit of the Greco Roman world had spent itself, and only after the acknowledgment of the individual had been submerged beneath an Oriental despotism. Christianity was married to and appropriated by the late empire, which was in all essentials a corporate state. Not only did it possess legally enforced class distinctions, but it organized its subjects by their trades and occupations, which they were compelled to follow by law and to which their descendants were likewise bound. The corporation was all; the individual was nothing. Such rights as a man had, he acquired by virtue of his class and trade, not by his existence or by his merits as an individual human being.

The Dark Ages and the Middle Ages thus were dominated by a collectivist philosophy. Christianity gave men and women moral individuality, but society took it away on the material plane. People went through life as members of sharply differentiated categories; they spoke and dressed as such, and they were judged as such in the courts. It was very difficult to change class, occupation, or even place of residence. People were locked into a system—for life; indeed, they were seen and saw themselves as mere living components of a collective social body. The image of society as a body or *corpus*, rather than a collection of individuals, each complete in himself or herself, dominated the thinking of the premodern world.

The concept is illuminated by the story of de Montfort's taking a heretic city during the Albigensian Crusade. Turning to his spiritual adviser, a Cistercian abbot, de Montfort asked him how his soldiers, who had orders to slaughter the heretics and spare the rest, would be able to tell them apart. "Oh, kill them all," replied the abbot. "God will know His own." Only God had the capacity to recognize the individual. Spiritually, the individual was paramount; in earthly terms he was buried in collectivity.

### The Rule of Law and the Freehold

Yet Christianity, with its stress on the individual, did carry with it the notion of inalienable rights, slowly though it matured. In western Europe, missionary Christian bishops collected, purified, codified, Latinized, and set down in writing the laws of the barbarians, thereby investing them with spiritual authority and sanction. By its work on these law codes, Christianity implanted the concept of the rule of law—a rule which, for the church's own protection, could be invoked even against the state. The Christian church needed a law that was even stronger than the state, and it got it. Of course, the church was thinking in terms of its own corporate rights, but the notion of the rule of law was inevitably extended to cover and underpin the rights of the individual.

By a similar process, the idea of freehold property was established. The freehold was unknown to barbarian Europe; indeed, it was only imperfectly developed in imperial Rome and Byzantium. The church needed it for the security of its own properties and wrote it into the law codes it processed—wrote it, indeed, so indelibly that the free-hold survived and defied the superimposed forms of feudalism. The in-strument of the land deed or charter, giving absolute possession of land to a private individual or private corporation, is one of the great inven-tions of human history. Taken in conjunction with the notion of the rule of law, it is economically and politically a very important one. For once an individual can own land absolutely, without social or economic quali-fication, and once his right in that land is protected—even against the state—by the rule of law, he has true *security of property*. Once security of property is a fact, the propensity to save—which, as Keynes noted, is exceedingly powerful in man—is enormously enhanced. Not only is it enhanced; it is translated into the propensity to invest.

We see, then, that the dawn of conscience—the idea that the indi-vidual has an absolute freehold in his own soul—foreshadows the dawn of capitalism. Capitalism is based on the system of possessive individual-ism, in which individual men and women, as well as tribes, crowns, states, and other political and social corporations, own absolute freeholds in property and manage and dispose of them freely. Likewise, the notion of equality before the judgment of God foreshadows the notion of individual equality before the law of man. These concepts are very much interdependent. Individual freehold is impossible without the rule of law, with its necessary implication of equality before the law, and its guarantee that the law will uphold individual property rights even against state prerogative. England and the Netherlands were the first states in which such rights were effectively established. Legal certitude, in turn, is the precondition of capitalist enterprise. As Friedrich von Hayek puts it in *The Constitution of Liberty*, "There is probably no single factor which has contributed more to the prosperity of the West than the relative certainty of the law which has prevailed there."

The establishment of the individual freehold is not the only way Christianity made capitalism possible. Like the Judaism on which it is based, Christianity is a historical religion, generated by a definite his-torical event and proceeding towards a definite historical goal. Its thrust is thus linear, not cyclical. Time is of the essence in its machinery, and it insists on preparedness; its constant exhortation is, "We know not the day nor the hour." Its morality stresses the principle of saving, of deferring worldly pleasures for the sake of future felicity, and it proceeds by a regular accounting of vice and virtue toward a final audit and celestial dividends. It is no accident that the monks of the West were the first to produce a system of regular working hours, governed by exact computation of time and the tolling of a bell. Indeed, most historians now agree that the roots of capitalism lay in the ethics of Christianity long before the advent of Calvin and his "salvation panic": the Merchant of Prato was inscribing "For the Greater Honour and Glory of God" at the head of each page of his accounts long before Protestantism was born. But, in my view, the notion of freehold possession was by far the most important Christian contribution to the emergence of capitalism.

Indeed, I would go so far as to argue that without individual freehold, a capitalist system cannot develop. Once you have individual freehold, however, with its concomitant developments of the rule of law and equality before the law, the development of some form of capitalism is not only likely but virtually inevitable. The connection between Christian morality and capitalism thus centers essentially on the role and importance of the individual.

### Historical Evolution of Capitalism

We can see this connection being worked out in history. In the later Middle Ages, especially in the towns, the Christian notion of the individual conscience gradually broke through the corporatist carapace of society. As the towns grew in size and importance, as people changed their class and occupation—and fortune—more rapidly, a new spirit of individualism was bred: people were increasingly judged and rewarded on their merits and efforts, not on their status. In art the true portrait emerges, and not just of the rich patron: the crowd scenes of a Hieronymus Bosch or a Breughel show a sharpening focus even on the faces of humble folk. In the sixteenth century we get the first true biographies and the first plays based on the development of character. Individuals leap out at us from the pages of the historical records. The moralistic writings of Erasmus for the first time link the Christian notion of individual conscience to the spirit of individual enterprise.

The new individualism inevitably threatened the social structure, based as that was on class privilege and the absolute right of status. In the English civil wars of the 1640s, the House of Commons, which represented the institutionalized individualism of property, overthrew the concept of the king as head of the body corporate. It was the end in

England of the medieval corporate state. But, in one sense, individualism threatened the political rights of property also. In the political debates— of which we have a marvelous verbatim record—between Cromwell and some of his generals, officers, and men in Putney Church in 1647, that was the point at issue. Did a man have political rights only by virtue of his property, his stake in the country, as Cromwell and his supporters maintained? Or did he have rights by virtue of his personality, the fact that he was a free, adult human being, a simple individual, as the radicals demanded?

At the time, the argument went in favor of property; but in the long run, the logical thrust of Christian moral individualism was irresistible. The civil wars, by dissolving the old corporate state, began a process of economic emancipation of the individual, which was just as important as giving him political rights. In the eighteenth century, as property triumphed over hereditary class and status, new ways of evaluating property and protecting it by law began to emerge. The law of industrial patents, which was now developed in England, made it possible for the first time for a man to obtain a true commercial reward for his inventive skill and investment in research—a notable and historic victory for the gifted individual. By introducing a new and dynamic element into the economy, the patent law was one of the principal contributing factors to the Industrial Revolution, which began to transform the world from the 1760s onwards.

Another important extension of the notion of individual property was the breakdown of the Laws of Settlement, which sought to control the free movement of labor and were among the last relics of the old corporatism. Adam Smith, in his great treatise on how wealth is created, *The Wealth of Nations*, was quick to grasp that this represented the economic emancipation of the ordinary working man. It allowed him to escape from the grip of a status society to one in which rewards depended on a freely negotiated contract, enabling him to realize the value of the only freehold property he possessed—his energy and skill. Throughout history, argued Smith, governments, lords, and guilds had sought to prevent ordinary poor people from seeking work in the best market. Yet, he added, "the property which every man has in his own labour, as it is the foundation of all other property, so it is the most sacred and inviolable. To hinder [a poor man] from employing his strength and dexterity in what manner he thinks proper without injury to his neighbour is a plain violation of this most sacred property."[1] As Smith grasped, the notion of the individual freehold embodied a political

---

[1] Adam Smith, *The Wealth of Nations*, bk. 1, chap. 10.

as well as an economic freedom: at bottom, political and economic freedom are inseparable. The political freedom to vote is largely meaningless without the economic freedom to work where you please. Once a man is free to make contracts for his own labor, he will soon begin to demand the right to make contracts with his political masters, too. It is no accident that the Industrial Revolution and the creation of the capitalist economy, based on freely contracted labor, were followed by the development of democracy in the West.

Hence it is a profound mistake, in my view, to see the rise of what Blake called the "dark Satanic mills" as the enslavement of man. The factory system, however harsh it may have been, proved to be the road to freedom for millions of agricultural workers. It offered them an escape from rural poverty, which was deeper and more degrading than anything experienced in the cities; in addition, it allowed them to move from status to contract, from a stationary place in a static society, with tied cottages and semiconscript labor, to a mobile place in a dynamic society. Long before he could vote through the ballot, the common man voted for industrial capitalism with his feet, by tramping from the countryside to the towns. This shift took place first in Britain, then throughout Europe. Tens of millions of European peasants moved across the Atlantic in pursuit of that same freedom, from semifeudal estates and small holdings in Russia, Poland, Germany, Austro-Hungary, Italy, Ireland, and Scandinavia to the factories and workshops of New York, Chicago, Pittsburgh, Cleveland, and Detroit. It was the first time in history that enormous numbers of ordinary, humble people were given the chance to exercise a choice about their livelihood and destiny—to move not as members of a tribe or as conscript soldiers, but as free individuals, selling their labor in the open market.

One might say that capitalism, far from dehumanizing man, allowed him at last to assume the full individuality Christianity had always accorded him as the possessor of a distinctive moral conscience and an immortal soul. Just as the notion of freehold property was implicit in the notion of the free will, so the wage contract was implicit in the Divine Contract. The advent of capitalism both reflected and advanced the emergence of the individual human personality. In the West, we are so used to being brought up and treated as individuals that we tend to take the concept of individuality for granted. Yet it is a comparatively modern idea—no older than capitalism, scarcely older than the Industrial Revolution. For most of history, the great majority of ordinary people have been treated by the authorities as if they were a congealed mass, without differentiating personalities, let alone individual rights and aspirations. For democracy to evolve, it was first necessary for society to recognize that it was composed of millions of individuals, not undifferentiated groups classified merely by occupation and social status.

It was with the rise of capitalism that ordinary people acquired names. Not, of course, the names they were given at birth, and by which they were known among the narrow circle of their family and neighbors, but hereditary family names which, in combination with their given names, provided them with specific identities. Family names were originally dynastic, reserved for kings. Only very slowly did they spread down to the aristocracy and then to the gentry. Most of those peasants who voted for industrial capitalism with their feet acquired names in the process, along with their residence and immigration papers. As recently as the First World War, soldiers in the Russian army below the rank of senior noncommissioned officer did not have names on the official record, only numbers. Only in the nineteenth century did most of the governments of Europe pass laws encouraging or compelling the adoption of family names. Denmark did not pass such a law until 1904; the Turks, until 1935.

## The Political Implications of Capitalism

More than to any other force, then, we owe the acknowledgment of our individuality to capitalism. The capitalist notion of what has been aptly called *possessive individualism* is rooted in turn in the Judaeo-Christian doctrine of conscience and free will. Free will implies choice; the moral function of society, its capacity to serve the moral needs of the individuals who compose it, is best executed when it facilitates the process of choice, when it permits consciences to inform themselves and so offers the individual the greatest possible opportunity to fulfill his or her part in the Divine Contract. That, essentially, is the moral basis of capitalism. As a purely economic device, capitalism is morally neutral. But based as it is on the legal rights of individual freehold, capitalism creates a multiplicity of power centers which rival the state. Hence, it is a matter of historical observation that capitalism tends to promote—and in my contention, *must* promote—liberal-democratic political systems. Such systems are not morally neutral; they are morally desirable, for they offer the individual the element of choice through which his or her free will matures.

By contrast, socialist societies, pursuing utopia and a positive moral framework, inevitably restrict this choice. I no longer believe, as I once did, that political freedom can be preserved where economic freedom is eliminated. As I have already argued, the existence of the right to own property makes capitalism inevitable; the state or party desiring to eliminate capitalism, then, must first destroy the property freehold. Without private ownership, there can be no effective and durable rival centers of power to keep the state in check. Monopoly must follow; and where there is monopoly, there is no individual choice. And without choice, the free will must live in an atrophied state, in hidden darkness and danger, as it did under the most hideous tyrannies of the past. Monopoly is the enemy of morals—and so, therefore, must be the collectivist societies that promote it. Ironically, the more such collectivisms proclaim or even acquire popular endorsement, the more dangerous they are. Lord Acton rightly observed, "It is bad to be oppressed by a minority, but it is worse to be oppressed by a majority. For there is a reserve of latent power in the masses which, if it is called into play, the minority can seldom resist. From the absolute will of the entire people there is no appeal, no redemption, no refuge but treason."

It seems to me that the authors of the mature Judaeo-Christian system of morals—the greatest such system the world has ever seen— were right to anchor it in the *individual* conscience. There is no intrinsic morality in majority decisions: far from it. All great moralists have rightly drawn attention to the horrors of the mass or herd in action— symbolized in the New Testament, for instance, in the image of the Gadarene swine. Sir Thomas Browne, in *Religio Medici*, warns us against "that great enemy of reason, virtue and religion, the multitude; that numerous piece of monstrosity which, taken asunder, seem men, and the reasonable creatures of God but, confused together, make but one Great Beast and a monstrosity more prodigious than Hydra."[2]

A true moral system must contain a self-correcting mechanism; for Christianity, it is the conscience of the individual. The strength of the system lies in its just estimate of man as a fallible creature with immortal longings. Its outstanding moral merit is to invest the individual with a conscience and bid him follow it. This particular form of liberation is what St. Paul meant by the freedom men find in Christ. For conscience is the enemy of tyranny and the compulsory society; and it is the Christian conscience which has destroyed the institutional tyrannies Christianity itself has created—the self-correcting mechanism at work. The notions of political and economic freedom both spring from the workings of the Christian conscience as a historical force.

In this process, I have argued, the decisive device is the notion of individual freehold. And individual freehold performs for capitalism the same role as the individual conscience in a Christian moral system— it is the self-correcting mechanism. So long as people can by law hold

---

[2] Sir Thomas Browne, *Religio Medici*, pt. 1.

property in the teeth of the state, or of any other large corporation, they will successfully endeavor to get such property and to hold it. Such people will be numerous, and the tendency will be for their number to grow. Where a multiplicity of citizens hold freehold property, political power must be divided and shared. And where power must be shared, and *is* shared, there can be no economic monopoly, either. Any inherent tendency in capitalism toward monopoly—and I am not so sure that there is such a tendency, despite Marx's arguments—is balanced by the undoubted tendency of capitalism to promote democratic liberalism and thus parliamentary checks on monopoly power. This is the self-correcting mechanism at work again.

I am not speaking of theoretical argument, but of demonstrable practice—of history. Take as examples the United States and Great Britain. Over the past 200 years, during which both nations have embraced capitalism, their societies have successfully reformed themselves from within—not by revolution and violence, but by debate and argument, by law and statute. When before in history has this been possible? That the first capitalist societies were rugged and ruthless, even cruel, I will not dispute. But the value of an institution lies not in its clumsy origins but in what it proves capable of accomplishing. The ability of capitalism to reform and improve itself is, I believe, almost infinite. This is logically so; for by its very nature capitalism is not a monolith but the sum of innumerable freeholds, vested in innumerable free minds—minds which reflect the infinity of human pressures, desires, and inventiveness. It is truly protean.

Indeed, capitalism's resilience, which has a moral quality because it is rooted in the free interplay of human consciences, is in marked and significant contrast to the rigidity of collectivist systems. They can be changed, too—but only by force. They respond—but only to revolution. They lack the self-correcting mechanism because they do not, and by their nature cannot, accord rights to the individual conscience. Such systems therefore lack a moral basis—not as ideas, perhaps, but as realities. Given that lack, they are doomed to revert to the chaos from which they sprang. Democratic capitalism, on the other hand, is destined to survive. Because it is protean, its more distant manifestations probably would astonish us, were we alive to witness them. But I suspect that it will always in some way retain the notion of the individual freehold; for it is this, the physical manifestation of the individual conscience, that gives democratic capitalism its economic and political strength and, not least, its moral legitimacy.

# Discussion

QUESTION: I would like to raise a question about your reading of St. Paul. If I understood you, your argument was that Paul articulates the notion of individual conscience and moral choice. I think a case could be made that Paul denies the possibility of moral choice, in the sense of free conscience that you talked about. He says in Romans that knowing what the good is, he cannot do it, even though he chooses to do it; so that his choice, even if he can make it, is irrelevant. And he does speak of freedom, but it seems to me that the freedom that he talks about is not the freedom to do what you will, but the freedom from sin, which is effected through baptism—as the believer is unified with the risen Lord, he is created as a new person, and therefore is not inclined to sin. It is difficult for me, from that reading, to see how one gets the notion of individual moral choice and individual conscience from Paul.

MR. JOHNSON: You have touched on very deep waters here. Paul's Epistle to the Romans, in my view, is not only the most important of all the Christian documents, but it is one of the most difficult to understand. St. Paul married a lot of the elements of Greek philosophy—because he was a member of the Diaspora, and he knew them—to some of the more modern elements of Judaism, as he got them from Jesus Christ; and he performed a very important operation there on behalf of the individual conscience. How you interpret the Epistle to the Romans is a matter, to some extent, of your own individual view of it. I take it as a great declaration of freedom—a freedom from the law, that is—though, of course, it can be read as a support of the powers that be, too.

But I think it is notable that Paul's Epistle to the Romans has come like a clap of thunder to one after another of the great conscience-ridden spirits of the church. St. Augustine—all of St. Augustine's really advanced thinking is based on Romans; Luther—who was reading Romans when he got it, just as I say, like a clap of thunder; or Karl Barth; or John Wesley. Time and time again, that epistle has taught great individual Christians to put their consciences first. That is why I say: even though it may be obscure, it has been read by a number of very powerful intellects in precisely the sense I have tried to give it today.

QUESTION: It seems to me that the relationship between capitalism and Christianity is a little bit more ambiguous, or uneasy, than you suggest. I agree that there is a lot to the connection between conscience and the capitalism of a liberal democracy; but I think of things like the Sermon on the Mount, or the First Letter to the Corinthians, or the Book of Acts, which don't strike me as emphasizing possessive individualism. And you hear Christian clergymen complain about the greedy acts of businessmen. There is a strong part of Christianity which, it seems to me, is very uneasy with the whole notion of possessive individualism, acquisitiveness, self-interest.

My other question is, when you emphasize the connection between Christianity and capitalism, how does one deal with the case of Japan?

MR. JOHNSON: One of the reasons why Christianity is the first great universalist religion—to my mind, the great universalist religion—is that it contains a whole series of different matrixes, molds as it were, for different types of human conscience. It is a religion in which both the activist and the contemplative can find inspiration, in which both the militant and the pacifist feel at home. Each of those people can find, in the words of Christ, text that inspires, phrases that are memorable and that become the whole heart of his philosophy. Somehow these phrases and these types of individuals live together, because the genius and, indeed, the divinity of Christ was that he saw mankind as consisting of groups of enormously disparate individuals, each group of which, each individual of which, had something to contribute to the rule of righteousness. Jesus gave what from one point of view might look like an inchoate and contradictory series of systems of guidance, which it is; but it can also be looked at as a series of perfectly compatible and internally consistent systems. That is how I choose to see it.

Therefore, my answer to your question is, I quite agree with you; there are lots of aspects of Christ's teaching that seem to work against capitalism. I was merely trying to point out that it is possible to construct a line of logical arguments showing that there is an ethical and moral basis for capitalism. I am not saying that is the only argument you can produce in Christianity; I am just saying it is a possible and tenable argument.

As for your point about Japan, I am not quite sure how it comes into this. Japan took fully formed capitalism from the West in the late nineteenth century. There was no independent development there of capitalism. But it is significant that you should raise the point of Japan, because the loss of Japan is the great tragedy of Christianity. I believe St. Francis Xavier and others of his Jesuit contemporaries were right in saying that the Japanese were the perfect Christian people—that somehow God had put in this obscure part of the world, which hadn't been known to exist fifty years before, a marvelously virile, enormously courageous, brilliantly inventive, gifted people, who were ripe for Christianity. And the way Christianity, though originally very well established there, quarrelled within itself and attracted the hatred of the state, and was then virtually stamped out for hundreds of years, is, as I say, the central tragedy of Christianity.

QUESTION: I have two questions. One deals with the development of capitalism in the eighteenth and nineteenth centuries in England. You can, of course, tell the tale of free contracts somewhat differently. You can tell it as the separation from their property of large numbers of at least semiindependent cultivators who held, if not freeholds, at least copyholds, and traditional rights in the land. That is one problem I welcome a comment on.

There is a second, more contemporary, problem that distresses me: capitalism has proved capable both of reversion to and of coexistence with very unpleasant authoritarian forms. It reverted most notably in Nazi Germany, which had a very high state of development and some advanced democratic institutions, to one of the most barbaric forms of authoritarianism in human history. In our own day, capitalism has coexisted with very unpleasant regimes in Chile, Indonesia, South Korea —a long list of societies that are not model democracies, by any stretch. So I wonder whether your optimistic case for the association of capitalism and human freedom is not really just two special cases, the United States and Great Britain.

MR. JOHNSON: Well, obviously those two cases are foremost in my mind, and I think, as a matter of fact, that they are actually the two most important cases. But I was careful to point out—at least, I hope I was careful to point out—that I see capitalism as a development of the individual freehold, the individual freehold being linked to the notion of the rule of law, and the rule of law being paramount. I don't believe that capitalism can long survive if those two are destroyed. Now, Hitler destroyed the rule of law completely. I don't think people realize the extent to which Hitler governed without a constitution during those twelve years. In my view, capitalism could not long have survived that, because capitalism cannot survive without the rule of law and the notion of the individual freehold. You can call it what you like, but it is not capitalism, as I understand it. So I would say that where there is tyranny imposed on and alongside a capitalist system, either the self-correcting mechanism will work, as I have tried to show, or else capitalism will be destroyed.

QUESTION: I am interested in what I see as the dialectic between the universality of the rule of law and individual freedom. At times, we refer to the conscience as the individual conscience; and yet, as you just said, conscience really has to be related to something more universal. How do you solve the problem of how the freedom of the person is related to conscience? And if you use this as a self-correcting mechanism, do you mean that a society of individually responsible Christians, seeing the problems of child labor or something, could put freehold capitalism in a box? That is, by making laws that would reflect their consciences, could they bring about a common law with regard to all kinds of social and political matters that would keep a very strict boundary on capitalism? Would you still see that as responsible free capitalism?

MR. JOHNSON: Yes, because I would argue that capitalism is by its nature a self-reforming system. But you have touched on what to my mind is the central and the most difficult problem of moral theology. What is a conscience, how do you define conscience, and when is my conscience right whereas yours is wrong? The answer is that nobody has found a satisfactory solution to this. All one can say is that a conscience becomes morally operative, as it were, as and to the extent that the individual endeavors to inform himself of the truth. And truth is an endless pursuit.

QUESTION: I would like to pursue this a little bit. It seems to me that had John Locke been asked to give an apologetic history of Christianity, he couldn't have given a better account. And yet, it is important that he didn't see it as his task to do that. It seems to me that if you look at the founders of modern liberal democracy—Spinoza, Hobbes, Locke —you see that they have in common what I think has been well expressed as an antitheological bias. They took it, apparently, as part of their task to destroy the hold that biblical religion had over the minds of men. And it seems to me that the legitimizing in capitalism of self-interest and acquisitiveness must have something to do with the delegitimizing of certain biblical restrictions and constraints. What Hobbes and others managed to accomplish was the creation of something you might call "morally autonomous men," men not bound by any historic norms. That's not quite the same thing as conscience. Morally autonomous man, in a rational sense, is a man who will choose what is right according to what seems to him right. And he need not choose Christianity; he need not choose religion.

MR. JOHNSON: I appreciate the distinction between conscience and the morally autonomous person. I would not claim that this is a watertight argument; it is a very tentative one, and that is why I am glad to have points like that made.

QUESTION: It would seem an assumption of this seminar that there is a value in mediating structures: neighborhoods, families, churches, corporations, the sorts of things that traditionally would have given one status, in a way, above one's private individuality. And there is a claim going back at least to Marx that one of the features of capitalism —which I think he took to be a positive feature—is that it eroded some of those mediating structures. I had a sense that you, too, have a positive appreciation of that erosion, and I wonder if you could talk about what you see as the connection between capitalism as a moral phenomenon and those institutions or those structures, which may also be moral phenomena.

MR. JOHNSON: I think you can build up quite powerful arguments on both sides of that fence. You can say that there were a number of powerful corporations within the premodern world which capitalism necessarily destroyed. Or you can argue that capitalism broke up what was, although composed of a number of corporations, essentially a static, a monolithic society—that the sort of society we have in a reasonably free, liberal, democratic democracy is capable of producing infinitely more structures, and infinitely more different varieties of structures, than the old corporatist society possibly could do. And I think you see the perfect example of that in the United States of America. It is a capitalist society in which power is very widely diffused, in which there are enormous centers of activity wielding all kinds of influence—not just the giant corporations, but public opinion expressing itself through churches and universities and independent colleges and societies and organizations and cranks and militants of every conceivable type, who all have the possibility of influencing opinion. I would say that this is a society infinitely more varied, and infinitely fuller of potential, than the old corporatist society capitalism destroyed. I think that if one has to make the choice between those two, there wouldn't be any doubt whatever in my mind or, I would have thought, in the minds of most free people.

# A MORAL BASIS FOR CAPITALISM?

QUESTION: I would like to turn to that part of your remarks from which, like everybody else in the room, I've learned a great deal, in which you stressed the Industrial Revolution in the United States and the rise of corporate capitalism here. It seems to me that you somewhat overstated that argument, or at least as I heard it. You said that at the time when corporate capitalism was emerging in the United States, laborers voted with their feet to come to this country. The capitalists, allowing workers to sell their labor in the open market, allowed them full free will, so instead of being treated as a congealed mass—I hope I am not misquoting you—suddenly the population was composed of millions of individuals.

Henry Frick's foreman at the Homestead Steel Company said, in talking to Frick, "What we really want are Bohemians"—that's his term—"Italians, Slavs, and a sprinkling of Buckwheats. Let us stay far away from the Germans, the Irish, and the native-born Americans." He was looking, of course, for the cheapest labor force. It was Frick who brought in south Slav scab labor, as it was considered by those on the other side, on barges, protected by Pinkerton's. These people were not considered individuals, certainly, by the capitalists at the time. You pointed out that capitalism goes through periods that are clumsy and brutal; but certainly these workers were considered, in a certain sense, the indentured servants of the new capitalist class. They did vote with their feet for it, and their children and their children's children would live better under it, but not necessarily because they found some new individualism in the capitalist system.

They were victims of monopoly, you could argue, and you argue that capitalism in the democratic system reforms itself. But Roosevelt and Wilson and the other reformers I take it you were referring to, who tried to deal with monopoly, dealt with the workers imprecisely, if at all. Roosevelt turned away from feeling that you could do anything about monopolies, and Woodrow Wilson, in his embracing the man-on-the-make, was unconcerned about that mass of workers. And how many times have we heard about the attack on the monopoly since then?

So why is it that you stress so strongly this triumphant discovery of individualism at what must be one of the darkest moments in the whole history of the United States—and Great Britain, for that matter?

MR. JOHNSON: Well, I think my answer to your point is that you have a lot of villagers coming to America who don't have to work for Frick. They come from a village where they had to work for von Frick because he was the only employer. They go to a country where there are in-numerable employers, where there is freedom of movement and freedom of labor. And, of course, there are the Pinkerton men, and all these kinds of abuses. But then I put the question to you, Does this exist today? The answer is no, because it is a self-reforming system, because it leads to democracy, and democracy gets the reforms through.

I don't believe for one second that people have given up hope over monopolies. Any tendency toward real monopolies' being created in free-enterprise societies is fairly swiftly met with legislation. Certainly, if this were a conference of senior executives in American enterprises, I don't think you'd have any feeling that the monopolies had overcome the legislative safeguards; quite the contrary. And that would also be true of most European countries.

What I am trying to get across is that a capitalist system is something that was very crude in its origins, but it did contain this ability to reform itself from within, peacefully, by parliament and by statute. And I think that is its great merit.

QUESTION: You have a view expressed in the Pauline letters that Jesus Christ, when he approaches the Almighty with the saved, will also bring social institutions—the state and economic institutions, also redeemed. The concept developing there is that Paul had a notion not only of individual salvation, of freedom, but also of social redemption and fulfillment. Here we have an element of continuity with the Old Testament prophets, who insisted that salvation comes through community, and who pointed to the necessity for institutional reform and not merely individual integrity.

Let's take another approach. Roscoe Pound's book of fifty years ago, on the spirit of the common law, makes a great contrast between what Pound calls the puritan element of Western thought, with emphasis on the individual conscience, and what he calls the feudal element. He sees changes in constitutional law, changes in the court decisions—first in England, but, after the Civil War, in the United States—more and more recognizing, emphasizing, articulating the responsibility of the whole community. This feudal element, says he, has brought about a correction you can already see in court decisions, indicating the responsibility of individual conscience for the character of the whole society.

Third, as I understand it, in the American culture—I don't know about the British—the proportion of people living below the poverty line has not changed in the last three generations.

So the question is whether one must not read a distinction between types of individual conscience, one type stressing the integrity of the individual and its freedom to ask for change, and another type that sees the necessity for social consensus for the transformation of institutions, so that more people can be brought into the process of enjoying freedom. Capitalism, so far in the twentieth century, does not have a conspicuous record in this latter direction. But I don't want to stress that. I want to raise the question of a possible distinction between types of— and, shall we say, jurisdictions of—moral conscience of the individual.

MR. JOHNSON: I accept all those points, and particularly the first point about welfare, because even the earliest Jewish theologians drew this fundamental distinction between justice, which dealt with man's rights, and righteousness, which dealt with his duties, and agreed that there were collective duties. I could equally well have presented a paper this evening showing that the welfare state is rooted in Christianity, because in my view, in my historical reading, it undoubtedly is. There again the bridge was the Jewish Diaspora, where these welfare institutions were created in the first and second centuries B.C., and where these voluntary welfare services were taken over by the earliest Christians. Welfare and duties toward society have always had a central place in the Christian doctrine of the conscience and in Christian teaching. I don't think that that necessarily contradicts anything I said. It's part of the same argument, but it was not the argument I was trying to develop today.

As for the third point, about poverty not having changed, it may be true that the proportion of the population classified as poor has not changed, but the definition of poverty has. That, I think, is the important thing. There cannot be any society, the human being being the fallible creature he is, in which there will not be poor elements. But we can try to make sure that the poverty the poor suffer from is bearable poverty. And that is what, over the past three generations, we have been, on the whole, quite successful in doing. The reason we can do that is that capitalism is the most effective wealth-producing system the world has yet known, in terms of producing actual wealth in enormous quantities and, on the whole, distributing it not unfairly.

QUESTION: Hearing about Henry Frick and the pitched battle in the Monongahela made me think about Frederick Taylor's and Max Weber's early assessment of large corporations and the role of bureaucracy in the way they were organized. It strikes me as an irony, if we grant your point about individualism, that the bureaucratic organization used the model of the machine, with people as cogs in the machine, not only as an organizational principle but almost as a justification, because it was the most efficient way of creating wealth quickly and distributing it. I happen to think that those probably are the two best justifications of capitalism; but you could hardly say that individual freedom was enhanced within the corporation.

My second question is born out of our seminar this morning, where Michael Novak noted, persuasively, that the weakest part of Christian theology has been the theology of economics. When you compare it to the theology of art, the theology of politics, the theology of marriage and family, et cetera, there has been virtually no systematic theology of economics—and, surely, no ringing endorsement of capitalism. I wonder how you would interpret that, given your own ringing moral Christian endorsement of it.

MR. JOHNSON: On the last point, surely what matters about an argument is not its uniqueness but its strength. Is it a good argument or not? On the point of the church not having a theology of economics, I think that is true. But the trouble with economics is that nobody has got any good theories of economics, least of all the economists.

The first point you raised, which is the important one in my view, is, of course, perfectly true. As I said, the essence of my argument is that the capitalist system, regarded technically as an economic system, is morally neutral. Morally neutral means it can be used to battle evil, and it can be used for evil; you do get the analogy of the machine and people being treated as cogs in the machine. But at the same time, you get the motion picture industry being created in Hollywood, producing a film called *Modern Times*, in which the analogy of the machine is used to lambaste capitalism. And you get a great publishing industry growing up in New York, producing a book like *The Grapes of Wrath*, which becomes a best seller, again lashing out at the bad sides of capitalism. There is a self-correcting mechanism at work, and I would say that, by and large, and making allowances for the frailty of men, that self-correcting mechanism does work, on the whole. Our holding this seminar is part of the self-correcting mechanism.

QUESTION: You have emphasized that capitalism is by nature a self-reforming system. I see a certain tension between that and your emphasis upon individualism. What you are really relying on is a system that makes it possible for reform to occur on the initiative of people who want reform to occur. The system doesn't do it as a system; it is the people who do it. But that shifts the game, in part at least, out of the economic sphere and into the political sphere. Would you want to settle the question of the extent to which government ought to be involved in the economy, or is that simply a matter of historical judgment at particular times and places?

MR. JOHNSON: Essentially the latter. I would think it was quite impossible to lay down any law about that. What one can say is that the role of the state becomes damaging to the whole concept I am trying to outline this evening, if it undermines the concept of the individual freehold. At that point, I think one has to resist the encroachments of the state absolutely, tooth and nail.

# The Church as Mediating Institution: Theological and Philosophical Perspective

*J. Philip Wogaman*

The church is sometimes considered to be a rather stodgy institution. It is generally taken for granted in American society—something everybody, or at least many, many people, participate in, but nobody talks much about. Yet it is fraught with all sorts of implications for social policy and the general shape of society. At a time when many categories of leadership in this country have fallen in public esteem, a beginning observation on the church might be that the most recent Gallup poll shows clergy persons at about the top of the list in the respect and trust of the American public.

But our present concern is with the church in its capacity as a mediating institution. The role of mediating institutions in a democracy is not altogether a new theme, of course. It has antecedents in political thought going back at least to Aristotle's criticisms of Plato's *Republic*, and it has reappeared wherever thinkers have criticized unrestrained expressions of idealism in political thought—in Edmund Burke's critique of the French Revolution; in the doctrine of subsidiarity in Roman Catholic encyclicals (which in some respects was also a reaction against the nineteenth-century climate growing out of the French Revolution and Marxism); in the Protestant doctrine of "orders" developed by Emil Brunner; and in various other places. Despite this history, though, the present state of national and world politics makes our topic peculiarly ripe for new reflection.

I am generally in agreement with Peter Berger's view of the importance of mediating institutions both empirically and normatively. I am fully persuaded that intimate association is necessary to authentic human existence, and that without institutions fostering such association, political democracy would not be long sustainable. This said, we must acknowledge that the concept of mediating institutions is more complex than it might appear at first. Such institutions cannot stand alone. Indeed, the very term "mediating" suggests the importance of linkages. That is, these institutions are mediate between what and what? How do they link people with one another and with other kinds of institutions?

I would like to begin by considering three important linkages involving mediating institutions, without which I think one can never understand the situation of the church.

## Linking People with One Another

The first of these three linkages is the primary one of people with one another. Without some nurturing association with other individuals, we could not exist as real human beings. At this most intimate level of society, where people interact face to face, the individual and social aspects of human nature are most fully joined. I want to stress this point, because it is commonplace in twentieth-century ideological debate for people to neglect either the individual or the social aspect of human life.

What we might call the individualistic heresy is illustrated in the writings of Ayn Rand. It appears also, to a lesser degree, in the philosophical writings of such economists as Milton Friedman, Ludwig von Mises, and George Stigler, who once wrote, "Our very concept of the humane society is one in which individual man is permitted and incited to make the utmost of himself."[1] Such individualism—heavily anticipated, of course, by John Locke—values society as the sphere of interactions for mutual benefit. We exist in society as traders; we do things for others in exchange for what they do for us, and we all benefit thereby. Now, this is a dimension of the truth, but it is only a half-truth, because it neglects the extent to which we *are* one another.

The opposite of this view we might call the collectivist heresy. It appears in various intellectual outgrowths of Rousseau's influence, including a good bit of Hegelianism, a good deal of Marxism, and ultimately, of course, fascism. One remembers the words of Mussolini: "The fascist conception of life stresses the importance of the State and accepts the individual only insofar as his interests coincide with those of the State, which stands for the conscience and the universal will of man as a historic entity."[2] That extreme view would seem to be very far removed from the spirit of, say, Cuban or Chinese Marxism; and yet wherever the claim is made that we are making a new socialist man, there are undertones of this kind of collective spirit, which need to be watched rather carefully.

Is human nature simply a function of the social collectivity? Again,

---

[1] George Stigler, "The Proper Goals of Economic Policy," *Journal of Business*, July 1958, p. 714.

[2] Benito Mussolini, *The Political and Social Doctrine of Fascism*, trans. Jane Soames (London: Hogarth Press, 1933).

there is a profound half-truth here. Aristotle was right: Man is, by nature, a social or political animal. There is a sense in which we exist only as we belong to society. The very forms of our thought are cultural, that is, socially derived. Even our personal identity, our sense of who we are, is based substantially on our perceptions of how we are perceived by those whose response matters most to us.

But the individual and social aspects of human nature are such that we cannot have one without the other. It seems to me a good deal of ideological confusion would be avoided if we recognized this polarity, that human nature is both essentially social and essentially individual. It is like the playground game of seesaw: you need a kid on each end of the board. Pure individualism flies in the face of all human experience; an unqualified collectivism lacks the generating personal creativities. Neither has ever existed in pure form, nor could they.

Furthermore, both individualism and collectivism ultimately reduce humanity to abstraction. As Karl Barth observed, we need to see "the man in humanity and the humanity in man."[3] This is really my main point: the fully personal and the fully social character of human life cannot be realized abstractly. They must find realization where we can know others and be known by them as we engage in social interactions. That can best occur on the level of the mediating institution. Thus, the first form of mediation these institutions can provide is links between and among persons.

### Linking People and Power Centers

The second important linkage in which mediating institutions can function is the one connecting people with the focal points of social power. A great temptation when we talk about mediating institutions is to overlook those centers of power, concentrating our sentimental attention instead on the humanizing functions of smaller-scale associations. The problem with that is that humanizing also requires a sense of participation in ultimate social power. When people feel alienated from social power, they may find some spiritual relief in group life, but it is the kind of relief Marx was referring to when he called religion the opiate of the people. Links between or among individuals cannot assuage the alienation that comes from being subjected to power one cannot affect. One may have a very fine neighborhood government or local community organization, but one feels alienated nevertheless when that government or organization is continually overwhelmed by outside powers over

---

[3] Karl Barth, *Christ and Adam*, trans. T. A. Small (New York: Harper and Brothers, 1956), p. 91.

which it has no control, such as city hall, the feds, large corporations, or other large collectivities. The local mediating institution takes on something of the character of a game—an interesting game to play, but one that lacks authenticity because it does not plug into the mainstream of important decision making.

This is a position I can speak of with some feeling because, as a citizen of the District of Columbia, I have no personal representation in the Congress of the United States. I can vote for a president of the United States, and I can vote for the school board, or take part in our well-devised neighborhood government. But when Congress meets to decide important legislative issues—for example, when the Senate discusses whether it will ratify the SALT treaty, or when the House of Representatives initiates tax legislation—there is nobody in the House or in the Senate who needs to worry one fig over the opinion of Philip Wogaman. And when I think of writing a letter to my congressman or to my senator, there is no congressman or senator to whom I can write.

There is another way of expressing the feeling of alienation that is generated by involvement with a mediating structure with no ultimate connection to the center of power. It is also a feeling of being unable to help determine the course of human history. I don't suppose many people give that much thought, particularly those who do not in fact participate in the disposition of social power. Yet this is precisely when we most lack a sense that our lives finally have contributed something enduring to the human enterprise.

Mediating institutions play a highly significant role in relating people to the centers of power, so long as those centers are substantially democratic. As part of a mediating institution, the individual can have a discernible effect on group policy, which in turn may have sufficient weight to have some discernible effect on the large-scale policies of the impersonal, remote political and economic institutions. One of the movement songs of the 1960s referred to the futility of any one person's efforts alone to bring in the new day of justice, but it went on to the refrain, "But if two and two and fifty make a million, we'll see that day come around."[4]

Besides the weight of numbers, mediating institutions also have the capacity to project their leaders onto a wider stage with a certain base of support behind them. And, of course, they are important schools for politics, too. Back in the 1940s, Harold Stassen—who was then a dominant figure in American politics—once remarked that he had

[4] From the song, "One Man's Hands," words by Alex Comfort, music by Pete Seeger (Fall River Music Inc., 1962).

never had to learn anything new about politics after he left college. Within that microcosm, where he was active in student government and served as student body president, he saw all the dynamics he later encountered on the much vaster scale of state and national politics. Most of the people who are active and effective at the summits of American politics today have résumés studded with participation in mediating institutions. These include church groups as well as political organizations.

As vital as mediating institutions can be, they can only work effectively if we attend also to the way the ultimate centers of power are structured, and to the way our activities within the mediating institutions relate to those structures. Although none of the large-scale institutions of economic and political power in modern society are very responsive to ordinary people, the greatest hope in a democratic society is for a sufficiently strong and sufficiently responsible government to control the other massive centers of power.

Some people contend that government cannot solve all of our problems because government *is* our problem. This view may not be altogether wrong; but I think it would be a mistake to place more trust in the automatic workings of those large-scale institutions that are not formally accountable to people than in those that could be, or are. It would be particularly ironic and tragic for us to allow our commitment to mediating structures to lead us to dismantle the basis of our power to affect human history through the state. The state remains the most promising agency for real social responsibility—more so, for example, than the free, but usually deeply biased, market, although that market has an important role to play. The great advances of the 1960s and 1970s in civil rights and environmental protection would never have been possible without the mobilization of power at the federal level, nor would the economic protections for individuals effected by the New Deal.

Mediating institutions, then, are not an alternative to the great centers of power; they are an important avenue into the responsible control of those centers. In marking off this avenue, we must be particularly mindful of the role of the democratic state.

### Linking People with Sources of Meaning

There is a third important linkage involving mediating structures: the system of connections between people and sources of meaning and value. Human fulfillment in small associations is not enough, and a sense of historical accomplishment is not enough, if people cannot believe that their lives have enduring purpose and that the values by which they live have some ontological status. We seek identity in our roots, in a

73

sense of heritage, but that heritage must have some relationship to ultimate reality. It is more than knowledge of our ancestry, more than affirming our ethnic background, and more than feeling comfortable in our daily interactions. I find it intriguing that people have had to create halls of fame for baseball and football to supplement the pleasures and meanings players and spectators can derive from a given game and season. Any social structure or social activity that lacks an ultimate point of reference can never be fully meaningful.

Here again the mediating structure is very important. Unfortunately, the ultimate frame of reference is not something we can reduce to an accessible scientific form. Our brains are not large enough, and our lives and history are not long enough, for us to identify and integrate indubitable metaphysical truth. We are continually forced to interpret the whole of reality on the basis of those aspects of experienced reality we consider decisive as clues to all the rest. This means we are also dependent on myth and story, the traditions centered on remembered and imagined events taken by the community to be enduring revelations of ultimate meanings and values.

## Mediating Structures and Theological Orientation

The mediating structures, then, are part of three important linkages: the interpersonal linkage, the linkage with social power, and the linkage with sources of meaning and value. We feel alienated from society when any one of these three linkages is weak or missing, and the more serious condition of anomie generally reflects trouble with all three simultaneously. Intimate group life based on common, universal meanings will result in alienation if the group experiences itself as powerless. Such alienation can only be overcome through political activity; or it can be bypassed if the group fosters some form of eschatology in which divine power is expected to intervene in behalf of a faithful, but politically weak, people. Alienation also can occur when politically active individuals pursuing broad social goals have very little interaction with other people at an intimate level. Or people can become alienated who have intimate associations with others and access to political power, but find themselves unable to believe any longer in the myths and traditions giving meaning to their existence.

All three of these linkages, as I have termed them, have theological importance. Theology is itself expressible in many ways; it depends on our particular traditions and on the insights we find most persuasive. Obviously there is not time here to outline a systematic theology for mediating structures; but several theological problems associated with the linkages are fundamental to the church, as it sees itself as a mediating structure.

First is the question of God. God-talk often has been greeted with faint embarrassment in discussions of moral and political philosophy—sometimes even in discussions of theology. When it appears at all, it is often received in the spirit of Voltaire's remark that you can kill a flock of sheep with incantations if, at the same time, you feed them enough arsenic.

The Marxists have gone further, regarding professed belief in God as a projection of the human essence in fantasy, in an alienated state in which the human essence cannot find concrete realization. Marx has written quite a poignant passage about the weakness of humanity and about its need for this opiate to provide some relief from the pain and suffering of its alienated existence. God is viewed as a pain-killing narcotic at best; at worst, God increases man's alienation by projecting the human essence out, away from the concrete.

All of us, of course—Marxists included—must own up to some epistemological limitations as we confront the ultimate character of reality. It is arguable that a view of man that sees reality centered in conscious intelligence, purpose, and benevolence is no less rational than one that sees blind, irrational, material forces at the center of things. Neither of these views, nor any other, can be proved conclusively on the plane of human reason.

Right now, though, I am less concerned with the truth or error of particular views than with their consequences in relation to meaning and alienation. I would dispute the Marxist view that God is an alienating projection, even though a good deal of theological expression and popular piety may be exactly what the Marxists describe. Instead, it seems to me that without God there can ultimately be only alienation. The Marxist can deal with the first two linkages, those representing interpersonal associations and power. I do not see how the Marxist can satisfactorily deal with the third. For, in a nontheistic universe, all is ultimately lost.

Now, the quality and character of the mediating institutions in any society seem to depend greatly on the theological meanings that society subscribes to. Some theological watersheds, of course, cut across religious and denominational lines. Perhaps most decisive for the mediating structures is whether the society's theological perspective is one based on grace or works, to use St. Paul's terminology. Some years ago, I asked a Christian acquaintance in one of the eastern European countries what she and her theologian husband considered to be the greatest theological flaw in the communism of their country. She remarked that they had often thought about this question, and their conclusion was that it was the communists' inability to accept forgiveness. I thought that was a really interesting observation. It suggests the importance to a society—Marxist or any other—of the moral orientation reflected in its mediating institutions. Are people relating to life on the basis of an anxious striving for salvation in some form, or are they responding to a gift of salvation?

A good deal would seem to be at stake, then, in whether a society's mediating institutions are the kind in which people can find human acceptance without worrying about whether they deserve it. One remembers Robert Frost's celebrated comment, "Home is the place where, when you have to go there, they have to take you in." Mediating institutions perform a profound theological role when they serve as places where people can find a basis for understanding and accepting grace—and also, then, a challenge to respond to grace.

### Christianity in the Political Sphere

The views I expressed earlier on linkages with centers of power are widely accepted today among theological ethicists, but they are being challenged by those who dispute human responsibility to manage history. A serious case has been made by John Howard Yoder and some other contemporary evangelical theologians that we should express our faithfulness to God primarily through the church and nongovernmental activity, leaving the final management of history to divine action.[5] Yoder is convinced that faithfulness to God will lead us into relevance, as it did Jesus; in fact, he points out, Jesus never would have been crucified had he not been relevant politically. If we are faithful to Jesus, we will inevitably act out our freedom from subservience to earthly powers. Perhaps we, like Jesus, will have to pay dearly for this challenge to vested interests. But we—again, like Jesus—should avoid those mechanisms of violence normally associated with the exercise of political power.

The implications of this position for mediating institutions would seem to be that Christians ought to concentrate all their efforts at the level of the mediating institution. We should live there the reality of the Kingdom of God, allowing the light, so to speak, to break forth from that order of life in such a way that the course of history will be affected in God's own time and in God's own way.

---

[5] John Howard Yoder, *The Politics of Jesus* (Grand Rapids, Mich.: Erdmans, 1972).

Although I am attracted by elements in Yoder's thought, I do not believe his case for Christian neglect of the centers of power is convincing. In the first place, he fails to address the question of God's purposes in creating our physical world. If we believe that fulfillment in this sphere is a decisively important aspect of God's purpose, we then must ask: What is it to God that millions of people in Bangladesh never even get a start in life, but suffer from malnutrition and die? Does it matter that vast numbers of people are frustrated politically, or are oppressed politically, or labor under other conditions that seem to be contrary to God's purposes? Insofar as those things are important, one must then ask: Should not Christians, faithful to God's purposes, act in this sphere? I am afraid that Yoder's rather extreme statement of pacitism may amount to a blank check for human suffering as a result of Christians' opting out of responsibility in the political arena. That is not his intention, but that may be the effect. I would argue that God's management of human history must be implemented pretty much by human hands. We may not understand the whole grand design, but we do well to try to understand and act on as much of it as we can.

Moreover, of course, we can hardly eschew the political order and still live and function within society. Society is too tightly wired together for that. Almost everything we do contributes in one way or another to the functioning of the state. Conscious participation in the political order by ethically sensitive people can help to humanize it, to make it more responsible, more sensitive, less violent.

## The Church as Mediating Institution

It should be clear from everything I have said that the church, at least in many of its manifestations, when it is true to its nature, is the quintessential mediating structure in society. Religious groups are by definition the bearers of human tradition concerning ultimate meaning and value; and, by common practice, they are organized in local, face-to-face, associational form. The second linkage, that with political power structures, has been established or neglected by religious groups in a wide variety of ways through history. But the opportunity is clearly present for the church to function in that linkage, and to fulfill the role rather well.

To play a mediating role in a democratic society, must the church be democratic in its own organization and modes of action? In a truly democratic society, in one sense it is and in another sense it is not required to be. It must be democratic in its membership: people can choose to belong and they can choose to drop their membership. But for this very reason, the leadership need not be democratic. Because a truly democratic state will not require any particular accountability from the church beyond the freedom of people to belong or not, even a very autocratic leadership can be taken to be democratically selected and sustained.

That said, I do not doubt for a moment that democratic societies are best sustained by mediating structures that are also democratic. For one thing, the structure of a church or other mediating institution tends both to represent and to reinforce the values of its members. This may be particularly true for churches, whose doctrine of their own nature has one foot in a central theological vision and the other foot in an order of discipline. For instance, it may prove difficult for the members of a church to accept a two-sided doctrine of human nature—Reinhold Niebuhr's "Man's capacity for justice makes democracy possible, but man's inclination to injustice makes democracy necessary"[6]—if their leaders fail to be accountable, thereby implying that they are exempt from the otherwise universal human inclination to sinfulness. In such a situation, the medium may prove to be the real message.

An undemocratic church also deprives its people of a valuable opportunity to develop the skills they need to participate in the democratic political process. When such a church encourages its members to enter the political arena, it may contribute more to social dissension and further alienation than to healthy political action, because the members' tendency is to move from the passivity and unthinking obedience they have learned within the church into unreflective support for some narrow political cause.

### Separation between Church and State

This leads us to the difficult issue of the church-state relationship. On this topic I would like for the moment just to make a few very basic points.

First, a good deal of nonsense has been written about the non-establishment clause of the First Amendment and about the supposedly absolute wall of separation between church and state. There is, of course, no way church and state can be separated in any literal sense where both are aspects of the same society. At times, the principle of separation has been taken to mean that the state is committed to secularism—that it is and ought to be hostile to religion. The churches could scarcely function effectively as mediating structures if that were the case.

In those societies where the state really is secularist—I mean mili-

---

[6] Reinhold Niebuhr, *The Children of Light and the Children of Darkness* (New York: Charles Scribner's Sons, 1944), p. xiii.

tantly secularist, as in most of the Marxist countries—the churches' mediating function is seriously impaired. I visited Czechoslovakia shortly after the "Prague spring" period; there, when the reform movement took hold and the spirit of creativity began to burst forth, one important expression of that was a great return to the church. People flocked back into the churches, correctly identifying them as the kind of institutional structure in which real creativity had a chance to flourish. The situation in that country is much less happy today, of course. This is not to say that the church cannot function as a mediating structure under adverse circumstances, but it is extremely difficult for it to do so where the state is officially and persistently hostile.

What the nonestablishment clause does assume is the religious equality of all this country's citizens. The state may not properly show favoritism, although I see no constitutional or philosophical reason why it should not facilitate religious expression where this can be done without favoritism. Allowing tax deductions for contributions to religious groups, providing meeting room space in public buildings, creating display space on public ground as a kind of public bulletin board, allowing religious groups to evangelize and solicit funds in public areas, providing a full range of religious literature in public libraries—all seem to me to be in harmony with the deeper meaning of American tradition.

A good example of the extremes to which the principle of separation can be taken is an incident I was involved in a number of years ago in Washington, D.C. I served as a witness in federal district court regarding the national Christmas manger scene on the Ellipse. It wasn't a matter of the government's allowing church groups to make use of the Ellipse, which would have been in keeping with a public bulletin board kind of idea; rather, it was as though the United States, having duly considered the matter, had concluded that the manger scene is an appropriate reflection of our common religious tradition. To make matters even worse, in response to certain litigations, the Park Service had erected a sign indicating that this manger scene was by no means in any way to be regarded as a religious phenomenon.

I pointed out on the stand that I as a Christian invested that symbolism with certain religious values, and I didn't want the federal government announcing to the public that my religious views or symbols were not religious views or symbols. In a curiously inverted way, that was an offense to my religious liberty.

The opposite extreme is a little more typical: the view that it is a violation of the First Amendment for any state building or property to be used for any kind of religious activity or expression. I think this is wrong.

When the Hare Krishnas or the representatives of the Unification Church solicit me in National Airport, I don't give them any money, but I am awfully glad, really, that the state allows them to be there. I believe the state should be affirmative about the religious expressions of all its people, provided it does not show favoritism among them.

This interpretation is not in harmony with all theological traditions. Whether one agrees with it depends not only on one's political views but on whether one's theology contains a basis of respect for divergent views and practices. Some religions, including my own, take account of possible fallibility and consider that God may relate in unique and unanticipated ways to other people and groups. But not all theologies see value in the expression of other religious traditions.

A second important point about the nonestablishment clause is that it does not deprive the churches of their right of political advocacy, a limitation that would undercut their role in linking people with centers of power. Indeed, I find nothing in the principle of nonestablishment that would keep a church from assuming the full responsibilities of a political party, if any church were foolish enough to take that on. Occasionally churches do come rather close to that: in Maryland, in 1966, when the voters were faced with choosing between a fairly unknown Republican politician and a well-known militant racist Democrat, many churches come out strongly in favor of the Republican—whose name was Spiro Agnew.

Certainly there are ambiguities in politics that the church must be aware of when it enters that arena. But I agree with Dean Kelley that it is quite improper for the state to threaten to remove the tax exemption of churches that are involved extensively in legislative advocacy. The democratic state is greatly aided by the thoughtful participation of religious groups.

The one caveat here is that although church groups should be free to advocate anything under the sun, a democratic state may not properly enact anything that is explicitly or implicitly designed to favor a particular religious group. Presbyterians might be free to lobby for a public subsidy for the salary of Presbyterian ministers, for instance, but the state could not properly approve it, even if a large majority favored it.

A third point about the separation between church and state is that churches do well to protect themselves from manipulation by the state. When the state uses churches to accomplish public ends, proper though the ends may be, the churches need to be on their guard lest their fundamental character and independence as religious institutions be compromised. This has happened so often in history—particularly, it seems, in such countries as the Soviet Union and Romania—that one cannot regard the warning as alarmist. It is for this reason that I am reluctant to subscribe to Peter Berger and Richard Neuhaus's maximalist principle for mediating institutions, much as I am in agreement with their minimalist principle.[7] What Berger and Neuhaus have done, in effect, is create a presumption in favor of government's use of mediating institutions for public purposes. In respect to churches, at least, I would rather reverse the presumption and give the burden of proof to those who favor such an arrangement. The churches' best contributions as mediating institutions are nurturing interpersonal relationships, transmitting traditions, and providing avenues of access to power, not implementing the state's purposes.

---

[7] Their "minimalist" principle is that "public policy should protect and foster mediating structures," while the "maximalist" principle is that "wherever possible, public policy should utilize mediating structures for the realization of social purposes." See Berger and Neuhaus, *To Empower People: The Role of Mediating Structures in Public Policy* (Washington, D. C.: American Enterprise Institute for Public Policy Research, 1977), p. 6. Chapter 4 of that book applies the maximalist and minimalist principles to the church.

# Discussion

QUESTION: I take some exception to your statement that in a non-theistic universe, all is ultimately lost. That, to my mind, dismisses the very real value structures to be found in non-Christian traditions, some of which are not specifically theistic. One of the vulnerable points of theism generally is that it is strong: It is subject to expressions of ego extension that nontheistic religions are not. That can mean that individuals participating in theistic religions can seek to be shapers of history in ways that often include considerable violence and aggression.

DR. WOGAMAN: I was aware in using that word "theism" or "theistic" that that was shorthand that probably would have to be explained during a discussion period because, of course, there are varieties of theism. To sharpen the issue, one might ask of any religious perspective, What would you consider to be enduring if a nuclear holocaust utterly destroyed the world? The answers that could be given wouldn't be restricted to my own particular form of theism; but if the universe is perceived as essentially impersonal, essentially material—energy, but without personality at the center of being—it is difficult to answer that question.

Now, I would immediately want to go on and say that I value the vast flowering of religious traditions, including many that are nontheistic. I value the contributions of sincere Marxists—that is, serious Marxists, and not Bolshevik opportunists—precisely because they are wrestling with those important value questions at the human level. But my own conviction is that the ultimate good news of the Christian faith is that at the center of being there is personal purpose.

QUESTION: In the two days I have been here, my main impression is that religious people today—I am not talking about every individual here —are not really believers. I don't detect any religious enthusiasm; I detect more of an intellectual enthusiasm and a political interest. And I see no future for the church in that situation. I see a future for the evangeli-

82

cals who have been criticized as fundamentalists. I read the other day that there is evidence of a good deal of superstition in society, because they sell 40,000 Bibles a month. What have you got, Dr. Wogaman, what have other people got here, that is going to attract me to self-discipline and humility and service in a Christian religion?

DR. WOGAMAN: You've asked for my standard evangelical sermon, which I must refrain from presenting here. But I will emphasize the integrity of the faith, the importance of allowing the faith to give us unity of experience and perspective. One of the problems I have with a good deal of religiosity today is that it has a lot of fervor, but it is essentially idolatrous fervor, based sometimes on very selfish interests. It seems to me particularly important to rescue the church as a mediating institution from bondage to interests of that sort.

QUESTION. Regarding your second linkage, when you were talking about mediating structures as something between people and social power, I wonder if in your mind that excludes the idea that there are many different levels of mediation. You used the example of the local community that can't really mediate, but one can have a powerful local government that is a highly effective mediating structure within a limited sphere. Does this conflict with what you were trying to say, or would you consider it merely additive?

DR. WOGAMAN: I think I would consider it additive. That is, the fabric of mediating institutions is very complex, and, indeed, the relationship between mediating institutions and the vast impersonal institutions does not correspond exactly with the relationship between private and public. Also, some centers of power that are needed do not currently exist. I referred rather briefly to the Catholic church's doctrine of subsidiarity. Essentially, the principle of subsidiarity is that higher levels of collectivity ought not to take over functions served by the more immediate levels. But when Pope John XXIII issued his encyclical *Pacem in Terris*, he observed that at the level of international politics, we currently lack the institutions needed to solve the problems at hand. Subsidiarity got turned on its head—or, more precisely, it was applied to a newly emerging historical situation. How are churches and other mediating institutions—and people, for that matter—to get their hands on the multinational corporations today? Can that be done at the level of any one nation's politics? I doubt it. There may be need for structures of power that are more international in character, which as yet don't exist.

QUESTION: I also wanted to address this matter of the church as a mediating structure between people and social and political powers, particularly with reference to the political expression of religious views. You mentioned that if religious institutions are to try to affect the political process, they must do this with tolerance for a variety of differing views. But it is my sense that one consistent and fundamental element of all religious positions is the conviction that what is believed is ultimately and finally true. That is, if you are right in your religious convictions, then I am wrong in mine; it is not possible for us both to be correct. So I am uncomfortable with your notion that churches ought to be free to express themselves politically, because, although you yourself and even your denomination may be prepared to acknowledge your fallibilities, I doubt that you would extend the possibility of fallibility to your notion that Jesus is the Christ.

DR. WOGAMAN: Your question has two levels, doesn't it? First is the level of what the state should permit. On that I argued that the state, if it is democratic, has no alternative: it must permit participation in the political process by people of any persuasion. It runs profound risks in doing so, but you can't have a democratic state without risk. But you are posing the question also at a theological level: How can the full thrust of theological conviction be combined with respect for the possibility of one's own error?

My central point is that if we believe in and worship the God who has created and sustained all that exists, we must also acknowledge that our own perspectives are very limited. We live by the truth we have, but God is greater than our ideas. It is interesting to me that while there is a certain strain of theological intolerance running through Hebrew-Christian history, there are also many witnesses to a theologically principled tolerance and humility. The Hebrew books of Jonah and Ruth, for instance, are on the side of intellectual and national humility, and Jesus reserved his most scathing criticism for self-righteous religious types who thought they had all the answers. In subsequent Christian history we have the intolerance of the Inquisition and the Puritans, but we also have St. Francis and the Quakers. I think the latter show greater respect for God by combining total commitment with intellectual humility.

(The rest of this discussion was not recorded, because of technical difficulties.)

# The Church as Mediating Institution: Contemporary American Challenge

*J. Philip Wogaman*

We are in the midst of great flux in the twentieth century. I suppose every century prides itself on being one of the turning points in human history; certainly ours does. That makes it all the more difficult to assess exactly where we are and where we are going.

Viewed in a wide historical perspective, it seems to me that religious institutions are in better shape in the United States than in most countries, certainly in most Western countries. The peculiar mix here of religious pluralism and the principle of voluntarism has evidently proved beneficial from the standpoint of institutional maintenance and broad participation. Of course, that is not exactly our question at this conference. We are concerned with how well the American churches are serving their functions as mediating institutions, which is a deeper issue than simply evidence of institutional success. We are concerned with diagnosing any problems and with working toward solutions to those problems insofar as we can.

## Orientation toward Social Issues

Thinking first of the mainline denominations—that is, most of the denominations in the National Council of Churches, the Roman Catholic church, and maybe a few others—it seems clear that, for good or ill, we are still in the era of a dominant thrust toward political relevance. This orientation, which dates from the early 1960s, began largely as a reaction against the religious materialism and subjectivism of the prosperous 1950s.

Up to a point, the churches' participation in the civil rights movement was a great success story. The churches had done their theological homework, in the main, and that was an important reason for the ultimate success of the movement. There came a point when the good conscience of the opposition to civil rights was gone; those who persisted were not able to oppose the movement with complete theological self-confidence. The churches contributed some of the outstanding leaders and a good deal of the institutional clout that undergirded that effort. They also deserve great credit for keeping it so largely nonviolent. That, I think, is an achievement of our period that will still be respected five hundred or a thousand years from now: that a vast social revolution was carried out with considerable success and with minimal violence—and, as a result, with a minimum of residual bitterness.

The churches' other great political involvement during the 1960s was in the reaction to the Vietnam war. The churches made important contributions to the American decision to withdraw from the war. This activity, too, was attended by considerable theological thought, although from the start it was more ambiguous than the civil rights movement.

Mainline church leadership, largely activated in the political sphere by these two efforts, has had to address a series of much more difficult and ambiguous political issues during the 1970s. The politics of ethnic identity, particularly black identity, has shifted from the rhetoric of integration of the 1960s to questions of black separatism. The women's liberation movement, which evidently has yet to peak, has deep cultural ramifications, even in the language we employ. There is a battle occurring right now over theological language, much of which is male-dominated. The gay liberation movement, too, has been a vexatious issue in several of the mainline denominations recently, and the abortion question is a great fly in the ecumenical ointment. These issues have proved as divisive within the churches as within society, sometimes more so. It has even been speculated that the eagerness with which church leadership turned to the world hunger problem owed as much to the quest for a unifying area for church activity as to the moral concern itself.

## New Trends in the 1970s

During the 1970s, a distinct reaction to this ferment over social issues set in in many mainline denominations. A number of the national social action agencies were drastically cut back or even eliminated altogether. The National Council of Churches dismantled much of its social action bureaucracy. Why has this happened?

In my opinion, two of the linkages I referred to this morning had been greatly weakened. First, the linkage between people and traditions of meaning and value was overshot in much of the political activism. The eagerness with which many people embraced biblical study and a new quest for spirituality during the 1970s is revealing on that point. A vacuum had been opened up that needed filling. But, second, the churches' nurturing, sustaining role—the linkage among individuals—had been neglected, in many cases even rejected in principle during the

1960s. When I was training young ministers in the late 1960s, I met a number who thought of ministry in terms of some detached form of service—that is, detached from the context of a congregation of people. The thing with great appeal to some of the more avant-garde was to seek out some missionary frontier, less "stodgy" than congregational life.

The effect of these changes was to undermine, a little bit at least, the morale and health of the communities of faith. This was not simply a result of the churches' political activism; it was also a reflection of their excessive institutionalism and of the remoteness of their leadership from local generating centers of church life. There was a resurgence in the 1970s of a fundamentalist theological tendency and, within several of the mainline denominations, of certain schismatic groups, which were essentially reactionary both theologically and in terms of the church's engagement with society.

Some positive developments also occurred during the 1970s. The biblical study movement and the quest for spirituality were rather positive, at least up to a point, representing a grappling with the sources of tradition. The "house church" movement has been of some importance—venturesome souls setting up a small church that can meet in a living room, sparing members the burden of maintaining church property, but sustaining a life of faith and mission. Also on the positive side is the liturgical renewal movement, which is still very much in force in many of the mainline denominations, as well as spilling across denominational lines. Although it contains a good deal of superficiality, the liturgical movement is designed to recapture the faith in the language of people today and, with that, to emphasize the sustaining character of the community, the celebration of the goodness of life through the faith, and the witness of the church for social justice. Even church architecture has undergone a kind of renewal. After years in which the typical church was a long, divided sanctuary with an aisle leading up to an altar, where people sat in rows and faced forward to be instructed, the current trend in many denominations is to strive for more circularity, for a sense of community and equality of participation.

Some of the most interesting church activity in the 1970s, however, has been outside the mainline denominations. The proliferation of religious cults and fads will doubtless continue to occupy researchers for years to come. Two clear notes are struck by most of these groups. First, they offer a deeply committed and very intimate group life. People are kept busy caring for each other and furthering the ideals and purposes of the group, whatever those may be. Second, and perhaps even more important, these groups provide their members with unambiguous schemata of meanings and values. Adherents no longer have to concern themselves about ambiguity in their linkage with meaning, or about alienation in their linkage with other people.

As for the third linkage I referred to this morning, alienation from the sphere of power still remains in many of these groups. Several of them, however—the People's Temple in Jonestown, Reverend Moon's Unification Church—have sought vigorously to advance political ends, sometimes using rather devious or unfortunate means to do so. I think it is very interesting that the failure to succeed politically was what finally evoked the crisis of the Jonestown group. The group still had its communal life, its theology, and its leader, but its political impotence had become unendurable. For the leader of the group, in particular, this was unbearable. Almost his last words were, "All is lost"—an implication that religious hope, too, had failed.

Now, while the mainline denominations are still doing rather well statistically, most of them have recorded numerical declines in recent years, while many of the sectarian and cult groups and the more marginal and conservative denominations have registered increases. Dean M. Kelley's judgment is that this is because the latter groups exact a greater commitment in a context of less theological insecurity. I think there is a lot of truth in that. These groups are havens of refuge for people who are having a very difficult time coping with a highly ambiguous era. Nevertheless, this is not quite the whole story. When Hendrik Kraemer was asked by American friends for an assessment of the health of the churches of Europe at the close of World War II, his cryptic reply was that the churches seemed to be doing very well, because attendance was down. He was referring to the popularity of the churches during the war, and particularly to Germany, where much of the church had cooperated altogether too fully with the National Socialist Party. We ought to remember that statistical success is not the final measure, either of the theological faithfulness of the church or of its cultural effectiveness.

## The Church and the Search for Meaning

My own interpretation of the present state of the church would be that we are still in the midst of a fundamental crisis of belief—that is, an alienation related to the third linkage. People find it desirable to participate in the churches for a variety of reasons, including sheer momentum, and participation in sects and cults clearly entails a flight from alienation and ambiguity. But neither may represent a wholeness, an integrity of faith.

To illustrate, I recall a story told by Ruth Benedict in her classic work *Patterns of Culture* about a conversation she had many years ago with an old Indian chief in California. The chief was reflecting on the dissolution of much of the old tribal culture: "In the beginning, God gave to every people a cup, a cup of clay, and from this cup they drank their life. They all dipped in the water, but their cups were different. Our cup is broken now. It has passed away."[1] With this striking metaphor, the chief expressed the insight that our cultural perspective, rooted in religious faith and tradition, is what holds our life's experience. When that cup is shattered, experience loses its coherence. The tragedy of this man's life, and his tribe's, was that their religious and cultural heritage no longer sufficed to interpret the new experiences to which they had been subjected.

Do contemporary American church members find their religion an adequate frame of reference for interpreting the range of experiences of modern life? Using the analogy of the broken cup, it is possible to cling to fragments of the cup, nostalgically or fanatically, and to make the cup itself the object of faith rather than the container of experience. This problem was posed strikingly by a character in Tom Robbins's novel *Another Roadside Attraction*:

> Christianity is dying of its own accord. Its most vital energies are already dead. We are living in a period of vast philosophical and psychological upheaval, a rare era of evolutionary outburst precipitated by a combination of technological breakthroughs. And when we come out of this period of change— provided that the tension and trauma of it doesn't lead us to destroy ourselves—we will find that many of the old mores and attitudes and doctrines will have been unrecognizably altered or eliminated altogether.
>
> One of the casualties of our present upheaval will unquestionably be Christianity. It is simply too ineffectual on a spiritual level, and too contradictory on an intellectual level, to survive.[2]

The same character in that novel, evidently reflecting the author's point of view, also remarked, "The discernible activity in the modern church, the modern ecumenism, social activism, militancy and debates about the state of God's health are merely the nervous twitchings of a cadaver. The handsome new church buildings, the plush pulpits, and the wall-to-wall carpets are no more than funeral trappings. It's all over. The Christian faith is dead."

---

[1] Ruth Benedict, *Patterns of Culture* (Boston: Houghton-Mifflin, 1960), pp. 21–22.
[2] Tom Robbins, *Another Roadside Attraction* (New York: Random House, 1971), p. 287.

Whether or not this is true—and I don't believe it is—it is a useful reminder that the important considerations for the church as a mediating structure go deeper than institutional prosperity. Indeed, a good deal of the energetic cult activity and spiritual renewal of the 1970s may be less a reflection of real renewal than an anxious reaction to the loss of an organizing religious and cultural perspective. Again, the key consideration is whether or not the religious perspective is capable of integrating the experience of people in our time.

### Faith and Scientific Rationalism

In addressing this question, one point we should consider is the encounter between religion and the scientific rationalism of our era. By this I do not mean simply the old problem of relating scientific discoveries and insights to religious faith. That problem is, in my judgment, no longer terribly important, except among fundamentalists who insist on the literal truth of biblical creation myths, miracle stories, and other aspects of Christian theology that are essentially metaphorical. There is another kind of tension behind the present crisis of religious faith: the conflict between religious tradition and life as it generally must be lived. When one's religious tradition, one's conceptions of meaning and value, are in conflict with one's existence, and one's existence cannot apparently be changed, then one's religious viewpoint can only be perceived as ineffectual. Paul Carter makes essentially this point in his *The Decline and Revival of the Social Gospel,* in which he attributes the secularism of the 1920s not to the visible conflicts between the scientific perspective and fundamentalism but to the failure of the churches to be deeply sensitive to humane values during the prohibition struggle and World War I. This failure led to the rejection of Christianity by numbers of cultural leaders, including some of the outstanding writers of the period, and to a dominant move toward secularism.

In the contemporary world, this conflict between religion and existence manifests itself in various aspects of our lives. One is the contrast between the egalitarian, communal American religious and political tradition and the seemingly unbridgeable gulf between the affluent and the desperately poor. If we believe that, as the Christian faith implies, all of humankind is one family, then the fact that vast numbers of people suffer extreme poverty while others live in prosperity is bound to suggest a gap between our existence and the implications of our faith.

Second, there is a built-in problem in what could be called the principled selfishness of the capitalist economic system. That is, the capitalist system is to some extent based on human greed and selfish

behavior, in contrast to the agape and community spirit that are fundamental to the Judaeo-Christian religious tradition. This is a dilemma
that must be faced by all of us who are attracted by the systemic values
of capitalism. Some of the system's defenders argue that capitalism is a
way of harnessing human selfishness, but it is also a way of enhancing
human selfishness.

Third, our attitude of rational control and our expectations of
progress, undergirded by a religious tradition of vocation and stewardship, have lately had a rather sudden and inexorable encounter with
the limits of earth. Just within the last decade or so, we have had to
reevaluate our faith in the immense wealth-creating capability of our
economic system, and also in our religio-cultural expectations of
progress.

Fourth, there is the conflict between the gospel of peace, love, and
community and the horrible violence of the twentieth century. How
easily we become desensitized to all the tragedies and evils of our time!
Yet our century has witnessed not only innumerable instances of man's
inhumanity to man, but the systematic destruction of a whole people in
World War II, followed now by active preparations for the hell of
thermonuclear war.

A fifth conflict has arisen between the missionary impulse of a
good deal of American Christianity, in particular, and the limitations
on that imposed by the realities of the world. In large measure that
may not be a bad thing, because a good deal of that missionary enterprise was rooted in cultural chauvinism. But its demise has certainly
caused a crisis of consciousness among American Christians. Think, for
instance, of the shock people felt at what was called the fall of China.
So much missionary activity had been invested in China in the 1930s that
when all that went down the drain, so to speak, and the Communists
won, and our man, Chiang Kai-shek, was relegated to Taiwan, it was
hard for a lot of American Christians to handle.

### Reconciling Faith and the Material World

All these areas, and perhaps others, represent points where modern
existence, to which we are committed, is at variance with our theological
idea of what life is, what its implications are. How are we to interpret
life in relation to the cup of Christian theology?

One obvious avenue is to spiritualize life, to say that the Christian
faith is, after all, a spiritual thing, and nothing can prevent you from
having the spirit. That involves you rather quickly in the Docetic heresy,
which involves treating God's purposes as though they were entirely

spiritual, and the material world as though it were the source of evil against God. Or there are eschatological possibilities, interpreting theology entirely in terms of the end of history: we are stuck in this vale of tears, but someday God will intervene, or someday we will find relief in death. Frankly, I don't think either of those avenues finally puts the cup back together. We still must live in this world; the question is, Can we live our experience in the light of our faith? not, Can we avoid the world of experience by running away to faith?

To be an effective mediating structure, the church must be actively engaged at this point of theological reflection, helping people come to terms with the existential realities they face. In pastoral terms, this may mean that dealing with human souls individually, by means of counseling, faintly modeled after psychiatric practice, is not enough. The church's pastoral role includes ministering to people in their existence, empowering them to grapple with their social environment. That may, in fact, be the more serious pastoral responsibility of the church. Christian theology does not promise us easy victories in this earthly existence, but it does summon us to engagement. To bring the disharmonies and injustices of the world into harmony with the gospel, so that one can live a life based upon religious insight, may be the most important pastoral task.

I don't want to leave this subject on a note of pessimism. For one thing, unless one has a sense of optimism about the future, it is not possible really to function; and for another, I think optimism about the capacity of the churches in the modern world is probably well-founded. Many churches really are nurturing, creative centers of life, a rich resource in American democratic society. Others are so heavily committed to formalism and to sheer institutional maintenance as to be virtually useless as mediating structures. As I indicated earlier, the growth of so many sect and cult groups is an important indictment of the impersonality of many aspects of American church life. Still, experimentation with new forms, which has been happening within as well as outside the mainline denominations, is a sign of hope.

### The State and Religious Expression

I think whatever renewal takes place in the church at this point must occur pretty much from within. This leads us to the question whether present church-state policies and constitutional interpretations are impeding important aspects of church life. Is there, for example, a de facto official secularism at work in our society which undermines the intellectual and moral self-confidence of the churches? Do church groups find themselves unduly inhibited from participating in public life, and thus relegated to the purely private spheres of existence? Are traditional functions of the church increasingly being taken over by the state?

It is worth remembering that the constitutional doctrines governing the separation of church and state were the product of a very different cultural era, one in which both governments and churches played vastly different roles from their present ones. At the time the Constitution was adopted, less than 10 percent of the population was churched. The whole population was around three million, at most, in a very spread-out agrarian society. Government was marginal to most aspects of life: it was not prominently involved in education; there was no radio or television for it to regulate; its fiscal policies, including taxation, were simple and pertinent to a rural society. In the main, I am in sympathy with the greatly increased role government has assumed in the twentieth century. But if church and state must be kept separate at every point, it is clear that government's expanding role will be a wedge driving the church out of contemporary social life. That, we may be sure, was not the intention of the framers of the Constitution.

In light of this situation, we may emphasize with Peter Berger and Richard Neuhaus, in their minimalist proposal, that "public policy should protect and foster mediating structures," including the church. Tax deductions for religious contributions, protection of religious access to the airwaves, access to public space, are all concrete ways this proposal can be applied. Inevitably, there will be difficult borderline areas; one such, to which Berger and Neuhaus have alluded, is the question of prayer in the schools. The Supreme Court did not, of course, outlaw prayer in the schools. Any child or teacher can pray silently more or less at any time. Indeed, the dicta of the Court that accompanied the prayer decisions suggest that a teacher may properly declare a period for silent prayer or meditation, to be used by each pupil in a manner consistent with his or her heritage and beliefs. What the Court did prohibit was public liturgy implying public endorsement of the religious faith of only some of the people.

From the standpoint of the churches, the problem here is also one of protecting the integrity of genuine worship. My wife encountered this when she was a teacher in Massachusetts a number of years ago. At that time, the schools of Massachusetts required the recitation of the Lord's Prayer at the beginning of each day. The class being about equally divided between Protestants and Catholics, a daily drama accompanied the prayer. When the Catholics came to the word "evil," they all shouted "Amen," while the Protestants loudly countered, "For thine is the kingdom and the power and the glory." So much for the intensely spiritual activity that was supposedly occurring in that classroom!

So perhaps the Supreme Court was not unwise. Even were there no problem of religious conflict, we would still have the implicit problem of possible humiliation of students of other faiths.

## The State and Church Political Activity

Now, what about impediments to church legislative activity or advocacy? First of all, speaking of the church's role as a mediating institution, I do not mean that the state ought to confer official status on the churches as political institutions or anything like that. Rather, the church, along with many other kinds of mediating institutions, should be considered a place where political dialogue can occur, where people can confer about what values are important in the political process and by what strategies their chosen policies might be implemented.

Regarding the interaction between church and state on particular issues, there are several areas just now in which policy making is bound to be difficult. One such is the abortion debate. There is a case right now in Brooklyn, *McRae* v. *Califano*, that is testing the constitutionality of the Hyde amendment, which denies Medicaid funding for abortions to women in poverty. The plaintiffs, who are supporting freedom of choice, claim that it is a denial of religious liberty and an improper establishment of religion for Congress to single out abortion, among the other obstetrical possibilities for poor women, for discrimination. The defendants insist that it is an issue of their freedom to function in the legislative arena. Both sides agree that the church may properly advocate in such political issues.

The decisive question, according to the plaintiffs, is whether the Hyde amendment's dominant purpose is secular or theological. Sabbath closing laws, for instance, very often were established ostensibly for reasons of community health and well being, when in fact the reason was that for commercial enterprises to open on Sunday was an offense against Protestant religious beliefs. Where that is perceived by the courts, they properly insist on the freedom of those who wish to use Sunday in secular ways. If a legislature did decide in good faith that closing businesses one day a week was in the interests of community health and that Sunday just happened to be the most convenient, that could pass the test.

Another aspect of the church-state encounter is the question of who speaks for the churches. To put it briefly: if, as is frequently alleged, church leaders do not speak for a majority of their people, then it is the business of good politicians to smoke that out and not to be intimidated by self-appointed spokesmen for large numbers of people. It may also be the business of the supposed followers of such people to bring them under discipline, but I don't think that is a problem of political philosophy.

Finally, I want to return to the maximalist proposition of Berger and Neuhaus: "Wherever possible, public policy should utilize mediating structures for the realization of social purposes." There are certain dangers if this is pushed too far, to the point that, in using the churches, the state thereby subtly—or not so subtly—remakes them in its own image. In my opinion, churches should not take on welfare functions that can be handled better on a larger scale by the government. For instance, if the government can run better hospitals, and the churches are concerned with good hospital care, they ought to leave that area to the government.

When churches do accept responsibility to conduct welfare functions with public funds, they should expect to meet public standards. In the school area, a whole series of cases has centered on this problem. In the 1960s, in Iowa, the Amish insisted—quite properly—on their right to educate their children; but the state insisted on the right of the children, for which it was in some sense a custodian, to an education that met certain standards. There was a loggerhead, because the Amish were not geared up to provide schooling on that level.

By no means do I disagree with anyone's right to private education, church sponsored or otherwise. It probably is healthy to have some mix in our educational establishment. On the other hand, I would urge us not to abandon what may be one of the greatest contributions of American civilized life. Looking beyond the horrors of some of the big-city school systems and the great, almost intractable difficulties we seem to find ourselves in, looking at American public education in the main and comparing it to education in almost any other country in the world, I think one has to be impressed. For one thing, on the most practical level, the high level of skills and general education of millions of Americans has contributed greatly to the prosperity of American business. My own concerns, though, have to do more with the character of democratic life. Apart from the rhetoric of the melting pot, I do think it is very important for there to be points in American life where our pluralism manifests itself in dialogue. The public schools have been centers where people have had to come to terms with one another. Henry Steele Commager wrote, perhaps a little euphorically, "This most heterogeneous of modern societies—profoundly varied in racial background, religious faith, and social and economic interest—has ever seemed the most easy prey to forces of riotous privilege and ruinous division. These forces have not prevailed; they have been routed, above all, in the school-rooms and the playgrounds of America."[3]

Finally, we need to ask whether church control of schools, hospitals, and other welfare agencies necessarily leads to greater personal concern and more humanization. Part of the church's role as a mediating institution is to underscore the human sensitivity and compassion of the people who work in such institutions. It ought to; I don't think it always does. Sometimes church institutions have been the last bastions of segregation, and of insensitivity to labor organization; they have, perhaps unwittingly, cultivated class privileges and helped to underscore division in American society. At their best, however, they have been a good influence, living up to their responsibility to challenge the vocational sense of their members as those members participate in the wider society.

---

[3] Henry Steele Commager, "Our Schools Have Kept Us Free," *Life* (October 16, 1950), p. 47.

# Discussion

QUESTION: There is a school of thought that the American public schools, far from being a meeting ground of minds, are in fact a tool that has been quite consciously used by the state for homogenizing the culture; that they have been used to create a certain type of American. If that is true, it would argue for parochial schools, among others, as a necessity for providing variety in our educational system.

DR. WOGAMAN: I wonder whether it isn't framing the categories too broadly if we speak of the public schools as offering only two alternatives, homogenization or enhancement of pluralism. A little bit of both is bound to occur, isn't it? I would argue that there is a necessity for homogenization, in the sense of socializing people into the disciplines of democratic society and acquainting them with the traditions of this nation. It is important for the people who are participating in the body politic to be acquainted with our constitutional tradition, our history of successes and failures, and the events of our common heritage. On the other hand, we don't want the kind of homogenization that lifts up Anglo-Saxon cultural history and events as being the really civilizing dimensions of American life, and plays down the vast enriching traditions of all other ethnic groups. The schools ought to be sensitive to that, and to work on it, in teacher education, for instance; a teacher can't teach what he or she doesn't know.

I am not opposed to a certain plurality of school structure, either My plea is rather that one not lightly experiment with dismantling the public school system. I think, in the main, it has served this country rather well.

QUESTION: This morning you cited the Gallup poll about the high respect Americans have for the clergy. I would suggest that that is partly because they are, by and large, a harmless lot. If you looked at the credibility of the clergy in terms of the affairs of life—political, economic, et cetera—it might come out differently.

This evening you raised the problem of the pastoral role of the church. I would suggest that, as a mediating structure, the church has been woefully remiss in its pastoral functioning to probably the most significant organization in contemporary society, the large corporation. Specifically, the church has not been a pastor to middle managers and upper-middle managers, who may find deep meaning in their vocations as marketing people, purchasing people, R&D people, personnel people, et cetera. One thesis relating to that is that the clergy, first, is ignorant of what goes on in life, and, second, has a latent and manifest antagonism to business, especially to big business. Virtually no seminary in this country has courses tying the pastoral relationship in practical theology to ethical considerations in business. Would you agree that the churches are remiss in that function?

DR. WOGAMAN: I should say first that I did not intend to link the word "pastoral," as I used it before, to the person of the clergyman. In describing the pastoral function of the church, I really was thinking of it as a function of the whole church. Another minor quibble would be that my statement about clergymen and the Gallup poll was not to be taken as a serious assessment, on my part, of the glorious triumph of American clergy astride the commanding peaks of American cultural life, or anything of that sort.

But I agree with you that the church's pastoral role with persons in business and in other areas of responsibility in American institutional life—going beyond personal ministry into the problems faced professionally by such people—has been deficient. That probably has origins on both sides; I have made some statements this evening about the dilemmas of capitalism as a system.

It seems to me the church, as it addresses economic life in general, needs to operate on two planes simultaneously, difficult though that may be. On the first plane, it needs what one might call "macroethics": it needs to be addressing broad systemic questions, policy questions at the general level. What kind of a society do we want to be? Where do we want power to be located? How should power be disciplined? How can the commanding institutions of economic life be brought into accountability? Those who are committed to the present institutions of American economic life need to know that the criticism of those institutions coming from the church is not trivial; it is serious.

But is there not also a microlevel, about which I think you are more concerned? Given the actualities of institutional life, how are people faithfully to function within the roles they find themselves in? How can business people, given the realities of the system, be brought into dialogue? And, indeed, that dialogue ought to pertain to the macrolevel issues, as well. I would agree with you that we haven't much started yet.

QUESTION: If Christian theology is sufficiently resourceful to allow enormous diversity—as I think has been demonstrated—then one might say the task today is simply to take into account whatever the realities of life are within the context in which we experience them, and to try to speak out of the resources of our tradition to that. That is the strategy I gather you favor. That is, the set of issues or conflicts you mentioned, in large outline at least, comes from the religious tradition of Christianity.

Schubert Ogden, however, in his book *Faith and Freedom*, has charged that all Christian theology today is flawed by beginning with some set of commitments and offering a rationalization for that position at which it has already arrived.[4] His contention is that it may not be a case of some matters' not yet having been faced by Christian theologians, but rather of the resources' offering insufficient material from which to work. It may be that we are so deeply into a crisis of meaning that we have to think radically about the adequacy, appropriateness, and resourcefulness of traditional Christian theology for the context within which life has to be lived today.

DR. WOGAMAN: There is a sense in which that is true, and I think a sense in which it isn't. Theology ought to be self-critical, but it has to have ground to stand on. You know, like Archimedes, you can't lever the world unless you have a place outside the world to stand. The question is, then, Is there a generating center in the Christian theological view that can serve that purpose? I think so; but I would have to be very honest and say that any statement of Christian theology is an interpretation. And there is also a sense in which it is rationalization after the fact.

Still, it seems to me there are two or three things in the Christian faith, certain central values or perceptions, that are at the very root of reality. First of all, to say that God is revealed in Jesus Christ is to make the point that at the very center of being, there is personal caring. There is no way that can be proved; in fact, there may be a good deal of evidence to the contrary. But if it is true that our grasp of the ultimate character of reality is metaphorical, always moving from some experiences or phenomena to an interpretation of the whole, then I don't think it is any more irrational to proceed from what may be perceived as the

---

[4] Schubert M. Ogden, *Faith and Freedom: Toward a Theology of Liberation* (Nashville: Abingdon Press, 1979).

higher in interpreting the whole than it would be, for example, to interpret the whole of reality in relation to scientific procedures of one sort or another. Besides, if you begin from a materialistic model of reality, you have the intellectual problem of accounting for the emergence of higher forms with no fundamental anticipation in the very center of being. So I think it is reasonable to affirm that at the heart of reality, there is God. One then can look biographically at Jesus Christ, at the drama of the crucifixion and at Jesus' ministry, and draw from that a qualitative understanding of the character of God. God is much more than Jesus Christ, but Jesus Christ is a basis for understanding God.

I have come to feel that, as this point of view suggests, the really tough questions aren't so much the ones posed by science as the old theodicy questions. How does one grapple with evil? The existence of certain kinds of evil, particularly moral evil, implies that God created human beings with freedom, a freedom that includes the capacity for sin and maybe even a propensity to sin. Perhaps even more difficult to explain is the suffering of other sentient beings, the way nature is structured for tooth and talon, for some to be the victims of others. Yet after a lifetime of wrestling with these issues, I still find myself driven to the faith that reality is good, that at the heart of being is goodness, and that all the beauties of nature are forms of God's infinite communication of goodness. I, as a person, am accepted; my life has meaning; and ultimately, in spite of life's difficulties, I need not fear. And I would make the further step that that kind of ultimate optimism is the best culturally unifying and generating and liberating form of faith. Religious pessimism does not help generate creativities; it is out of gratitude that the heart sings, and that the great poetry emerges, and the great symphonies.

The theodicy question remains the tough one, and that brings me back to what I think was your starting point. Why did I emphasize these conflicts? I think it is because I agree with Paul Carter's thesis, in his book *The Decline and Revival of the Social Gospel*, that the secularism of the 1920s owed more to the failure of the churches to be sensitive during the era of Prohibition and the First World War than it did to science. The church was not responsive to the human tragedies at work in modern Western culture. The more sensitive poets and novelists of that period saw these tragedies all too clearly, and as a result they were turned off to the church. I want to emphasize this: that our capacity to be engaged with the tragedies and the suffering and the evils of our time is what helps people or hinders them from being able to grasp and understand and accept the faith we proclaim.

QUESTION: I have two questions. First, you referred to the fundamentalists as people who believe literally in the biblical myths and miracle stories. Do you then regard as a fundamentalist one who believes in the miracles of Christ? Do you regard such people as theological reactionaries, with the pejorative tone that has?

Second, you suggested that capitalism institutionalizes human greed. Would you be prepared to entertain another proposition, that perhaps human greed will find expression equally in all political-economic systems, including socialist systems?

DR. WOGAMAN: Regarding the fundamentalists, I don't want to be misunderstood; I think all people are God's children and are loved by God, and need to find self-acceptance. But fundamentalism as biblical literalism seems to me to be seeking to prop up a shaky faith with objective external support.

As far as the miracles are concerned, one might say that the healing miracles are consistent with general human experience, to some extent. But do I literally believe that Jesus turned water into wine, or that he walked on water that had a temperature higher than thirty-two degrees? No, I don't; and I think that to insist on that belief, which flies in the face of all observed experience, is a movement away from interpreting life on the basis of our common experience and faith. By the same token, I think the Resurrection is a central Christian doctrine, but the form of it is not; one need not insist on a literal interpretation of stories concerning the empty tomb, and so on. I do think it is crucial to Christian faith to say "Christ is risen": that is, God has not permitted this life to perish, with all that that means in terms of what life is.

Your other question, whether socialism could not leave as much room for human greed as capitalism does, is a very good question. In my book *The Great Economic Debate* I tried to pose the problem of centralization of power implicit in socialism. In most models of socialism, there is indeed a danger that the unity of political and economic power may overwhelm institutions of responsibility. But I am not going to retreat from my criticism of capitalism. The cultural effects of a system that challenges people to grasp need to be watched. More than productivity is at stake; more even than equal distribution is at stake. The cultural genie that is let out of the bottle, that has to do with defining people's values, that is important.

Now, I think we are all sinners, and I cannot conceive of any economic or political system that would not be afflicted with problems of sinfulness. We are dealing with relativities. The relevant debate, so far as Christians are concerned, is probably between a modified capitalism

—social-market capitalism—and a modified democratic socialism. Pure laissez-faire capitalism, I think, is discredited, as is Marxism, for reasons I tried to explore in my book. The advocates of capitalism need to make their case, not rhetorically, but in terms of results: can we begin to overcome the great disparities between the prosperous world and the third world, and create greater economic justice? And those who favor socialism need to do more than talk about equality of distribution; they need to show results in terms of real creativity—what is happening in the arts, in freedom of expression, and in the general health of the political life of the people. The returns aren't in yet; and those who support one or another basic ideology need to bend their efforts to concrete historical results because, in the long run, that is how the world is going to judge the question.

QUESTION: I believe your comments about the state and corporations show an asymmetry, in that you have not addressed the evils of the public sector to any comparable extent. I think it is worth mentioning that millions of Christians on this planet, while we are sitting here, are limited to one act of political relevance alone: saving their immortal souls. They are reduced to maintaining a fidelity of conscience—according to Solzhenitsyn, 30 million of them in the Soviet Union alone. I think we have paid far too little attention to the importance of saving one's immortal soul; and in failing in that, we have failed to pay attention to the underpinnings of our institutions. The fundamental social motive of capitalism as a system is, as Adam Smith designated it, the wealth of nations—not the wealth of individuals, not the wealth of Great Britain, but the wealth of nations, the betterment of humankind. You have said that the acquisitiveness, the self-interest of capitalism, needs to be watched. But this rational self-interest is far from being the most evil of human motivations; in some aspects it is even a virtue—it becomes a means of producing the greatest good for the greatest number of people. The amount of giving and generosity I have seen in capitalists and corporations is quite astonishing; yet there is no theological theory even noticing it, let alone rewarding it or encouraging it. A tremendous number of our fellow Christians working in corporations, because all they hear is negative things about corporations, find themselves living in a world of bad faith. They are publicly reprimanded for work about which they personally feel good; and there is a terrific disjunction in their lives, between their own knowledge of what they do and society's castigation of them for a greed they don't feel.

And that Gallup poll, I think, should not be made fun of. It goes along with other studies, which show that persons who go to clergymen for counseling report a higher rate of satisfaction at the changes in their lives than those who go to psychiatrists, counselors, or anybody else. I believe the high respect for clergymen is very well earned. It is carried even for people with little education, who out of a wisdom older and deeper than themselves can minister in times of death, bereavement, marriage, birth.

Last, I do not believe in optimism. It seems to me that one of the great forces of creativity is the most ruthless pessimism. I believe we are entering an exceedingly dark age; I believe that the superiority of Russian military might is the beginning of the end. I think Solzhenitsyn is right: we are moving into an age of tyranny the likes of which the world has never known. And I think we ought to prepare people for the only kind of political activity they are going to have, which is not to change the system, but to save their immortal souls. God permitted Jesus, His son, to be crucified, and we have no greater hope. I don't believe that in order to be creative you have to believe you are going to be successful or have any effect at all. I think it is quite enough to press on and do what you consider to be the right thing even under the most hopeless of circumstances. That is what, in a concentration camp, constitutes saving your soul, remaining faithful to God where there is no hope. To me, it is vitally important to see that people can go on without hope. Hope is not nearly so important as we make it out to be.

DR. WOGAMAN: I am, as you have indicated, in deep disagreement with much that you have said. But most of all, I wish to reiterate my feeling of hope about the historical era in which we are living. The times are difficult and challenging, but much can be accomplished by people of good faith and high vision.

QUESTION: I feel I have learned a lot, as a corporate businessman, in the last several days of these sessions. I am sorry to see, though, that so many of the people here seem to mistrust democratic capitalism. I hope people attending this seminar will make an effort to understand how the large corporation really works, because I think many of the questions that have been raised here reflect a lack of such understanding. Theologians should be debating the authenticity of the large corporation, what the corporation does well and poorly, and become involved so that it can be improved. I am deeply convinced that it *can* be improved— but not if we just sit here and say, "Well, that's the wrong side," and deny its reality.

103

DR. WOGAMAN: I greatly appreciate that statement. I begin to sense here and there around the country some reaching out from business in exactly that direction—conferences, for instance, sponsored by corporate leaders and religious leaders, designed to further some serious dialogue. I think that is terribly important.

Regarding the feeling you expressed that there is a fundamentally anticapitalist, antibusiness attitude here, I would rather my own remarks were interpreted as simply posing some of the searching questions and saying that the results will have to register historically. Maybe the questions that I, as a lay person from a business standpoint, have been asking are not the right ones. If so, we need to pursue that. On the other hand, people in business need to see that the criteria by which their performance is being judged by the world may not be the same criteria that are being posed in the boardroom.

QUESTION: I would like to raise a question about your view of the church as a mediating institution. I thought I heard you say the state should not make the church a political institution, but the church should be a place where political dialogue can take place. By this do you mean that church members and leaders should look at major problems, and use church facilities so that the discussion can go forward? Or do you mean something more? Should the Methodist Church of the United States, for example, take a position on the question of the gospel of peace and love versus the arms buildup of the twentieth century? Where matters like the Soviet Union, the arms race, and the implications for the future of the West are concerned, I don't think I would be very comfortable if I knew that these questions were being debated and formal positions were being taken in churches on the basis of some analysis of the gospel of peace and love, as the parishioners examined it. What are you really saying about the church as a mediating structure? Is it a debating society for important questions, or should it take a position?

DR. WOGAMAN: Well, I think the church does well to struggle toward a position when it has done its homework, but not on everything that comes along. When it does take a position, it ought to be reasonably concrete. For instance, I think the churches ought to be doing a good deal of thinking now about the pros and cons of ratification of the SALT II treaty, which according to its most enthusiastic supporters is only a modest bit of progress, and in the lips of its detractors is maybe part of a major decline. That needs to be sorted out, because it pertains to the awesome threat of thermonuclear war.

May I make one final comment before we conclude? We have, many of us, expressed ourselves vigorously tonight, and we have not blanched at the expression of disagreements. We all need to understand that our debates are under the ultimate aegis of forces and theological realities that are greater than any of us. And we ought to continue to love each other!

# The Large Business Corporation as a Mediating Structure

*Richard B. Madden*

Humanity seems to be inextricably involved with conflict. King and commoner, church and state, capitalism and socialism, economy and environment, society and the individual, government and industry—the list is endless. Many of these conflicts are between the individual and forces one cannot control alone. It is here that mediating structures come in. Peter Berger and Richard Neuhaus, professor at Rutgers and senior editor of *Worldview Magazine,* respectively, in their study *To Empower People,* have defined mediating structures as "those institutions standing between the individual in his private life and the large institutions of public life." Their definition excludes corporations, but I believe the corporation should be included.

The purpose of mediating structures is to serve individuals, to help them to realize their own objectives more completely, to allow them freedom of choice. An individual has a number of identities. From the corporate point of view, he can be a shareholder, an employee, or both. He can be an investor, a customer, a supplier, or simply a citizen of a community that is affected by a corporation. In these various roles, an individual can find resolution of many of his own conflicts through the mediating forces a corporation can provide in the social, economic, and political areas.

That large corporations can act as mediating structures between individuals and the many other forces in society is a thesis that is not widely recognized. Because it is not, corporations, our society, and— even more tragically—individuals are the poorer. I believe it is to the advantage of all of us for large corporations to become more active as mediating structures. I hope I can begin to persuade you of this view, and I hope more corporations will see the same advantages I do in expanding a role they already fill.

To focus on the large business corporation as a mediating structure, we first need to review certain aspects of four concepts: the business corporation, the individual, the state, and mediating structures themselves.

## The Corporation: An Organization of Individuals

Hardly anyone today can picture the "company of friends" that was the ancestor of the modern corporation, yet the concept of friends was inherent in those early business associations: individuals pooled their savings, and often their efforts, in a joint enterprise. Today, a corporation is defined as an association of individuals created under the authority of state laws that recognize it as a separate entity having its own rights, privileges, and liabilities, distinct from those of its members. We often forget that this definition emphasizes individuals, just as the earlier definition emphasized friends. I mention it here because I want to return to the importance of the individual later on.

By recognizing the business corporation, the states have helped create vehicles in which individuals can join together for a particular venture, while limiting their personal liability for the venture to the amounts of money they have invested in it. The corporation thus is a way for individuals to undertake commercial risks none of them could handle alone. This kind of risk taking is beneficial to society, and the corporation has proved itself to be a most efficient mechanism for encouraging it and for minimizing those risks. Furthermore, bankruptcy can make the system self-correcting.

The purpose of the business corporation is specific: to earn a growing profit and a reasonable rate of return for the individuals who have created it. The essential element here is the reasonable rate of return, for without it the corporation would eventually wither and die. This rate of return must, at a very minimum, equal the corporation's cost of attracting capital. The profits generated by the return can be distributed to the individual shareholders or retained in the business for further investment. To the extent that adequate funds are wisely reinvested, this reasonable return will generate a growing profit. Thus the growing profit and the reasonable rate of return are closely related. Both hinge on the willingness of the original participants to make and to retain their investment, the willingness of new investors to join in, and the willingness of various lenders to provide the funds the corporation may need to maintain its capacity to earn a reasonable rate of return.

## The Concept of Profit

The word profit is misleading in common usage, because so-called profit seldom exceeds the normal cost of capital. Profit in the sense of net gain really is an accounting term. In any relatively free market, over time, if the rate of return exceeds the cost of capital, competition will enter the field, and the return will decrease. If the return drops below the cost of capital, new competitors will not enter the field, and existing competitors may reduce their involvement. Then the rate of return gradually will increase until it reaches a level at least equal to the cost of capital. The cost of capital will, of course, vary, depending on the relationship of risk to reward; but over time, there is seldom anything left over— any true economic profit. Rather, there is a cost of capital which will be equated with the reasonable rate of return expected under the circumstances. Therefore, when the accounting profit equals the corporation's cost of capital, the true economic profit is zero.

These concepts may sound elementary, but they seem to be widely misunderstood. In a market-oriented system of democratic capitalism, individual participation is fundamental; it is therefore essential both to the health of individual business corporations and to the overall health of our economy that people comprehend the system and feel confidence in it. At Potlatch we have written a corporate philosophy that starts with our sole objective, namely, to earn a growing profit and a reasonable rate of return. We go on to say, however, that this objective can be effectively achieved only through talented, well-trained, and highly motivated people, properly supported by a sound financial structure, and with a keen sense of social responsibility to all of the publics with whom the corporation has contact. Each of these supporting principles for our corporate objective is based on people: individual employees, individual stockholders and lenders, and the individuals who make up the many publics with whom we deal.

### The Importance of the Individual

This leads me to the second of the four concepts I want to cover: the importance of the individual. Alexis de Tocqueville, in *Democracy in America*, observed that equality of opportunity was the concept that gave promise to a young land where hard work and ability, not accidents of birth, were the hallmarks of rising expectations. Economic and political freedom in the United States was rooted in the firm belief that the individual possesses rights and dignity that the state does not confer and cannot take away. Politically, this concept provided the foundation for our popular representative government and our constitutional guarantees, including the Bill of Rights. Economically, it meant that the individual was considered to have the right to own property, to make his own economic decisions, to pursue his own interests, and to enjoy the fruits of his labor. The concept of individual rights unchained the most powerful of human motivations, the self-interest of a free individual responsible for his own success or failure. It also offered another great motivating force, the opportunity for self-fulfillment.

It should be obvious that it is individuals who work, create, and save. Society can only distribute what individuals produce; and what society provides to one individual it must obtain from another. The literature of the human race is full of warnings against excesses and abuses in this area. King Midas repented of his greedy wish. The dead goose could lay no golden eggs. The camel refused to budge under the weight of the last straw. We are seeing the same thing today on a national scale in Sweden and Great Britain, where productivity by individuals has collapsed under a tax burden that simply became too great. Some percentage of what individuals produce must be available for redistribution by society, but society suffers if that percentage becomes so high as to discourage individual initiative. Productivity falls, the expenditures of government exceed its income, and inflation occurs.

If we really are concerned about society, then, we must focus first on the importance of the individual and what will create wealth. Simply stated, we must realize that we cannot distribute what we do not have, and we cannot have what we do not create. Since individuals create and society can only distribute, we must develop a rational economic and political philosophy with the individual as its cornerstone if we are to keep our society healthy and growing.

## The Role of the State

The third concept is misunderstood, too, or at least it is conceived of in far too many guises. That concept is the state, which my dictionary defines as the supreme public power within a sovereign political entity, or an aggregation of individuals united under a single government.

The objective of the state generally should be to do for its citizens only those things they cannot do for themselves, either individually or through voluntary organizations they select and control. This approach goes back to the critical importance of the individual. The state is almost never able to act impartially; whenever it acts, it is bound to favor some individuals and impinge on the rights of others. The individual works, creates, and saves, and the state can only distribute what individuals produce. It follows, then, that the activities of the state should be limited to those areas where the majority of individuals who make up society agree on a goal but cannot or will not act—as individuals or through a mediating structure—to achieve it.

Tocqueville, writing about an earlier, but still strongly recognizable, nation, said, "In America, the people are enlightened, awake to their own interests, and accustomed to take thought for them. I am persuaded that the collective force of the citizens will always be better able to achieve social prosperity than the authority of the government." This is in direct contrast to the thesis Franklin D. Roosevelt presented to Congress a hundred years later, which has since become almost an article of faith in the development of public policy. Roosevelt said, "As new conditions and problems arise beyond the power of men and women to meet as individuals, it becomes the duty of the government itself to find new remedies with which to meet them. . . . Government has the definite duty to use all its power and resources to meet new social problems with new social controls." Political debate over the past four decades has largely revolved around which part of government—local, state, or federal—should accomplish these goals, rather than whether there might be a better and more efficient social mechanism for achieving them. In a sense, we have accepted the premise that society consists of the individual and the state, with nothing in between.

### Mediating Structures: A New Concept

The fourth concept is the mediating structure, a label I used in the title of these remarks, and an entity that is just beginning to gain recognition under that name. Mediating structures have been defined as "those institutions standing between the individual in his private life and the large institutions of public life." The state is the classic large institution of public life; the individual we have also discussed. Mediating structures generally are considered to include the family, the neighborhood, the church, and the many varied voluntary organizations that appear to be especially vital in our American social climate. They take in everything from private schools, museums, and hospitals to organizations for the arts or public welfare. Even today, there are tens of thousands of separate, identifiable organizations of this kind in the United States.

Berger and Neuhaus, describing the reasons for their interest in this topic, argue that the mediating function of these structures is "crucial to democracy" and that the "understanding of mediating structures is sympathetic to Edmund Burke's well-known claim: 'To be attached to the subdivision, to love the little platoon we belong to in society, is the first principle (the germ as it were) of public affections.' " This presupposes the individual's freedom to choose his or her subdivision, and that choice requires alternatives. Size has relatively little to do with whether or not an organization can serve as a mediating structure; however, if large size improves the ability to offer alternatives, then size can

110

be an advantage. The community orchestra versus the large city symphony would be an example of the phenomenon.

It often has been argued that the functions appropriate for mediating structures can be handled equally well by the state. This is the attitude and practice in most totalitarian nations. I believe this approach has two serious flaws. First, the state cannot, in our present complex society, react equitably to all citizens, on a general rule-making basis. The state must be autocratic in the sense that it must decide among alternatives: when it selects certain choices, it must eliminate others. It can never be as responsive to all the individuals who make it up as can the tens of thousands of mediating structures. Second, the state has consistently proved itself to be a most inefficient vehicle for accomplishing the objectives of the mediating structures.

These points have been proved time and time again over the centuries in every nation where the state has taken over the activities of the mediating structures. Two recent examples come from our own society. One involves private colleges, a system of mediating structures that certainly has a legitimate place in contemporary America. Religious denominations would argue strongly for their survival. Private colleges for black students, designed to help members of a disadvantaged minority prepare themselves to compete in society, serve a special purpose. For them, some federal assistance is virtually a necessity. Yet the conditions under which these funds are available puts pressure on black colleges to reverse the policies that made them especially valuable mediating structures, for discrimination is illegal, even in a good cause.

What is happening to "Meals on Wheels" is equally disturbing. Founded twenty-five years ago to provide nutritious meals to shut-ins and the elderly, this nonprofit, all-volunteer movement had over a thousand independent groups by 1977. Congress decided this was such a worthy program that it deserved federal funding; but the money also brought a 105-page policy manual, federal administrators, and proposed requirements that many of the unpaid volunteers cannot meet, such as professional training and use of approved bookkeeping methods. The organization also would be forced to meet minority quotas, to add elements to its program such as recreational opportunities, shopping trips, and counseling, and to meet various other federal requirements.

Substantial state support of any mediating structure invites this kind of difficulty. Domination of a mediating structure's finances most often will lead to control of the structure itself. Since the objective of the mediating structure is to provide an intermediate institution between the individual and the state, the state cannot dominate or the individual will lose the mediator.

No one questions the need for the services mediating structures can provide. However, it is my thesis that for the mediating structure to be effective, it must represent the individual, offer an alternative choice, and be relatively free from state control, including financial domination. This thesis starts with the family and the church and includes all of those private organizations providing mediating services for the individual, including the business corporation, large or small.

## The Corporation's Mediating Role

The corporation, as it originally evolved, meets the definition of a mediating structure. For the owners, the corporation is a means of seeking mutual financial benefits while limiting the individual risks they might otherwise incur. A large, healthy corporation also provides security for numerous employees. As their numbers grow, it gives them the further opportunity to pool their resources in group insurance, pensions, credit unions, and even more unusual benefits—day nurseries, for example. In addition, the corporation provides alternatives for suppliers, customers, and investors in the communities in which it operates. Finally, the resources of a corporation can be used to support other mediating structures that improve the social climate in which the corporation exists and from which it must attract the kind of people it needs to excel. This might mean helping financially with the creation or maintenance of a senior citizens' center, a school for retarded children, or a center for the performing arts.

It is quite clear to me that if we, as a democratic capitalist nation, are to succeed, then the private sector must succeed; and the private sector cannot succeed if any important part of it fails. Mediating structures are an important part of our private structure; they should be encouraged to flourish.

Labor unions and business corporations have grown to a size where, according to Berger and Neuhaus, they are no longer mediating structures, but megastructures. By definition, these megastructures are assumed to have lost their ability to reflect the needs and desires of the individuals they were created to serve. I believe it is erroneous to include the large business corporation in this category. My major thesis, in fact, is quite the contrary:

- that the large business corporation is a mediating structure of the utmost importance to our nation
- that unless it succeeds, first, in its sole objective of a growing profit and a reasonable rate of return and, second, in its role as a mediat-

ing structure, this nation will pass, as have so many great nations in the past, into a twilight of mediocrity or, even worse, into a dark age.

The recent work by Professor Yale Brozen of the University of Chicago and the American Enterprise Institute entitled *The Concentration-Collusion Doctrine* describes why the large corporation creates efficiencies far beyond what philosophers of the last two centuries could have predicted. Because of cost efficiencies, corporations create savings and jobs that are not possible for smaller, less competitive enterprises. Brozen concludes, "Industries have become concentrated where that was the road to lower costs. It is these lower costs that have created temporary above-average profitability in concentrated industries when it has occurred. Where concentration was not the road to lower costs, industries have remained unconcentrated. The market has worked surprisingly well, where it has been permitted, to conserve our resources and maximize our output."

For any nation to achieve its societal goals, productivity must improve. Individual productivity can improve only so far; then machines and large-scale efficiencies must take over. The Chinese have finally realized the inevitability of this shift. Self-sufficient local economies cannot produce the efficiencies of scale of great industrial concentrations and technological advancement. These efficiencies can only be created by companies of great financial strength, and they can only occur with huge modern facilities.

Efficiencies of scale make it possible for the large corporation to tackle the challenge of the mediating role. Any organization has to guard against diverting resources that are necessary for its own survival, and the smaller the structure, the more critical is each of its parts. Corporations with large resources can afford to devote more attention to subjects unrelated to bare survival than smaller ones can. For only after survival has been assured can attention be given to perfecting the structure and its environment—including a social climate that encourages the development of the individual abilities a large organization needs to continue to be efficient.

What if we can rekindle the flame of productivity? What if we can open people's eyes to the need for a reasonable rate of return and capital formation, the need for the cost efficiencies of huge capital- or technology-intensive industries? Do we then have a societal vehicle that can act as an adequate repository of this vast trust? I believe we do, and it is the large business corporation.

The corporation is not perfect: it is run by humans, and it is prey to all their faults as well as all their strengths. If we as a nation are to achieve continued well-being for our people, however, I believe we must be competitive in our productive sectors. Productivity depends on the wise use of capital in vast amounts. This capital is initially created by the savings of individuals, and it will be managed by individuals who are entrusted with it as were the three servants in the Gospel of Matthew who received talents from their master. The two faithful servants, whose honest work returned a profit on the talents entrusted to them, were rewarded, each according to his ability. The unprofitable servant was cast into outer darkness, and there was weeping and gnashing of teeth.

The parable spoke only of profit, but much more was meant. The servants who were entrusted with their master's talents and the servants, or managers, of today's corporations know there is more to business success than one-time earnings. The perceptive manager quickly realizes that to achieve the sole objective of a growing profit and a reasonable rate of return, the organization must act as a mediating structure.

Let me use another example: Jonas Martin, living in a small western village in the nineteenth century, is a very good cobbler. He wants to earn more money for a better home, a college education for his children, and, in general, a better way of life. He goes to his friends, and, since they trust him, they invest their savings in his businesss. With these funds and a loan from the local bank, which in turn is entrusted with the savings of various individuals, Jonas buys some shoemaking equipment to increase his productivity.

Now Jonas is able to produce enough boots and shoes to supply other nearby towns. But he still has to make the shoes and sell them. This means he has to deal with the local ranchers, his employees, the various communities in which he operates, and his many prospective customers. Each of these publics creates potential pitfalls for his fledgling enterprise. If Jonas alienates the ranchers, they will not sell him hides; if he does not offer a going wage, his more ambitious employees will leave; if he locates his factory next to the church, he will antagonize the neighbors; and if his shoes are defective, his sales will be short-lived.

Can Jonas survive all these obstacles? He will if he can react appropriately as a mediating structure to all of his publics. If he does a satisfactory job, he will return to his friends a growing profit and a reasonable rate of return. If he does not, his customers' or suppliers' or employees' retribution will be quick, and it will be apparent how and why he has failed. This assumes, of course, that everyone Jonas deals with has a choice—that competition exists. Where there is no competition, you must sell your hides to the only buyer or not sell them at all; you must buy your shoes from the only cobbler or go without. If there is only one employer, you work for him or you are unemployed. Providing there is competition, it is in Jonas Martin's self-interest to recognize his responsibilities to everyone with whom he deals, for the success of his business depends on it.

## The Corporation in Today's World

Our modern industrial world is much more complicated than Jonas Martin's village. Many times a failing business is not immediately perceived as such, but can live for a while off the accumulated wealth of the past. The principles remain the same, however: over time, the business corporation must be a mediating structure to all its publics if it is to achieve its sole objective of a growing profit and a reasonable rate of return. If it does not, it will fail, and our failures are legion. We must not destroy this possibility of failure, if as a nation we are to succeed. Competition guarantees that possibility. Yet we must also recognize the need for a climate conducive to success.

While the cobbler Jonas Martin is imaginary, his story has been replicated throughout the United States over and over again. At Potlatch we say that our growing profit and reasonable rate of return can only be achieved "by talented, well-trained, and highly motivated people, properly supported by a sound financial structure and with a keen sense of social responsibility to all of the publics with whom the company has contact." That is, we must be a mediating structure to succeed in our sole objective. There is, furthermore, no question in my mind that we do act as a mediating structure, although failures do sometimes occur, since we are only human.

In the employee area we strive to provide competitive wages, regular, steady work, safe and attractive working conditions, opportunities for personal growth, respect for the dignity and integrity of each employee as an individual, opportunity for open, two-way communication, and affirmative actions which fulfill not only the company's legal but also its moral obligations to provide equal opportunity for all employees. In the financial area we deal fairly, honestly, and openly with all our lenders, recognizing that they represent many individuals who have entrusted funds to them, yet we also recognize our primary financial obligation to our own shareholders, just as did that early "company of friends." In this sphere we mediate directly for our shareholders and indirectly for our lenders.

With regard to our publics, we not only recognize, as Jonas Martin did, the importance to us of suppliers, customers, and all the various communities in which we operate, but we also frequently mediate for them. Such mediation can vary from advocacy of a fair inheritance-tax bill for small timberland owners who supply us with fiber, to the support of uniform standards for our customer home builders, to advocacy of an improved school system in a community where we operate. Finally, we contribute directly and indirectly to other mediating structures. These contributions run the gamut from partially financing a local private hospital wing and supporting numerous private service organizations to lending bulldozers and their operators to remove the debris caused by a tornado or to build a Little League ballpark.

We all know of businesses that do not serve as mediating structures but that somehow continue to exist. Most of them eventually fail, because their competitors serve people's needs better. Competition provides a climate that will give an advantage to the business that best serves all the individuals involved with the corporation. Thus it stimulates corporations to pay more attention to individuals.

Competition also permits talented employees to choose among employers. A company's reputation is the deciding factor to many potential employees. Reputation also directs the choice of potential investors or shareholders wondering whether to entrust their funds to one company or another, and it can help a community decide whether to support a company in its efforts to expand, or even to locate in a desirable area. To give itself the best opportunity to grow, then, a corporation must give individuals the same opportunity. It must mediate.

### "Altruistic Egoism"

The large business corporation is needed today more than ever because of its efficiency in producing jobs, capital, and the reasonable rate of return its owners have a right to expect. Simultaneously it can afford to be and it must be a mediating structure if it is to succeed over time. It must be selfish with regard to its shareholders' reasonable objectives, yet it must be sensitive to its social role. It will not always succeed at this complex task, because it is composed of fallible individuals. But a failure in one area does not mean the entire system is wrong, only that one manager or group has not understood that the corporation's need for a growing profit and reasonable rate of return cannot be separated from its role as a mediating structure.

I believe the large business corporation frequently was a fundamental mediating structure in the past, and it can continue to be one today. It would be overly optimistic to say that most corporations today have achieved this potential. Many of them are working toward this goal, however, with some promise of success.

116

Self-interest and mediating structures: Are they compatible? I contend they are. Let's look at two examples.

In the field of medicine, around forty years ago, Doctor Hans Selye of the University of Montreal made discoveries about human reactions that led him to create his famous theory of stress. He summed up the essentials of stress avoidance as "altruistic egoism": first know yourself —be selfish—then apply yourself to altruistic aims.

In the field of religion, some two thousand years ago, Jesus of Nazareth discussed humankind's responsibility for financial stewardship and for charity. Many religious leaders since then have said roughly the same things.

Why should the large business corporation not take the same approach? First, know your corporate self, your economic reason for being; develop your corporate talents; don't be ashamed to be selfish for your shareholders. Recognize and seek the engineered efficiencies of scale and productivity that are possible in the corporate context. Second, apply this selfishness to altruistic aims, to charitable purposes, to worthwhile goals—that is, make a good competitive product; create opportunities for unprejudicial employment, worthwhile work, and personal growth for your employees; deal fairly with your customers, financial backers, and suppliers; aid the communities in which you operate—in general, be a mediating structure.

If the large business corporation can do all this, I contend that it should be supported in achieving its sole objective of a growing profit and reasonable rate of return, as well as encouraged to contribute to the welfare of our society by remaining a most valued mediating structure.

# Discussion

QUESTION: You stressed that the state should not attempt to do the job of mediating structures, that it should stick to its job and let them do theirs. My question is whether the government should undertake this policy of noninterference on the corporation's terms. As you said, the corporation's job is to make a profit: that is the primary goal, and its mediating role helps it achieve this. Now, surely, a family doesn't exist to make a profit; a school doesn't exist to make a profit. I hope families exist to make love and schools exist to make knowledge, and all kinds of other institutions have other mediating roles. Shouldn't the state be concerned to see to it that families and schools have room to perform their functions? Shouldn't it protect individuals from bad air and water? You mentioned how the corporation ought to carry on its mediating role in a nonprejudicial way, aiding the healthy atmosphere of workers. My recollection is that, historically, most of those pressures for benevolence —for keeping young children from working, and so on—were not initiated from within the corporation, but came precisely because the larger community was interested in having other interests served besides profit making.

It sounded to me almost as if you were arguing for business not simply to be given room to be a mediating structure, but to be trusted with the major mediation of all public goods. It can be trusted; the state can't be trusted. It is efficient; the state isn't efficient. It can work with all kinds of groups and persons; it can look after hospitals and farmers and cattle ranchers. In other words, if we would just let the government wither away and allow the business corporation to become the largest mediating structure, all would be well.

MR. MADDEN: I think I agree essentially with the thrust of your comments. However, I did not mean to imply that the corporation can do all good things for all people, nor should it. But I do think there are many things a large corporation can do and should do to be a mediating structure. It can be used for the good of mankind. It is the most efficient

118

proven capital-formation mechanism in the world today, or in the history of the world, as best I can study it. The small corporation doesn't have that advantage. It's on the razor's edge. In a small business, you are wondering every day if you can meet the payroll. You can't afford to think about giving money to help a senior citizens' home. How many small corporations have pensions, let alone any kind of health plan? Most don't; they can't.

I tried to say there is no such thing as profit in the sense that we talk about a profit. There is a return on capital. So, in one sense, the corporation is neutral relative to its sole goal, which is an economic goal. Now, the state, I feel, must create a set of laws within which the game will be played. At Potlatch we have spent over $50 million fighting air and water pollution alone in three of our plants. No one is going to do that sort of thing without someone—the state, I would contend—saying that this is a rule, this is how we as a society have decided we are going to play the game.

QUESTION: First, you put special emphasis on the fact that the corporation is made up of individuals. But what institution is not made up of individuals? It seems to me that to focus on the individual is to take away from the importance of the institution, which is what we are trying to understand. But that is a relatively minor point.

Second, if size is irrelevant, as you insist, to whether or not an industry might serve as a mediating structure, then I think we must dispense with the whole concept of a mediating structure. The reason, of course, is that a liberal might—and, I think, would and does—contend that the state is a mediating structure. If we go back to the origins of the modern state, it was indeed intended to be exactly that.

MR. MADDEN: Two very good questions. First, you are right; every organization is made up of individuals. The reason I stress it is that I have sensed, a number of times when I have given papers, that many people think of the corporation as some type of monolithic structure that has an existence outside of people.

Your second point is a good one as well. To me, the word "mediate" means you mediate between something and something else. Ultimately, this could even be done by some supraworld organization. I think in some ways the state does mediate indirectly between, say, a corporation and individuals, insofar as it creates rules within which the corporation is to operate.

With regard to the size argument, I would contend that as you study a large corporation, what you find is that it is not just a behemoth;

119

it is made up of a whole lot of small groups. Size is not really all that relevant to the corporation's ability to mediate, because its structures can be set up to work in a delegated, segmented way. Getting to the heart of your question, then, Should we forget mediating structures? I would say no. One needs to be able to mediate between two extremes. The corporation can mediate between the state and the individual irrespective of its size.

QUESTION: One of our previous speakers suggested that democracy is best served when the various mediating structures are themselves democratically constituted. You have defined the large corporation as a mediating structure, but you haven't really spoken to the question of its democratic qualities. I refer particularly to the shareholders. You did say that the corporation mediates for the shareholders, but that is, it seems to me, more a paternalistic claim than a democratic one.

As an example, a certain large insurance company sends me, as a small policyholder, an annual report, as the Securities and Exchange Commission requires that it does. In it, the company tells me it is trying hard to centralize, and I am assured that bigger is better, so I will be better served as a shareholder through that. Second, there is a litigation underway; the federal government feels the company should pay more taxes than it has been paying over the last six or eight years, and they tell me they think they have a good case. And the other thing the SEC asks of them, and they of me, is that I send in my proxy vote. What I feel when I read all this is that, as a shareholder, my democratic level of participation is not nearly so real as my democratic participation as a citizen in the political structure. Employees and members of communities in which such large corporations find themselves might feel differently, but for shareholders, I think the democracy is quite limited.

MR. MADDEN: I can't deny that as you have more people and as things become more complex, the mechanisms to handle them become more complex. We could do away with all the problems we have with credit cards if, as Charles Schultze says, we did away with people, or if we did away with credit cards. But to the extent that we want credit cards and we are a nation of over two hundred million people, we have some complexities built in. Going back to your question, there is no doubt that as you get larger, you lose some of the personal touch that existed in the past. However, do we worry about shareholder reaction? Yes, we do. The proxy vote seems impersonal—it is impersonal. But it is not meaningless. I tell you, my job is on the line once a year. Members of the House complain about their job being on the line once every other year.

QUESTION: But I don't have an option that says no, you cannot have my proxy, unless I choose not to send the thing back.

MR. MADDEN: Oh, yes, you do. If it is a stock-owned company, you vote for or against the board of directors, the slate, and so on, and so I am up for election every year.

QUESTION: If I vote for or against the Communist party in the Soviet Union, are you as a party official up for election?

MR. MADDEN: Yes, that is a good point. We usually do win rather handsomely, because more people are inclined to say yes than no. But this is not always true, and if dissents begin to reach 10 to 15 percent, a significant point is made. This is why I advocate that people study the corporation, get involved somehow. You know, do some weekend work, or offer your services in any way you can. Otherwise it's hard to understand the tensions, the interaction, the group situations that occur in a corporation. This is why I keep coming back to people; so often people think either, well, it is a monolithic organization that we can't understand, or, yes, it is made up of people, but everything is made up of people. But pragmatically, it is people interacting at a gut level, on things that have all sorts of implications for society. Furthermore, the freedom to buy and sell shares in the ownership of a company can dramatically affect the price of those shares and the management of the company.

QUESTION: I agree with you that size is probably not as significant in defining a mediating structure as some kind of qualitative concern is. It seems to me that an important feature of Berger and Neuhaus's definition of a mediating structure is that it has something to do with providing people with a personal identity and meaning in human life. That is part of the definition I haven't heard you address. How do you see the corporation providing a locus of identity and meaning?

MR. MADDEN: The qualitative issue is most important. First, let me say that any organization, large or small, can have this qualitative feature or not, depending really on its leadership. That leadership may be the first-line foreman, the professor, the manager in a corporation, the vice president, or, in my own case, the chairman. At any level, individual

121

leadership is where it starts. The corporation that will survive, I believe, is the one that provides the qualitative opportunity to people within it; and that is the one that is sensitive to decentralization. The corporation's officers have to delegate authority; they have to believe in career development, giving people the opportunity to develop in whatever way is appropriate, anything from a fairly simplistic job-rotation program at a supervisor's level up to something much more sophisticated, like an advanced business course for a junior officer. And when people join the company, or change jobs within it, they should feel that they are joining a group of friends.

If you go through the plant of a corporation that is managed that way, and you talk with the man at a machine, he is proud of it and of his friends in the organization. They go out and play ball on their lunch hour. They like to fish together. They are, in fact, a team of friends. And they feel challenged; they feel they have opportunities. So, I think, in that sense, there is the qualitative side to a corporation as a mediating structure, if it is managed properly.

QUESTION: Are you suggesting, then, that you want to use a theory of work as a theory of meaning in human life?

MR. MADDEN: Well, that is a hard question. I wasn't implying that work is the only thing on the qualitative side. I think you are asking about a deeper issue, which doesn't relate to the fact that people need to work for a livelihood and therefore they come into the Potlatch mill. I am contending that the Potlatch mill creates an ambiance where people are not only working for money, but they also enjoy the people, they feel a challenge, they have opportunities for personal growth, and so there is a self-fulfillment opportunity as well. I don't want to deny the work ethic, because that is important, but I am saying there is this additional factor that is also important, that goes back to your qualitative side.

QUESTION: There has been a movement since 1970, when Ralph Nader formed a committee to make General Motors responsible, called the corporate-responsibility movement. Although there are many directions from which corporations have to take flak, this one is rather concentrated. And it's theological, at least superficially. That is, Christian activists are insisting, at corporate meetings where they may go with one share of stock, that the company follow a rather specific interpretation of Christian ethics in making decisions—decisions dealing with corporate operations in South Africa or Chile, or with the environment. The bottom line for these people is people, not profit. What do you think when these people speak to you, and what are your reactions to the movement?

MR. MADDEN: I think that is a terribly important question. First, we welcome criticism at Potlatch. That does not mean we accept each criticism at face value; we try to analyze it, find out if it is based on facts, if it's worthwhile or not, and see what can be done with it. I mention this because it is not necessarily true of all corporations, especially in the past. The corporation still is not way out front; it reflects society, just as the state does, for good or for evil, and we can do with it what we want. It is a relatively neutral organization.

But you say, "People, not profits." Well, one of the most important messages I was trying to get across today is that we must have profits. In an economic sense, of course, profits don't really exist; the point is to have a reasonable rate of return. If we forget that, the corporation goes bankrupt. So I would contend that people are not incompatible with profits or a reasonable return, because it is people who produce it and who benefit from it.

Now, finally, you talked about specifically religious attacks. So long as you are receiving attacks from knowledgeable people or well-intentioned people who are attempting to improve the corporation and its objectives, then I feel those attacks may well be warranted, and we had better listen. If the attack is aimed at something outside the corporation's methods and goals, then that person should take his or her case to the state government, to the local government, to the federal government for resolution, depending on what it is. If we are going to decide, as a people, on certain standards for air and water, then, to the extent that Potlatch can meet those standards and still remain competitive, we should do so on our own initiative. To the extent that if we did this we would lose our competitive position, then the case against pollution really should be presented for solution to the state, because one has to maintain the competitive ambiance within which the corporate wealth machine, if you will, can continue to produce.

Now, I happen to serve on the board of Del Monte, and in the past we received quite a lot of flak about investments in South Africa. No one denies that Del Monte is among the most progressive companies in South Africa. The blacks they employ are living better than most, and they have an open policy for employment, and so on. Still, the advocacy is, pull out of South Africa because South Africa is wrong in many of the things it is doing. But what happens if we do pull out? Is it going to change? No, not really. Del Monte is doing something good in the employment area; it is setting an example that can be copied by others.

It is making a reasonable return for its shareholders. And it can't affect the social situation in South Africa more than it is already doing. So I don't know why it should pull out.

International laws have tried to get at this kind of problem, but they are inadequate; so largely has been the United Nations. Until humankind has a better way to handle this, I think you have to take it case by case on the issues; appraise it, listen to the people that chastise you, and then try to determine whether it is appropriate for you to take action, or whether it should be done by some other group. This is the minimalist doctrine.

# Organized Labor as a Mediating Structure

*Tom Kahn*

We seem to be entering a new era of political posturing, in which words have more importance than content. This being the case, I feel the need to renounce a label that was pinned on me by *Esquire* magazine, which referred to me as a neoconservative. I am not a neoconservative because, to the extent that I want to reexamine critically the nature of the welfare state, I prefer to do so from the point of view of one who favored its construction in the first place, and not from the point of view of one who was against it. I thought, then, that I might use the label "neo-liberal" to convey that sympathetic, though critical, attitude toward the welfare state. But that also causes confusion, because you have to ask what kind of liberal I am "neo" to. An old-fashioned nineteenth-century liberal? A New Deal liberal? What I really am, perhaps, is a neo–social democrat—that is, a social democrat who has learned something over the last fifteen or twenty or twenty-five years, who starts out with a basically egalitarian attitude toward society but has recognized that the nationalization of the economy is not the answer, and that between complete private control of the economy and complete nationalization of the economy there is a wide field for experimentation.

## The Essential Role of Unions

One of the reasons I was interested in coming here to talk about trade unions as mediating structures was that for so long now we have been attacked by our critics—most recently, the occupants of the White House—as but another special interest group. I would like to suggest that the phrase "mediating structure" is a synonym for special interest group, and so I come to talk about the labor movement as a mediating structure in our society.

When I read the Berger-Neuhaus booklet, while preparing these remarks, I was struck by the reference several times to big labor. In fact, the term "big labor" was used more often than "big business"—business being the other word "big" is supposed to go with. "Big" seems to be the first name of labor and business, just as crusty old George Meany's first two names are "crusty old."

The authors even went so far as to compare us to HEW. That reveals, I think, how little is understood about unions, even among people who approach unions somewhat sympathetically. HEW, as I understand it, is a very large, multi-billion-dollar, highly centralized bureaucracy. The AFL-CIO has a budget considerably smaller than HEW's, and it is a highly decentralized, not centralized, operation.

What the labor movement is really about is some 60,000 local unions in the United States. That is what the trade union movement is to the worker. He doesn't belong to the AFL-CIO; he doesn't send his dues in to Sixteenth Street in Washington. He belongs to a local union. That means there are hundreds of thousands of individuals who are union officials, union leaders, in the United States. A good portion of them are part time and unpaid, and they are rather average people, with roots in their communities.

Those 60,000 or so local unions negotiate some 150,000 collective bargaining agreements. That is a rather extraordinary thing. If we did not have collective bargaining agreements, then what alternative mechanisms would we have for setting wages? Basically, two: wages could be determined unilaterally by the employer, or wages could be determined by state decree. Yet, very few people seem to think of collective bargaining as part of the central function of a mediating institution in our society. We tend to look on it as either a dull affair or a nuisance. When collective bargaining breaks down, and the result is a strike, that is a problem for everybody. But, fundamentally, collective bargaining is the institutional arrangement by which we avoid having state control of wages or unilateral employer determination of wages.

### Unions' Double Role

It is an immensely complicated business, the consummation of 150,000 agreements. Each one results from people's sitting down across the table. Here is where the trade union reveals itself as a kind of double mediating structure: that is, it mediates between the worker and the state, protecting the worker from state fiat, state-decreed wage levels; and it also mediates to protect him from the employer.

So long as these mediating trade union structures exist, there is no way the state can have complete control over our economy. That is a very important thing. There are many other mediating structures in

126

society that could go out the window, and although we might miss them sorely, the economic structure of the country would remain pretty much the same. Not so if trade unions did not exist. Totalitarians understand that. That is why trade unions are the first institutions that are destroyed in a totalitarian seizure of power, whether it be fascist or communist, from the left or the right.

As I say, collective bargaining is a very messy process, and consequently, it has its critics. They just find it too messy; they would prefer that some neater formula be established for governing wages and for working out disagreements between the worker and his employer.

An incomes policy would be a lot neater than collective bargaining. We would just have a government decree saying all wages shall be restricted to 7 percent increases, no more. It would save a lot of time. People wouldn't have to sit down at the collective bargaining table and scream and yell at each other, as they do now. We wouldn't have to hire all the lawyers we now have to hire to go up against management's lawyers. We could simply sit back and collect the dues and run social affairs.

But that is a very dangerous business. This is why the AFL-CIO went to court against President Carter's threat to cut off government contracts to companies that exceeded the 7 percent voluntary wage guideline. We were not interested in protecting the companies, maintaining their access to government contracts, so much as in defending ourselves against the principle that under a *voluntary* program of wage guidelines, the state could employ coercive power. We won the case in the lower court, we lost it in the higher court, and the case will go on.

I can't think of a clearer and more direct illustration of the role of the labor movement as a mediating structure between the individual and the state than this case. Not because we take the view that we would never allow wages to be subjected to government controls—we have said again and again we would accept controls, if all forms of income were subjected to the same controls—prices, profits, dividends, executive compensation, interest rates, and all the rest—but because only in such a case, where some kind of equity is built in, would we be willing to allow the government to step into the collective bargaining process and say, This is what you must settle for. And I want to suggest to you that the position the AFL-CIO has taken ultimately redounds to the benefit of all citizens, whether they are workers or not, whether they are in the trade union movement or not, because democracy requires some clearly defined limits to state action.

## Unions in Public and Private

Berger and Neuhaus talk about the double role of mediating structures in another sense—that mediating structures address themselves to the fact that we have public faces and private faces. Trade unions offer, I think, a uniquely rich example of that double mediating role.

The public face is clear enough. Our trade unions are engaged in collective bargaining which determines the division of about 70 percent of the national income of the American people. Not that that percentage of the work force is in unions, but 70 percent of the national income is in the form of wages, and trade union agreements set the pace for nonunion as well as union wages. The trade union movement also engages in intensive legislative lobbying through which we try to have an impact on national economic and social policies. And we have effective political action programs through which we try to elect to office the candidates we want. In all these ways, we affect national policy.

But the trade union is also a social institution. It cuts across, and at the same time reinforces, certain ethnic, racial, religious, and neighborhood lines. In some parts of the country, the local union hall is as important a social center as a fraternal organization, a neighborhood club, a political party, or an ethnic social group. In some cases, it is essentially synonymous with one of these other groups. In such a situation, the trade union reinforces existing homogeneous ethnic, racial, and religious units at the local level. We have had an Italian local of the ILGWU [International Ladies Garment Workers Union] for years. It conducts its meetings in Italian. Anyone who is not Italian has a hard time in that local union understanding what is going on.

Through his local union, the worker is also affiliated to a national union. That larger organization cuts across geographic lines, and it also cuts across these racial, religious, and ethnic lines, so that the total labor movement includes people of every conceivable size, shape, color, creed, and ideology. I cannot think of many institutions that function quite the same way. We share with the neighborhood, as a mediating structure, some element of territorial jurisdiction; that is, we are based on place— not where your house is, but where you work. For that reason, too, the local trade union tends to be a socially cohesive force, at the same time that it brings members into contact with a much wider variety of people.

## The Participatory Aspect

Berger and Neuhaus also speak of communities as running the gamut from communities of cohesion to communities of anonymity. They say the important thing is to defend freedom of choice, although I detect in their book a certain bias toward the communities of cohesion—a subliminal bias, almost. In any case, they emphasize freedom of choice. That is true for unions also. This relates to a criticism one often hears of unions, one which especially was heard from the New Left around ten years ago: that is, that unions are empty shells, because they really do not have a great deal of worker participation. Someone going to a local union meeting sees a handful of people sitting there, and they elect the officers and make the decisions. That means that unions are not democratic, according to this view, because institutions are only democratic if they are participatory, that is, if they get everybody aroused and involved.

I have always felt that that contains the germ of a totalitarian idea. Participatory democracy as an idea has totalitarian tendencies, because it doesn't recognize the right of people to be left alone and not go to meetings. There are some people who love to go to meetings, who really would rather be out there at ten or eleven o'clock at night making motions, following parliamentary procedure, and so forth, than staying home with their families, watching television, going to sleep, going to the bar, or whatever. And that is fine for those people. But other people have the right not to go to meetings. Just as we say the individual has the freedom to choose whether to live in a community of cohesion, a community that imposes on him certain communal obligations, or to move to the big city and live in a community of anonymity, where he can do what he wants to do, so too does the union member have the right to go to a meeting or not go to a meeting. I don't blame union members who do not go to meetings, because often meetings are boring. All meetings do not take strike votes. When strike votes are coming up, when the contract is being debated, you will get full participation. There are very few unions I know of whose members do not turn out to fill up large halls when something important is happening. The point is that to be effective, unions and other mediating structures do not have to be participatorily democratic in an agitated way.

It may sound like a cliché, but for many people in society, unions really are schools of democracy. They are the place where workers, many of them with relatively little formal schooling, learn how to raise their hands, be recognized, get up, say something, and sit down. They learn how to organize and run a meeting; and they learn about parliamentary procedure, which is important as a formalization of the rules of where your rights stop and someone else's begin. That is, parliamentary procedure teaches us that the other person has rights, too: no one has the right to talk all night without giving others a chance to speak, and a speaker cannot be hooted off the platform or out of the hall by those who disagree. That is a pretty basic lesson of democracy. Our meetings are not always conducted according to *Robert's Rules of Order.* Trade union democracy is imperfect, like other forms of democracy, but it is the only place many people ever have a chance to learn about democracy at all.

### Racial Integration in the Union

I want to say something else about the union as a mediating structure and as a social institution, something that, no matter how often it gets said, never seems to be understood, or accepted, or remembered. The trade union movement is the most racially integrated institution in American life, bar none. By that I mean that both in absolute numbers and in percentage terms, there are more blacks in the trade union movement than in any other comparable institution. By comparison, the churches still tend to be segregated. There are black churches and there are white churches in the United States. There are far, far fewer black local unions and white local unions.

Second, the percentage of blacks in the trade union movement exceeds their percentage in the population as a whole, and the proportion of blacks in leadership positions—on executive boards, as vice presidents, or whatever—in the trade union movement is far higher than in any comparable institution in American life. By "comparable," I mean large institutions: the universities, the churches, the corporations, the media.

I cannot believe that this can continue to be a fact for a long time without its having a beneficial effect on society. The television crews don't come running out to take film footage of black and white workers attending a union meeting together; that is not news. It is news if they go out on strike and close down one facility or another. But although the normal day-to-day intercourse among people in a union is not news, I think it has to be affecting our racial attitudes in this country, and affecting them, on the whole, for the better.

I want to make another point that is difficult to formulate without lapsing into the language of Karl Marx. Marx spoke about classes existing in two forms: classes in themselves and classes for themselves. A class can be a class and not be conscious of itself as such; that is a class in itself. But when a class becomes conscious of itself as a class with interests separate from those of other classes, it is a class for itself.

What a trade union does to the individual worker is elevate the quality of the demands he makes on his fellow citizens. Individual workers may be racists; yet the trade union movement as a whole has been in the forefront of the civil rights movement. It pressed for civil rights legislation, and it even pushed to get the fair employment practices provision into the civil rights bill in 1964. That provision enforces equal opportunity not only on employers but on unions. Whether the individual white worker is a racist or not, it is not in the interests of white workers as a group to have blacks outside of the trade union movement earning lower wages and constituting a permanent threat to the whites' wage structure.

## Unions and Centralization

Politically, the trade-union movement has a very decentralized structure, although you wouldn't think so from what you read in the papers. Cigar-chomping George Meany did not sit at his desk deciding who was going to be the next senator from South Dakota. That decision is made by our state labor federation in South Dakota. The endorsement of congressional candidates is done by our local federations, our local central bodies. (In addition to having a state federation in every state, we have central labor councils in every major city, some seven hundred of them.) The only decision that is made on the eighth floor of the AFL-CIO is the presidential–vice presidential decision.

This is important to bring up because it has a bearing on the role of the union as a mediating structure. In days gone by, if we had problems in Chicago, for example, George Meany would not call Mayor Daley, but the head of the central labor council in Chicago could pick up the phone and get right through to Mayor Daley. There are many cities in which local labor leaders have that kind of relationship with the politicians. Sometimes it is an embarrassment, frankly, but that is their role. In order to represent the workers, they must have an in to city hall, an in to the state house, to the local political parties, and so forth. If we were to try to direct that from Washington, from a centralized national source, not only would it not work, not only would it come apart, but the role of the labor movement as a mediating structure between the worker and the politician at the local level would be weakened.

In some parts of this country now, given the demise of the old political machines, the trade union movement is the closest thing there is to a structure through which workers can influence what happens at city hall. The fact that the labor movement in the United States is independent of the political parties—unlike the Trade Union Congress of England, which is the owner of the British Labour party, and unlike other unions in Europe that are affiliated directly with political parties—enhances our ability to perform a mediating function. We are able to speak for the workers' interests as they see them, without having them muffled by, or filtered through, a political party and its bureaucracy or its officials, its needs of the moment. Some filtering takes place in our own bureaucracy, of course; that is inevitable. But for the interests of the workers to have to go through a political party bureaucracy would, I think, make things a lot worse.

### The Future for the Unions

Let me throw out some random and perhaps controversial thoughts about the future. I think the trade union movement is in great danger now. Its ability to serve as a mediating structure is in danger for several reasons.

The most immediate and obvious, although not necessarily the most important in the long run, is the current business and New Right campaign against the labor movement. This has cropped up in place after place, with some success. We have lost decertification elections in more places than we would have liked to. There is a lot of steam left in the right-to-work movement. And the fact that not a single prominent businessman in this country broke ranks with his colleagues and supported a piece of legislation as mild as labor law reform has convinced large numbers in our ranks that the trade union movement in this country still has not acquired the legitimacy, let alone the respectability, that it has in the European countries, for example. A large segment of management has not yet made its peace with the fact that unions are and should be here to stay. This has created a very bitter attitude through the leadership ranks in the labor movement. But that is a problem that can be turned around, and I think it will be turned around, even if it takes a decade.

There are other tendencies more deeply rooted in our political democracy that worry me more. Mediating structures are important for democracy. Democracy doesn't always know that, and sometimes it makes trouble for itself.

In order for structures to be mediating, they have to be structures. That is, they cannot be liquid; they cannot just float. They must have a shape, they must have a form, a leadership that is recognized in the society. There has to be somebody who can be talked to in that structure, if the structure is going to mediate anything. These days, there is a tendency among American politicians to go over the heads of the leaders of mediating structures, including the labor movement, directly to the rank and file, directly to the mass. We have this problem with President Carter all the time, but we had it before him, with Nixon and Ford. I think it is not a matter of party so much as a new attitude—an attitude that all institutions are illegitimate, that they don't really have anything underneath them. They are just empty shells, hollow inside. The leadership doesn't represent the rank and file—look at the polls! The polls show the people don't have confidence in the leaders of any institution. So politicians go directly to the ranks—and sometimes that is effective.

This sounds like special pleading, and I suppose it is. After all, if all the politicians do that, and if everybody does that, we will have a hard time keeping the labor union together. But that will be a problem for you as well as for us, because if it can be done with the labor movement, it can be done with other institutions. The result of that kind of behavior is to atomize everybody. That is, if all of us can be appealed to directly by the president of the United States over the tube, never mind what our institutional leaders may think, then we are all rendered equal and impotent. At that point the force of organization goes out of our lives, and democracy gets into real trouble, because there is no greater threat to democracy than atomized individuals. That is why totalitarian states have to destroy institutions like the labor movement, the churches, and academic institutions, and create fakes in their places, to keep the population atomized.

We could perhaps deal with this problem by exercising our right to change political leadership from time to time. I am more worried about an even longer-term problem which I don't have any solution to, and that is the media. I think that of all the forces in American life, the communications media are the most corrosive of mediating structures. They have a vested self-interest in the erosion of all such structures. Why? Well, partly to disguise their real character. That is, they are part of the corporate world, with corporate interests, but they never portray themselves that way. They portray themselves as champions of the public interest. And to speak for the public interest, they have to convince themselves and everybody else that there is something out there called the public—John Q. Public. Well, John Q. Public does not exist.

The editorial writers continue nonetheless to talk about strikes or about other activities they say are against the public interest. Unions don't know what the public interest is; corporations, churches, universities don't know. Only the press knows what is in the public interest. Some people think the maintenance of that fiction is essential to the maintenance of a free press. I doubt that, but, frankly, I don't know the answer to this problem, unless it is that we all have to figure out ways of fighting back, of saying to the media, "We understand your role. We don't accept your definition of your role—or your definition of ours. We know why you do what you do." But we need to arouse the citizenry to the problems that the media pose for mediating structures. This is not incompatible with protecting freedom of expression.

# Discussion

QUESTION: If a Democratic president uses the media to speak over the head of a labor union leader to the rank and file, that seems to me to say more about the state of the Democratic party than about the role of the media. The media have lucked into this. They are the only instrument, in the absence of a Democratic party with some strength and vigor, by which the president can get a political consensus for his programs. So, my question is not about the media so much as about how the labor unions see the present state of the political parties.

MR. KAHN: On the first part of your question, I am not suggesting that the president of the United States doesn't have the right to go over the heads of union leaders and speak directly to the rank and file through the media. Of course he has that right, and it may even be, from his point of view, a politically wise thing to do. What I am suggesting is that if that continues to be a politically wise thing to do over a period of time, it will have a corrosive effect on whatever institution is subjected to it. We ought to bear that in mind as we look with dismay on so many polls that show an ever-plummeting public confidence in our institutions and in their leadership. Yes, it is a problem for the Democratic party, the Democratic president, and the labor movement.

As to what our feelings are about the present situation of the parties—What parties? There are no parties in the United States. That is one of the reasons we are in the difficulty we are in now.

If a man wants to run for president of the United States, the first thing he does is to form a corporation: the X for President Corporation. He appoints a treasurer. There is a board. And then he sells stocks; they are called contributions You buy a share in his campaign. The product is the man himself, competing with other products, trying to corner the market. Senator Jackson had a corporation whose object was to get more people to buy Jackson than McGovern, or whoever. The political party becomes merely the backdrop against which this battle is fought; the party has nothing to do with the character of the nominee. These corporations compete with each other to sell their product. Don't mis-understand me—this is not a sly attack on corporations. I am using the word "corporate" in the more generic sense. That is the way we are now electing the president of the United States, thanks to this idiot primary system we have got ourselves into in the name of participatory democracy. I think political parties are one of the mediating structures we need to reconstruct. I am for back-room deals for the presidency—it is more democratic. I am for a party's taking responsibility for what it offers the American people. We have not been able to get either of the political parties to do that for some time now, it seems to me. The Democratic party, as it surveys Carter's problems, shrugs its shoulders and says, "Don't blame me. You elected him in the primaries. We had nothing to do with him." Well, that is ludicrous. The party should have a program and candidates, and the leadership of the party ought to know how to engage in some good old-fashioned ticket balancing, how to draw votes from here and there, and how to win behind a program and candidates. Then it should go before the American people and take responsibility for its decision, instead of doing what it now does, which is throw it open to the people themselves. That process destroys two important institutions.

One of the results of the disintegration of the Democratic party is that the most powerful political machine in the United States today belongs to the labor movement. As that fact has become more apparent, we have met increasing competition from the business community and New Right groups who are also getting into this game. They are coming in mainly with money; they don't have, by and large, the bodies that we have in city after city. So, we now find ourselves under attack because of the disintegration, really, of the Democratic party. This is not the role we wanted to play. We want to have a strong political machine, but we didn't expect to be the only political machine in the country.

QUESTION: What have you done to organize the South?

MR. KAHN: We have not succeeded in organizing the South. We have poured millions of dollars and thousands of people in there, and it is simply tough. But one could have said to blacks only twenty years ago, "Why don't you give up on the South and just move north? At least you have the right to vote in Chicago." Then, all of a sudden, the whole thing in the South came tumbling down like a house of cards. The ancien régime collapsed, assaulted by small numbers of people engaged in direct action. The whole thing collapsed because it was rotten from the inside. That is what is going to happen in the South with the labor movement. There will be years and years of hacking away at it. A whole new industry has developed in this country, law firms springing up that not only defend corporations in legal conflicts with unions, but also advise them during organization campaigns, write their leaflets for them, tell them how to defeat the union in elections, how to harass the union once it is recognized, and how to evade good-faith collective bargaining with it. These firms are very highly paid, with large budgets. What do you suppose the AFL-CIO's budget is? About $16 million. Of course, that is just the bureaucracy on top. But we are the ones who often have to bear the brunt of the criticism: Why aren't you organizing more successfully in the South? Why can't you break J. P. Stevens? Once Stevens is broken, I think we are going to see the whole South go union, and so fast that it will be comparable to the civil rights movement in the 1960s.

QUESTION: In European countries, the labor movement tends to be socialistic, yet its proponents are working with their capitalistic counterparts in management. In this country, the labor people tend to be fiercely capitalistic, yet there is a continuing antagonism. It seems to me that management and workers in this country have a number of commonalities. Both of you have a fierce antagonism toward the media; both are fiercely capitalistic and in favor of profits. You both have a strong stake in democracy. You both are suspicious of the academic community. In practice, you both rely on structures rather than individuals. How do you explain the continuing antagonism on both sides? Is there, in fact, a deep antagonism between locals and plant managers, or is it more rhetorical?

MR. KAHN: It completely depends on the company and the industry. You can run the whole gamut from relatively cordial, peaceful relations to extremely hostile relations.

But I will try to address the logical point you make, because it is interesting that there is not as much ideological incompatibility between labor and capital in America as there is, let us say, in Europe. That is partly because we have never developed in the United States a socialist movement to which a labor movement could commit itself and thereby find itself in an ideologically antagonistic relationship to capital. But more fundamental is that the class struggle in the United States—if I may revert again to the Marxian vernacular—historically has always been fiercer, more violent than in any European country. We never experienced feudalism; we never had a society in which people had to accept their place, except because of race in the South. American

137

workers never really felt inferior to their bosses. They never felt it was their place in life to be deferential, obedient, and all the rest of it. Get into a taxicab in New York, and then get into a taxicab in London, talk to the cab drivers, and you will see the whole history unfold right before your eyes. Deference? You can't teach a cab driver in New York—or anywhere in the United States, I suspect—deference to anybody. If anything, he is your superior.

It is that, and the strongly individualistic tradition in the United States, where the worker says, "Don't tread on me," that has accounted for the extreme violence of the class struggle in the United States. The fact of blurred ideological differences may make even more problems. The American worker is favorably disposed toward capitalism for one reason: he hopes that he will someday become a capitalist. When those hopes are not realized, and he can't get even a 7 percent wage increase, he can become a lot angrier than the worker who never expected to be anything more than what his father was, and his father before him.

QUESTION: You mentioned that the unions defend freedom of choice. But are they really voluntary in practice? Within the last fourteen years, as a professional musician, I have come into contact with the AFL-CIO many times. I never got a call from George Meany, but I did get calls from the local enforcers, or whatever, many times, and if I didn't have two lawyers, I would have been out of business.

Furthermore, Walter Williams and Thomas Sowell, black economists, have shown that blacks suffer from the minimum wage increases that are periodically supported by the AFL-CIO. The white unions keep blacks not just in lower-paying jobs, but out of work entirely, because of the exceptionally high cost of entering into the labor market owing to the continually escalating minimum wage. Would you care to comment?

MR. KAHN: On the question of involuntary membership in the union, that is a difficult moral problem. I know only one fair answer, and that would be to withdraw the requirement for involuntary union membership and also withdraw the requirement for nonunion members to share in whatever benefits are won by the unionized workers. Unfortunately, that idea has been ruled illegal by the courts again and again. That being the case, what you are arguing for is that some members should belong to a union and pay dues, that their union dues should be used to try to win higher wages and other benefits from employers, and that people who are not members of the union and did not pay their dues—who in fact are antagonistic to the union—should get all these benefits. Isn't free-loading a moral problem? There are certain forms of coercion we accept because we recognize that in some cases, individual rights have to be curbed for other purposes. For example, I often don't like the way my tax money gets spent, but I have got to pay it anyway. The labor movement presents a unique problem here, because most other institutions do not require us to join but do not require us to share in their benefits, either. I have to join the church to get the benefits of the church. To get education, I have to go to school. I don't know how you get around the particular problem of the unions. Of course, you can also argue that a weakening union membership would mean a lowering of the wage standard across the country for all workers, union and nonunion, which I, at least, would look upon as a bad thing.

I also want to say something about this minimum wage business. Let's assume you are right, that if you were to lower the minimum wage, you could suck more people into the labor market—unemployed teenagers and so forth. That is exactly what goes on in the Soviet Union: you accept lower wage rates and productivity rates in order to bring everybody into the job market. You have five people doing what three people could do, or what two people could do. I will tell you how to get even more people in: lower the wage rate to practically nothing, and employers will go out and recruit off the street. They will offer room and board. The cheaper you make it, the more people. I just don't think we want a society like that.

And isn't it ironic?—we finally get the building trades integrated, so that we have a larger percentage of blacks in the building trades today than in the rest of the work force, and there is an assault on Davis-Bacon and on the wage rates in the building trades! Why did blacks want to go into the building trades? Just because they like to make bricks and pile them up? No, it was the wage rate that was so attractive—those fancy plumber salaries that everybody makes fun of, because everyone thinks that lawyers and doctors are worth more than plumbers, which I think remains to be proved.

So we got blacks into the building trades, and now we want to lower the wage rates. What we are saying by that is that, for those who are still unemployed, our interest is in getting them off the streets and into jobs. We don't care so much about what kind of income level they have, or how well they are able to live. Well, I think the minimum wage is too low. It ought to be raised.

(QUESTION INAUDIBLE)

MR. KAHN: Samuel Gompers would have enjoyed this discussion about unions as mediating structures. The early AFL, you know, was

139

opposed to such things as federal unemployment compensation because it felt that if the worker began to look to the government to solve his problems with the boss, he would stop looking to the union. It was not until a little before the New Deal that the AFL began to accept the idea of government intervention on behalf of the worker without the labor movement as a mediating structure.

The AFL-CIO is governed by the dominant philosophy of America, which is pragmatism. I can assure you the executive council does not sit down and say, "Do we want to move to the left or the right?" Our positions are taken on the basis of what our members seem to want, what we think is in their best interests. The AFL-CIO has been in favor of busing. We disciplined and reprimanded our Louisiana local officials when they participated in antibusing rallies. The AFL-CIO is for national health insurance along the Kennedy lines. The AFL-CIO has a strong national defense posture; it is a hard-line anticommunist organization, and I think that is going to continue. Many people find our domestic and international policies ideologically divergent—that is, according to the currently prevailing definitions of liberalism and conservatism.

But I would like to take your question another step forward. You raised the question of socialism. I think it can be argued, and some have argued, that the reason there is not a mass socialist movement in the United States is that an equivalent to it did arise. It just never called itself socialist. It didn't take the form of a political party, but it adopted programs that are not terribly different from those of the social democratic parties of Europe. That movement is the labor movement. On foreign policy issues, I think we would have great differences with the European social democrats—with Willy Brandt's Ostpolitik, for example, but the attempt to expand the public sector, to put floors under everyone, the tendency toward some kind of socialized medicine program, all have been social democratic. Now, in other respects, no. We have rejected the idea of an incomes policy unless it is across the board; and we are not going to get bogged down in a discussion of socialism versus capitalism, because that doesn't tell us what to do tomorrow—it doesn't tell us how many votes there are in Congress for our bill on this, that, or the other thing.

(QUESTION INAUDIBLE)

MR. KAHN: I did not mean to say that we accept the European unions as a model, not at all. Specifically, we do not go along with the idea of codetermination. We believe that employers have their jobs to do and workers have their jobs to do. It is not our job to run the company. There is also evidence that the wave of strikes in West Germany recently is the result of the weakening of workers' identification with their union leadership and their willingness to accept direction from the union leadership, because they see the leadership now as sitting on the boards of directors of the corporations. If I had to say in one word or one sentence what idea George Meany holds to most fiercely about the labor movement, it would be that separation between workers' and employers' responsibilities.

QUESTION: I wonder if you would be willing to reflect on what you see as some of the chief reasons for what we are coming to see this week as a general crisis of confidence and meaning in American life today. Let me cite some illustrations to get at what I mean. Every public-school teachers' group I have listened to is convinced beyond a shadow of a doubt that they have the answer to what America's children need. Yet American families are deciding in quite large numbers to take kids out of public schools. We are hearing from businessmen that one of the greatest things for Americans and for the world is our capitalist system's production of wealth. Yet business is under attack from many sides, including the media and labor. What I hear from you is that one of the greatest contributions to community nurturing, to ethnic sense, and to democracy is the union movement. Yet the union is losing members; you yourself outlined some of the crises it faces. And from you and many sources I hear that the media are the great villains. Yet the media's story is that they are under attack: the freedom of the press is going to be taken away from them, and the freedom of confidentiality. Most government officials are convinced that the greatest thing that can happen is getting some sound management in government, getting things worked out. Yet people are failing to vote in droves, and the party is defunct. How does one get hold of all this?

MR. KAHN: It is easier to list all those phenomena than to explain them. The chief cause of all of this, it seems to me, is that society is changing rapidly. That is our chief problem in the labor movement. Our percentage of the labor force is not declining because we have become incompetent, fat, and lazy, but because the work force itself is undergoing a tremendous change in composition. It is moving into areas that have been traditionally nonunion. A growing portion of the work force is female. Workers are coming in who have no union background. We have to appeal to a whole new group of educated workers, and to workers whose employer is a nonprofit governmental or voluntary association.

141

The demographic changes also have produced drastic upheavals in the culture, so that parents do not recognize themselves in their children, and children do not recognize their aspirations in their parents. There is a crisis in both aspirations and expectations. I believe that that is largely rooted in technology.

There also have been other social changes in the country which we realized at the time were serious and yet didn't react to. Busing is one example. People perceived busing as something the government was doing to them, moving them around, saying you have to do this and that. And the courts seemed to be making decisions that nobody voted for. But instead of rising up in a revolution and kicking out the government, disaffected people just began to withdraw. I think a number of things happened domestically of that character to produce a sense that our leaders and our institutions were not working for the people but somehow against them, against their wishes. This has to be combined with truly catastrophic developments in the international field which we still are not willing to face. The United States surrendered in Vietnam. We had a massive defeat, our first one. And everybody went home and stuck his head in the sand and pretended nothing was going to happen. "Dominoes are not falling," they said. I think the dominoes are falling all over the place, including in our internal spirit. We have never faced what that did to us in terms of loss of confidence, that our leaders lost a war that most Americans have to believe we could have won if we had really wanted to.

We have problems perceiving what is going on. In the 1950s, you had this tremendously hopeful sense that technology would bring us everything; we were in a new era. Such a glut of material abundance was going to fall down on our heads that 98 percent of the population would no longer have to work. Well, where is it? I was in a gas line two and a half hours to get gas so I could come out here. There is no abundance falling down on our heads. We are in a recession. I worry about our inability to get a grasp on reality as it is in the world, a steady grasp on the long-term reality, and our tendency to be swept off our feet by fads and images. I get back again to the media as a central part of this problem. I don't know how to deal with it.

(QUESTION INAUDIBLE)

MR. KAHN: There is no such thing as a public interest, because there is no such thing as a public. What doors do I knock on to find the public? If I knock on your door, I find a worker, I assume. You earn a living; you work for somebody or for yourself. You are also a consumer. Your attitude as a consumer may conflict with your attitude as a worker. You may also be a member of a political party. You have other roles. And what is the public except an abstract notion of an aggregate of people in all their roles, with various roles canceling each other out?

Invariably, it is against the public interest to have a strike. I have never read an editorial in the *New York Times* that said, "This strike is in the public interest." Is it conceivable that an action that people have been engaging in for hundreds of years cannot produce one good example to justify itself? In a world of four billion people, where there are strikes taking place all the time, not one commends itself to the *New York Times* as worthy of support, or as being in the public interest. Oh, you might find an editorial saying, "Cesar Chavez has a point. His workers are very badly off." So long as the union is poor, weak, badly organized, then it is worthy of support. As soon as it succeeds in lifting its poor workers into a modicum of respectability, economically, then it is unworthy of support, even retroactive support. I don't know of any other institution that is treated that way, where when it succeeds, it fails.

QUESTION: One thing we haven't talked about is the way mediating structures can serve to fragment individual identities and generate confusion in individuals as to what their genuine allegiances are. It is interesting that the dominant theme of so many of these self-help groups, to which people are turning in massive numbers now, is to try to recover some sense of wholeness.

MR. KAHN: I think you are right. And I think the real problem in history is not how you pull it all together at once, or return to some earlier "together" time—we can't remedievalize ourselves—but how you survive periods of unusually rapid change. You need, you expect a period of consolidation afterwards, and then you can absorb larger changes in the future. I think we are all adapting almost biologically to this pace of change, which I can see no way of impeding or turning back. We have to learn to live with tensions, and we will. There is tension between capital and labor; there is also tension between freedom and totalitarianism. That is the tension that bothers me the most, because that is the one I am afraid we are going to cop out on. I gave a talk to some young people a couple of weeks ago on the future of democracy and human rights, and I had to tell them what I honestly feel: that if they are really interested in preserving and defending and extending democracy and human rights, they are talking about locking their generation and the next one into a period of great tension in the world, between the United States and the Soviet Union. I think that is the price we have to pay for the protection of freedom.

# The Family as a Mediating Structure

*Brigitte Berger*

A mediating structure carries out necessary functions for the individual as well as for society and stands as a link between the two. The family is the single most important mediating structure around. Within the democratic pluralism of American society, the family has traditionally been embedded in a network of voluntarist institutions. And, again traditionally, both voluntarism and pluralism have been closely intertwined with a free-market economic system. Those who view the family as the preeminent mediating structure emphasize its continued importance for the individual in a period of rapid social and economic change, and they also seek mechanisms to permit the continuation of the voluntarism and pluralism that have distinguished American society in the past. Since questions pertaining to the values informing public policy are of special concern in this volume, I shall concentrate on the public policy interest in the family. Public policy is concerned primarily with the child-rearing and child-caring functions of the family as an institution and much less—if at all—with the many other functions in which the family serves the individual.

My argument on behalf of the family as a mediating structure in child care is guided by two separate yet related considerations. The first pertains to the defense of the family as the single most important agent and locale for child care. After summarizing the issues and debates that have surfaced in the recent "rediscovery" of the value of the family after a prolonged period of attack, I will establish the basis for a defense of the family in the first part of this chapter. The second part is concerned much more directly with the understanding of the family as a mediating structure. I will try to show how a mediating structures approach to the role of the family differs from the currently dominant trend in policy discussions that is informed by the rediscovery of the value of the family. I will also try to indicate *why* a mediating structures approach is imperative, particularly if the value and hopes of ordinary people are to be taken seriously and if individuals and groups are to have the widest possible freedom to express their unique values, practices, and hopes.

## In Defense of the Family

The family has always been an object of intense interest and concern. In recent decades, as virulent antifamily sentiments seemed to be running rampant in American society, it has been the source of violent controversy. For some time predications of doom were flaunted from every newsstand. The unmasking of yet another aspect of family life became the order of the day for a variety of vocal special interest groups. At least in the opinion-making sector of American society, the American family tended to be judged as an outmoded, if not indeed a harmful, institution. In the words of David Cooper, the family is "a lethal chamber destroying human personalities."[1]

Just when the wider public has come either to grieve for or to celebrate the "death of the family," it is surprising that the value of the family as an institution for the individual as well as for society is being rediscovered. The order of the day is now to *reverse* gears. The general public is asked to revise its reluctant perception of the family as a destructive and ultimately undesirable carry-over from the past, and instead to understand it as an endangered species that is in need of protection and national support.

How could such a reversal come about? Throughout the period of gloom, there was a paradox few cared to grapple with. At the same time as the institution of the family was under attack, marriage statistics showed that people continued to marry just as much as previously. Although admittedly the divorce rate was up, so was the remarriage rate. Moreover, if the information about groups that practiced alternative life-styles was reliable, it indicated a profound longing for and search for something that resembled the conventional family to an astonishing degree. The contradiction between the continued social practices of the majority, who kept on getting married and having families, and the persisting attacks on these practices, accompanied by an all-pervasive malaise, should have given pause to the cultural pundits who quickly jumped on the bandwagon of currently fashionable opinion. Again I am reminded of the general tendency among opinion-making intellectuals to overlook the practices, values, and hopes of ordinary men and women. Even in the presently emerging "postreformist" mood that seeks to legitimate proposals and policy suggestions in more populist

---

[1] David Cooper, *The Death of the Family* (New York: Vintage, 1970).

terms, this tendency—as I shall try to show—persists. This persistence is probably not accidental, but it is a subject that cannot be pursued in this context.

In the past three years a number of books on the family complex have attracted considerable attention. In spite of their different orientations and emphases, these books directly challenge the apocalyptical prognoses of yesteryear, just as they challenge more extreme indictments of the American family as fostering all sorts of real or assumed individual and social pathologies. All across the country, study groups, foundations, universities, religious groups, government agencies, and commissions are virtually competing with one another in their desire to assess the "crisis" of the family and in their exploration of ways and means to strengthen the family. A call for public policy measures, governmentally designed, sanctioned, financed, and executed, seems to unite in rare harmony the newly declared champions of the family. Even the popular media are today inclined to pay more attention to the virtues of family life and to give proportionately less space to radical attacks on the traditional family. Clearly, the family is again a topical subject, and nearly everyone—or so it seems—is expressing concern and willingness to come to the aid of this oldest of all social institutions. The problem, however, is: Will the family survive its newly declared champions?

As the nation is about to respond to this rousing call to support the "endangered" family, there is a need to explore more carefully what we are asked to battle for and why. Whether we want to or not, we will have to address not only questions pertaining to the family complex but also the equally important issues concerning the nature and purpose of American society. These are questions that I find strangely absent from the current discussion. We must discover the specific values and practices that ordinary Americans associate with the family, and we must learn how each of these relates to the distinctive aspects of American society. We must be concerned with the desirability of continuing the historical "American experience," which has grown out of the practices, values, and compromises of a democracy, a culturally pluralistic society, and a market economy. Above all, we will have to understand what this society essentially stands for and wishes to stand for in continuity with its past and in its hopes for the future. I would suggest that the values of ordinary men and women offer a meaningful frame of reference and point toward the kind of political and economic system necessary for the realization of these values. This explicit awareness of operative values, in my opinion, is the basic challenge that faces American society at this juncture in history. No other institution is better

146

suited than the family to illuminate problems we are facing and to help us meet this challenge successfully.

A brief look at some of the most significant books on the family published in recent years will lay the groundwork for this discussion. These books reflect the changing assessment of the situation of the American family and, in turn, help reshape public perception. An example of the curious reversal that has taken place with regard to the understanding of the role and function of the modern family is Christopher Lasch's *Haven in a Heartless World: The Family Besieged*. Lasch, undoubtedly one of America's most brilliant Marxist historians (author of the much acclaimed *The Agony of the American Left*), makes an unabashed defense of the traditional family—that is, the "bourgeois" family customarily maligned by the left—that even the most conservative member of the Vatican hierarchy would find hard to fault. As such, Lasch's *Haven in a Heartless World* is not really a study of the American family, but a study of the study of the family. His basic premise is that the American family is not in crisis, but is in fact already lost. He deplores and grieves this loss and explicitly concurs with Max Horkheimer that "the bourgeois family not only educates for authority in bourgeois society, it also cultivates the dream of a better society."[2] Lasch categorically states that the traditional family produced healthier and better adjusted individuals (a statement he will have to argue with such historians of childhood as the psychohistorian Lloyd DeMeuse, who has tried to show that the history of childhood has been a nightmare).

The "integrity of the family," Lasch claims, has been lost by the onslaught of imperialistic professionals. America's social scientists, the legions of anthropologists, sociologists, psychiatrists, psychologists, and their offshoots in counseling, teaching, social work, and the like—in short, all the experts of our mental and social welfare—have "expropriated" the traditional family. These "guardians of public health and welfare" have unwittingly engineered the American family into a position of impotence, ultimately robbing it of its most vital functions for individual and social well-being. During the past century, according to Lasch, America has gradually come under the spell of the therapeutic. The authority of the family has declined under the concerted attack of experts, psychiatric reformers, and cultural relativists, the "advocates of 'nonbinding commitments,' " who tragically misunderstood the nature

---

[2] Max Horkheimer, "Authority and the Family" (1936) in *Critical Theory: Selected Essays*, trans. Matthew J. O'Connell et al. (New York: Seabury, 1972), pp. 58 ff.

of authority and the most basic components of socialization. This triumph of the therapeutic was further facilitated by the surrender of the traditional guardians of morality, the clergy and the churches. To quote Lasch:

> The medicalization of religion facilitated the rapprochement between religion and psychiatry. Advocates of existential and humanistic therapies pointed out that Martin Heidegger, Martin Buber, and Paul Tillich had redefined religion as a form of psychotherapy. Neurosis, in the view of these existentialist theologians, reflected a pervasive modern anxiety, and religion, like psychiatry, had to enlist in the organized effort to undo modern society's dehumanizing effects: to equip men to tolerate anxiety and thus to make them whole again, self-accepting, authentic, and capable of achieving a state of "being."[3]

In this fashion the cure of the soul gave way to mental hygiene, the search for salvation to the search for peace of mind, the attack upon evil to the war against anxiety. As Leslie Farber, the social psychologist, once said, "morality itself was turned over to the psychiatrists, along with philosophy and religion."[4] Lasch observes that liberal clergymen participated with gusto in the campaign to transform religion into moral and mental hygiene.

This devastatingly critical analysis spares no one—on the right, the left, or in between—who has ever dared doubt the rights of the traditional family. In Lasch's mind, the crisis—nay, the "loss"—of the family is due not so much to the vast social transformations of the past two hundred years, as to the intervention of the imperialistic professional guardians of public health and welfare and the social scientists who inform them. Together they seek to replace the nourishing family with the "nourishing mother of the state." Of course, as a committed Marxist, Lasch eventually has to make a connection to the "substructure," the economic-technological order from which this professionalism flows. He does this by viewing these professions as lackeys of the capitalist system and the giant corporations that dominate this system.

Much can be said in support of Lasch's interpretation of the devastating effect of the intervention of the "helping professions," the "friendly intruders"[5] upon the affairs of the family. This theme is

---

[3] Christopher Lasch, *Haven in a Heartless World: The Family Besieged* (New York: Basic Books, 1977), p. 98.

[4] Leslie Farber, "Martin Buber and Psychiatry," *Psychiatry*, vol. 11 (1956), p. 119.

[5] To use the term coined by Carole E. Joffe, *Friendly Intruders: Childcare Professionals and Family Life* (Berkeley: University of California Press, 1973).

emphasized by almost every analyst of contemporary society. Lasch, however, makes a direct connection with other trends, which he sees as a "giant conspiracy" resulting from the growth of corporations and of the bureaucratic state that serves them. In the end, the mental acrobatics in which Lasch engages to reconcile his conservative, if not reactionary, sentiments with his radical political agenda devalue the importance of his insights. As it stands, the book may well go down in history as an exercise in what the historian Fritz Stern called "the politics of cultural despair,"[6] a favorite pastime of many American intellectuals. Lasch writes as if all compassion, all intelligence, all energy, all positive and creative features had vanished from the face of this country. And that is blatantly untrue.

Nonetheless, Lasch has pointed to a real problem, namely, the need to weigh and, if necessary, to counter the encroachment of professionalization upon the affairs of the family. If professional services for children and the family are indeed of dubious value, the question will have to be asked, What alternatives are there? A further question centers on the possibility of intellectually rehabilitating parenthood and the family. Considerations of this kind are strangely absent from current discussions. The staying power of the family is recognized, but few commentators look to the family as the major agent to care for the nation's children.

The family's return to its child-caring function is the dominant theme of Kenneth Keniston and the Carnegie Council on Children in *All Our Children*. Neither Keniston nor his coauthors can be accused of a lack of liberal or leftist sentiments. They, too, perceive that the major problem is not so much "to reeducate parents but to make available the help they need and to give them enough power so that they can be effective advocates with and coordinators of the other forces that are bringing up their children." This is good news, for until recently, most took the position that parents lacked not only the resources but also the technical knowledge to provide adequately for their children's needs. In the past, the consensus was that the efforts of parents were doubtful, if not harmful, and had to be supplemented, if not supplanted. Keniston and his colleagues, however, belong to an emerging consensus that is inclined to believe that parents are still the world's greatest experts about the needs of their own children.[7]

[6] Fritz R. Stern, *The Politics of Cultural Despair* (Berkeley: University of California Press, 1974).

[7] Kenneth Keniston and the Carnegie Council on Children, *All Our Children: The American Family under Pressure* (New York: Harcourt Brace Jovanovich, 1977), pt. 1, "Children and Families: Myth and Reality."

At first sight, it is encouraging to have the family—and that means the old bourgeois type of family, though the authors are careful not to commit themselves—accepted and defended in circles that have hitherto been loath to entertain such ideas. Could it be that the liberal left has at last come to appreciate the values and practices of the common man and woman? But, alas, the analyses and policy proposals set forth in *All Our Children* do not warrant any such hope.

The authors set out to describe the dilemma of the modern American family. In a rapidly changing world, they argue, families have been shorn of traditional child-rearing functions such as providing schooling, the opportunity for health care, and economic production. At the same time, parents have acquired new roles, the most significant being that of the executive or coordinator, albeit with very little authority, who deals with the all-powerful outside forces encroaching upon the life of the children. In particular, they argue that the deck is stacked against a large minority—the poor, the nonwhite, and the parents of handicapped children. The odds are overwhelmingly against their achieving a decent life because their reality is determined by an unfair distribution of economic goods and resources. The old liberal dream of achieving greater economic equality through equal educational opportunities is diagnosed in *All Our Children* as having failed. The authors then propose that the nation deemphasize education and liberal reforms; instead, they suggest that the government provide jobs, income, and services to parents. The overriding target for this camp is economic equality; the family is of ancillary concern.[8]

Lasch and Keniston close ranks in viewing the major enemy as modern technology in the industrial world of the free market. Keniston and his associates see great perils for the family stemming from television, which promotes consumerism, aggression, and nonrealism in children. Generally unsafe and unhealthy nutritional habits are peddled under the pressure of a consumer society in a free-market situation. The chief villains in this environmental nightmare are rampant technology and a generally laissez-faire economy.

The recommendations flowing from this type of analysis are predictable. The central policy proposals made by Keniston and his associates would imply not only more services and therefore more professional intervention—so much lamented by Lasch—for the family, but also a total revamping, if not replacement, of the present welfare system. These proposals would amount to a profound transformation of

[8] Richard Delone and the Carnegie Council on Children, *Small Future: Children, Inequality, and the Limits of Liberal Reform* (New York: Harcourt Brace Jovanovich, 1979).

the American family and the American society as we know them. In practice, it would constitute a massive interference by the state in the affairs of the family to make the latter into an instrument for income redistribution.

I agree that the family has lost some of its power, particularly among the poor, the minority groups, and the handicapped. But if indeed we wish to empower people to direct their own lives, if indeed the goal is to make the family more self-reliant and less dependent, is the road suggested by Keniston and the Carnegie Council the reasonable one to take?

The authors of *All Our Children* seem to be persuaded that the causes they espouse and the measures they propose are on behalf of the weak against the strong, the poor against the rich. But have not the events of the past decade shown that many of the interventions sponsored by the liberal left, however admirable in intent, however earnestly promoted and advocated, have had rather a dismal record? Busing and affirmative action are examples of programs that, at best, have brought about little improvement for those on whose behalf the whole machinery was put into motion. Many programs aimed at the poor in recent years amply demonstrate this point. Most claims to equality—social, economic, racial, sexual, intellectual—serve only to intensify these inequalities. And now the family is to be enlisted to battle for a more just, more equitable, more brotherly society. In this battle all forms of real and unnecessary human suffering are jumbled together with wickedness such as economic exploitation, unemployment, the nuclear threat, and bad nutritional habits. All these evils presumably are manifestations of free-market capitalism.

In the great shift of gears that is about to take place, those who once thought too little of the family, even to the point of seeking its destruction, now think too much of it. The family is to become the vehicle for the redistribution of income, for tax reform, and for a guaranteed full-employment policy. At the same time, the family is to be enlisted in the battle against such fashionable evils as consumerism, the laissez-faire economy, and modern technology. In short, the institution of the family is to be made a tool for changing the American system.

It has become obvious by now that the rediscovery of the family must take into consideration its relation to wider society. Both Lasch and Keniston have made this requirement dramatically clear. The need for such considerations is further highlighted by the lopsided understanding of this relation that emerges from their books. What is more, to a large degree this interpretation is fairly typical of the general confusion that reigns. In spite of the general shift in gears, public discussion of the family continues to be dominated by the same elite intellectual perception of the world that has monopolized the interpretation of modern society since the Enlightenment. It seems that old dreams are slow to die. It is precisely this kind of mind-set, in its proclaimed support of expert knowledge and higher consciousness, against which the poor and the working class have been helpless for so long.

To sharpen our focus we have to turn to another book that has gained wide attention recently: Sheila Rothman's immensely readable *Woman's Proper Place*. It traces the changing role and self-understanding of women in America during the past hundred years. To a large measure, Rothman has written the "official" history of the forces that have led to the emergence and dominance of the women's liberation movement and its consequences for the American family.

As a careful cultural historian, Rothman also records the revolutionizing effect of technology on the lives of women and their families. Her inquiry into the role of technological innovations beginning at the end of the nineteenth century clearly demonstrates the liberating effect of modernizing industry and its mass-produced consumer goods on the life of American families. Modern sewage systems, electricity, and hot and cold running water improved sanitation and health care, and at the same time the advent of the washing machine, refrigerator, and hosts of labor-saving devices, spewed out by a fiercely competitive industry, immeasurably benefited not only the rich but, above all, the working class and those in poverty. "These conveniences," says Rothman, "are so much a part of our lives that we may easily forget their significance to the first generation of women who enjoyed them: they reduced—almost eliminated—an extraordinary amount of menial tasks."[9] Rothman shows convincingly that it was precisely the much maligned modernizing technology developed by the free-market system that allowed for the mass production and widest possible distribution of these products. Better health and living conditions and, above all, the widest array of choices are the products of a specific political-economic system that allows freedom of the individual to a degree previously unknown.

This system also fostered public tolerance of different life-styles and provided the economic basis for the women's liberation movement. In bemoaning the consumerism of American society, the radical critic fails to understand that affluence and the diversity of available goods provide what a Marxist would call the "material substructure" for

---

[9] Sheila Rothman, *Woman's Proper Place: A History of Changing Ideals and Practices, 1870 to the Present* (New York: Basic Books, 1978), pp. 14 ff.

liberation from want and drudgery. As Rothman shows historically—though this is not her professed aim—liberation means above all a quantum jump in the number of choices open to individuals. To add to Rothman's analysis, there seems to be a crucial correlation between the polity and the economy, that is, between political freedom and economic freedom, in a pluralistic democracy. This correlation has been widely recognized by social thinkers of the past, such as Max Weber, but is in disrepute today. Empirical evidence demonstrates the superiority of the free-market economy in improving living conditions and opportunities for the majority. It is a paradox that in the face of the outstanding achievements of the free market, the capitalist system is perceived to be the cause of all evil.

According to Rothman, after a succession of changes in the definition of womanhood in America ("virtuous womanhood," "educated motherhood," and "woman as a wife-companion"), by the late 1950s the new definition of "woman as a person" carried the day. The new self-definition of women came into sharp conflict with the needs of their children. As women began to leave home in large numbers in order to find their true "selves" in paid occupations, governmental agencies came under pressure to find solutions to the child-care problem, which many observers believed to be urgent. A combination of forces seems to have been at work to increase state intervention in the affairs of the family—and it was not, as Christopher Lasch argues, solely the result of the expansionistic self-interest of the professional complex. Regardless of the cause, it is generally agreed that there has been a significant expansion of the power of the state. Rothman's description of the paradoxical and, at times, even tragic consequences of this shift is persuasive indeed.

A second important point gleaned from the Rothman book is that defining the woman "as a person" outside the household and the family is very much a class phenomenon. For the educated middle class, the values and meanings derived from what the sociologists call "the private sphere" (that is, family, neighborhood, and religion) are denied and denigrated, while success in "the public sphere" (work and politics) is considered the only way for a woman to achieve true "personhood." It is not generally recognized, however, that work means entirely different things to different social classes. Indeed, for highly educated middle-class women it may well be that the problems of "uncertain identity" can be solved only in the world of work outside the family—and I in no way wish to belittle this problem. Different social classes, however, and different personality types regardless of their class origin, have quite different priorities and values. For most working-class women, the pressing desire during the child-bearing and child-rearing period of their lives is to be with and to care for their children. For many, at least in this period, work is more of an economic necessity and a burden than a means for achieving personal identity. If given the option— which most women are not—they would prefer to participate in the family, the household, the neighborhood, and the many religious and voluntary organizations that have traditionally contributed to the variety and richness of cultural life in America.

It is at this point that a fundamental policy dilemma opens up. As Rothman fully recognizes, public policy is shaped largely by vocal groups, anchored in the middle class, which seek solutions to their own problems by trying to legitimate their own interests under the guise of helping the poor and downtrodden. The fact that different social groupings may have different needs—just as they may have different values —is blatantly ignored. This disregard has had drastic consequences. For when middle-class intellectuals invite government action to improve the quality of life of the poor, as they perceive it, they often have merely supplied the state with yet one more means of manipulating the poor.

Selma Fraiberg, the eminent child psychologist and therapist, entered the arena of controversy with *Every Child's Birthright: In Defense of Mothering*.[10] In this book, Dr. Fraiberg presents an unequivocal defense of the needs of children, which she believes are woefully and dangerously disregarded today by those who seek to separate the needs of women from those of their children. She summed up the most important insights of her book in an interview with the *New York Times* (December 11, 1977):

> Statistics tell us that there are about 14 million working mothers who need substitute care for their children, and 5 million of them have over 6 million pre-school children in need of "day care." But licensed day-care centers and day-care homes don't provide a numerical answer to the problem. There are about a million available places, maybe a bit more, in day-care centers. I have to say it: many of these centers, even the ones licensed, are not providing for the real emotional needs of infants.
> . . . What kind of care do these children get? . . . I have to be critical of many of those arrangements; I have to speak out against the way thousands and thousands of children are treated—handed from one virtual stranger to another in the name of "day-care." Even *licensed* day-care centers or pre-school nurseries often fail to meet the child's needs for a

[10] New York: Basic Books, 1977.

sustained, close involvement with a caring person. Young children who get to know such a person then lose that person, show anxiety, agitation, tearfulness. When those children keep meeting someone, then losing someone, and meeting someone and losing someone, and so on; or when (and that isn't rare at all) they don't for hours each day really know anyone well enough to feel close, to feel trust—well, there are going to be emotional consequences: lack of confidence in the future: a degree of withdrawal from the future, a degree of withdrawal from the world.

Aside from astronomical economic resources that would be needed to supply governmentally licensed mother substitutes, Dr. Fraiberg, from her vast experience, coolly points to the fact that no such substitutes are to be had today, licensed or not. This very unpopular though honest position brought Dr. Fraiberg under heavy attack. Her own solution to this problem is one I personally sympathize with: instead of appropriating billions of dollars of federal money to create at best a dubious, and at worst a harmful, system of child care, we should use federal funding to assist those mothers on welfare who want to take care of their own children.

The question now arises: What are we to do with all the new interpretations and propositions that have emerged during the recent rediscovery of the family? Can we now move forward to search for a more adequate recognition of the needs and values of ordinary American people? Are there any empirically verifiable data that describe the family practices currently engaged in by most American people, and their pervasive values, needs, and hopes? In short, is there available any nonapologetic, nonideological information on the family life of Americans today? Fortunately, there is: Mary Jo Bane's important book *Here to Stay: American Families in the Twentieth Century*.[11] Bane's credentials are impeccable: a coauthor with Christopher Jencks of *Inequality*,[12] coeditor with Donald M. Levine of *The Inequality Controversy*,[13] and an associate director of the Center for Research on Women at Wellesley College, she is an experienced survey researcher, relying heavily on demographic indicators and the interpretation of quantitative data. Politically, she can hardly be accused of a conservative bias. In her research, she is ruthlessly honest. She tells us quite candidly that when she began her study of the contemporary American

---

[11] New York: Basic Books, 1977.

[12] Christopher Jencks et al., *Inequality* (New York: Basic Books, 1972).

[13] Donald M. Levine and Mary Jo Bane, eds., *The Inequality Controversy* (New York: Basic Books, 1975).

family, she expected to be able to verify the dimensions of its sorry state and to conclude that we should develop "public institutions to replace [it] with other forms of living arrangements and other methods of child care."[14]

Contrary to her expectations, it became evident that the staying power of the American family had been grossly underestimated. In fact, all the indicators that she used demonstrated that the American family is neither lost nor in crisis. Bane laconically labels as myths the predictions of doom and crisis—the so-called new reality—that have dominated the public arena.

*Myth I. The disrupted family.* Bane's data indicate that there is no foundation for the widely held beliefs that the home has become little more than a boarding place, that the family is unable and unwilling to care for its young, that parent-child relations are disrupted. True enough, the family has become smaller in size, but the family structure of America has not changed much over the past hundred years. On the contrary, the bonds between parents and children have become prolonged and intensified, and although many mothers have joined the labor force, there is no evidence that this has measurably affected the quality or quantity of mother-child interaction.

*Myth II. The decline of marriage.* Here again Bane demonstrates that 90 to 95 percent of Americans marry at least once, and although the divorce rate has increased significantly, those who divorce tend to remarry promptly. The proportion of singles, historically very small, has risen only slightly. Married men and women in general rate themselves "happier" than the single, divorced, or widowed. The death rates for married men and women are significantly lower than for their unmarried counterparts at all ages. Marriage as an institution continues despite indications of increased conflict and tensions between husbands and wives.

*Myth III. The isolation of the nuclear family from the extended family.* Much has been said about the emergence of the isolated nuclear family in recent decades. It has been argued that the American family, increasingly deprived of wider family ties, has become isolated and turned inward on a self-centered and often destructive course. The shrinkage of the American family from an extended to a nuclear structure is also shown to be a myth by Bane. The extended family seems never to have existed in this country, and far from being isolated from its kin, the contemporary nuclear family maintains close ties with many relatives. Although there is a trend for the young and the old to

14 Bane, *Here to Stay*, p. xiv.

live in their own independent households, they nonetheless interact frequently with the other members of their family.

*Myth IV. The isolation of the nuclear family from the community.* Bane also exposes the myth that the modern family, bereft of ties with the wider family, faces loneliness and increasing isolation from the community, particularly in the urban setting. This perception, incidentally, was instrumental in reviving the movement to establish communes. In sorting out the scattered data underlining this assumption, Bane concludes that in spite of greater (though limited) geographical mobility and architectural and bureaucratic obstacles, Americans are amazingly resourceful in finding friends and forming new relationships. Americans, it seems, continue to be moved by altruism to assist each other, and an astonishingly high proportion of Americans today are involved in community and other cooperative activities.

To sum up Bane's findings, whatever changes may have taken place during the past hundred years, in all likelihood they are less catastrophic than most analysts make them out to be. The point is best expressed in Bane's own words:

> Assuming that the family is dead or dying may lead to policies that, in their desperate attempt to keep the patient alive, infringe unnecessarily on other cherished values and prove once again that the cure can be worse than the disease. . . . Too hasty concern for replacing the "dying" family may, in fact, bring about its untimely death.[15]

One of the foremost problems today is that unfounded assumptions have guided public policy in the past, just as they are continuing to shape the present battle for the rediscovery of the family. The Bane data convincingly demonstrate that American men, women, and children continue to be committed to the family; marriage as an institution continues to be central to the lives of individuals; wider family ties have not weakened; and American families are no more and no less isolated from the community and wider society than at other times in American history.

As I have tried to show, the trend in family analysis and policy making is no longer to seek to replace the family, as was the fashion only a few years ago. Instead, the family is judged to be in urgent need of more help, more attention, extraordinary measures—all governmentally determined, financed, and delivered. It is puzzling that the barrage of analyses of this kind seems to be diametrically opposed to

---

[15] Ibid.

the individual practices, values, and hopes that are shown to exist by the data presented by Mary Jo Bane.

It is precisely at this juncture that the concept of mediating structures offers an alternative to governmental intervention. This approach seeks to reconcile in a common-sense way the continued private practices and commitments of Americans with the new public values flowing from a variety of pressures and demands in today's world.

## A Mediating Structures Approach to the Family and Child Care

In outlining the mediating structures perspective on the needs of the American family, I shall try to demonstrate how this differs from other approaches to the family and child-care complex and why the mediating structures perspective is imperative. Since public policy—as pointed out before—is interested primarily in the family's relation to its children and its capacity to care for them, I shall restrict my considerations largely to this aspect.

From a mediating structures perspective the central problem of the American family today is its loss of autonomy. It may well be—as Mary Jo Bane has shown (to my mind, convincingly)—that the family remains central to the lives of individuals. Nonetheless, the situation of the family has changed fundamentally with the expansion of the power of the state into the family's relations to its children.

It can be said with a fair degree of certainty that a number of forces both outside of and within the family have caused the growth of state intervention into family affairs. Most of the external forces are deeply rooted in the modernization processes that have transformed all important sectors of contemporary society. The most visible among these changes are the ever-increasing differentiation of institutions that has stripped the family of its earlier functions such as education; the technological growth and bureaucratization of the economy that have made the family dependent on the overall system of economic production, and thus robbed it of its traditional and integrative role as a self-supporting economic unit; and urbanization, the modernizing process that seems to have had the greatest consequences for the patterns of human habitation and interaction.

These forces of modernity seemed to change the world with cataclysmic speed. As a result, they were perceived to have a devastating effect upon the family. Not only did they remove the family from its traditional educational and economic functions, but these external forces were above all seen to be instrumental in eroding the family's traditional sources of cohesion (in the jargon of sociologists, "the organic bonds of solidarity") as well as its traditional sources of authority. Schools, for example, have not only offered academic instruction but also shaped the individual's values and morality independent of the family. These changes were not entirely negative, however. For instance, it could be argued rather persuasively that economic progress and specialization helped to liberate individuals and their families from economic struggle and want. The rise of the educational system can also be seen as an aid to individuals, families, and a modernizing society. In both instances, modernization liberates the individual from the narrow confines of the family, just as it liberates the family from having to be everything to the individual. While the family may have lost its traditional functions, it gained new ones, such as providing for the individual's emotional and affectional sustenance. These new functions were viewed as more than psychological and were celebrated by some as developing truly "independent" individuals. To many observers the expanding educational institution in particular became an attractive and powerful reality invested with a quasi-religious meaning (Ivan Illich called schools the "new church").[16] Education was sometimes believed to be almost a panacea. What is important for our argument is that modernization was not—and should not be—seen *only* as a negative force, robbing the family of its functions and authority and throwing the individual into anomie and loneliness. It certainly may do that, but at the same time modernity can also be seen as a liberating force.

Liberation is a singularly Western concept derived from Rousseau's view that "men are born free, yet everywhere they are in chains." The supreme task, according to this philosophy, is the liberation of human beings from the prison of traditionality, from cultural barriers and oppressive social practices. Above all, Rousseau insisted, the family, the most powerful generator and reinforcer of wretched traditions, must be broken. Rousseau's indictment of the family provided an effective philosophical basis for subsequent social thinkers to attack the institution of the family as a barrier to social progress and individual liberty. This general disregard of the family has led to the willingness to trust outside "experts" more than family members and has culminated today in the women's liberation movement, as well as in the children's rights movement. Both movements can muster strong support, and it is not easy to prejudge either.

This Rousseauean tradition underlies the proclivity in modern society to look in the political-juridical arena for the primary mecha-

---

[16] Ivan Illich, *Deschooling Society* (New York: Harper and Row, 1971).

nisms to facilitate the liberation struggle of all individuals. For if the authority of tradition is to be torn asunder, if the leaden cage of the family is to be pried open, individual and social life must now be anchored in the public realm, which is perceived to be more just and better suited to provide for equality and the realization of individuality. For Rousseau and those standing in this tradition, the answer is simple: "public" authority is to supplant the authority of tradition, and this is to be done at the expense of the "domestic" authority of the family. The Rousseauean vision, entailing the rise of the "public" as the guarantor of liberty, is confirmed by modern events. It is ironic that even as this vision is penetrating every niche of life and every corner of the globe, the economic order that has made it possible is outrightly denied.

By far the prevailing assumption today is that the political units of society are the individual and the state, not the state and the family. This kind of society requires a large bureaucracy, because when there are no social units to mediate between the state and the individual and to meet individual needs, administrative units have to be created. In sum, state intervention into the affairs of the family and the concomitant development of state and professional agencies that challenge family authority have two sources: the transfer of functions from the family to other specialized institutions and the new consciousness of individual liberation. Moreover, these developments are a general result of modernization, regardless of the political and economic system under which the modernizing process may unfold. The situation is not, as Christopher Lasch wants us to believe, primarily the product of a quasi-conspiracy of professionals who are unwitting instruments of an economic system based on private capital and dominated by large corporations.

It can, of course, be argued that, once established, a trend continues on its course independent of the forces that made for its emergence, impelled by its own dynamics. This argument pertains to the dynamics of professionalization, as well. Yet, this is an exceedingly complicated process driven forward by many imponderables. To be sure, an imperialism of the professional complex is clearly visible in our society. But other forces such as values and ideals have to be taken into consideration. The well-known dynamics of professionalization become a genuine social problem, however, when those who formulate public values and ideals are the same professionals who benefit most from this formulation. I am referring here to the role of social class in the formulation of public policy—a problem that cannot be overemphasized.

For some time the general public perception, under whatever tutelage, has been that the family alone is no longer able to prepare and protect its children adequately in a modernizing world. The deficiencies of the family, it was argued, were dramatically visible in the case of immigrants, migrants, and poor ethnic and racial groups. In the absence of any counterclaims it was rarely, if ever, asked to what degree this perception was correct. Certain types of families were seen to be in growing need of the help and assistance of knowledgeable and trained professionals. A broad public, perceiving this need to be urgent and real, was willing to subsidize the cost of these services from public coffers. It is not surprising that professionals were eager to oblige.

It would fill volumes to trace the efforts and vacillations of "the mandarins of child care" in their quest for legitimate and "scientific" methods and tools that would not only supplement the child-rearing and child-care functions of the family but would increasingly move them away from the family. But no clear-cut answers and guidelines could be found. Controversy proliferated as fuzzy studies, dubious theories, and competing and contradictory intellectual orthodoxies consumed time and energy in the battle for the family.

While the morass of notions and claims surrounding the family and child care has created disarray in middle-class families, its influence on the non-middle-class segment of the population has been devastating. It is still possible for strong middle-class parents to prevail and survive the onslaught against the family—at least they have the financial means, the verbal skills, and the bureaucratic knowledge to navigate around the most blatant dangers to themselves and their children. The poorer classes, however, are lacking money, status, and verbal know-how and thus are particularly vulnerable. More than anyone else, they became the powerless victims of "friendly intruders," the experts and agencies who ever more began to run their lives. The paradox of the dynamics of professionalization is accentuated by this class difference. Instead of being given the means to cope and succeed, instead of liberation and the enhancement of their individual choices, poor families frequently receive exactly the opposite: more intervention and the loss of choice and individual freedom. The effect upon the black family has been particularly disastrous. It is this tutelage of the poor that leaders such as Jesse Jackson are trying to break through. To look for a way out of this situation by creating *more* professional services and interference in the affairs of the family—as Keniston and his associates do —seems to me to be absurd in light of the poor performance of many of these programs. The targeted problems have persisted, if not multiplied, in spite of massive intervention and the immense sums spent from public coffers. Whatever the arguments may be, the loss of the autonomy of the American family is evident, particularly (but not only) in the case of poor and lower-class families. Clearly the American family has lost its function to serve as a mediator between the child and the state.

In the present debate concerning the family and child care, those who, like Keniston, seek a total restructuring of the American social, economic, and political system are joined by liberal theoreticians and old practitioners of "doing good," who fear that fiscal considerations may in the end hurt the opportunity of the poor for greater equality. In the mind of David Rothman, coauthor of *Doing Good*, America is moving into a postreformist era, and the commitment to paternalistic state intervention in the name of equality is giving way to a commitment to restrict intervention in the name of liberty. This is a serious allegation. As the old liberal reforms are being discredited, as a general disenchantment with professional and state intervention becomes manifest, we must, indeed, ask whether these two fundamental American commitments, liberty and equality, are mutually exclusive.

At this point it becomes strikingly clear not only that a mediating structures perspective on society presents a genuine alternative to the views that have so far carried the day, but also that such a perspective is imperative if we wish to continue to seek liberty and equality. To my mind the need for this much neglected mediating structures approach becomes nowhere more obvious than in the debate concerning a national family policy. When all is said and done, the perceptions of the American family and proposals for alternatives and aid to the family are tackling the issues from the wrong end. It is important to recognize that the American concepts of democracy, freedom, and equality are not merely abstractions, but are rooted in the practical realities of the everyday lives of individuals in a highly pluralistic society.

An adequate knowledge of the life of ordinary people, their practices, and hopes hence becomes the first imperative. As indicated above, Mary Jo Bane's *Here To Stay* collects empirical data that cast doubt on many of the clichés hitherto taken for granted about the contemporary American family. These data are helpful in formulating a concept of the American family for use in developing a policy model that takes ordinary people seriously.

Such a conceptualization is the proclaimed task of the Mediating Structures Project of the American Enterprise Institute for Public Policy Research. According to its originators, Peter Berger and Richard John Neuhaus, the Mediating Structures Project aims to identify "those institutions that have been neglected and have come into disregard," sometimes even to the verge of destruction, but that have continued to be of primacy in the lives of ordinary American citizens.[17] Berger and Neuhaus perceive the institutions of the family, neighborhood, church, and voluntary associations to be vital for the future of democracy. This perception and its emphasis on ordinary Americans has been missing from the present trend toward rediscovering the significance of the family.

Among the mediating structures that continue to order the lives of most individuals in contemporary society, the family clearly holds a primary place. But what is meant by "the family"? I would suggest that it is inaccurate to speak of *the* family as if there were only one type, for it does not exist in a pure form. Empirically, there are considerable differences in families in terms of class, ethnicity, and race, and a variety of new forms have emerged recently, such as single-parent and grandparent families, that more often than not are products of necessity rather than choice. Families can also be differentiated by their values. There are and always have been strong value commitments in American society deriving from religious and quasi-religious systems that have a pronounced impact on the kind of family individuals seek to establish. This dimension of values and morality is often ignored, however, in current discussions. The political, cultural, and value pluralism of American society has great significance for the pluralism of the American family; all sorts of family structures and contents have traditionally coexisted side by side and continue to do so.

America is not only one of the most complex societies in history, but also perhaps one of the most heterogeneous. Nathan Glazer and Daniel P. Moynihan have illustrated this point:

In 1660 William Kieft, the Dutch governor of New Netherland, remarked to the French Jesuit Isaac Jogues that there were eighteen languages spoken at or near Fort Amsterdam at the tip of Manhattan Island. There still are: not necessarily the same languages, but at least as many, nor has the number ever declined in the intervening three centuries. This is an essential fact of New York: a merchant metropolis with an extraordinarily heterogeneous population. The first shipload of settlers sent out by the Dutch was made up largely of French-speaking Protestants . . . British, Germans, Finns, Jews, Swedes, Africans, Italians, Irish followed, beginning a stream that has never stopped. . . .

The census of 1960 showed that 19 percent of the population of the city were still foreign-born whites, 28 percent were

---

[17] Peter L. Berger and Richard John Neuhaus, *To Empower People* (Washington, D.C.: American Enterprise Institute, 1977).

children of foreign-born whites, another 14 percent were
Negro, 8 percent were of Puerto Rican birth or parentage.
Unquestionably, a great majority of the rest (31 percent) were
the grandchildren and great-grandchildren of immigrants, and
still thought of themselves, on some occasions and for some
purposes, as German, Irish, Italian, Jewish, or what not,
as·well as of course American.[18]

Since the 1960 census the ethnic heterogeneity of New York may have
increased even more as new groups have streamed into the city, with
Hispanics, Indians, and Southeast Asians among the latest arrivals. Almost every country in the world is represented by enough people in
New York to make up communities of thousands and tens of thousands
with organizations, churches, a language, and a distinctive culture. Nor
is New York unique. Other cities and even many rural areas, which
once were characterized by ethnic homogeneity, are today turning into
polyglot conglomerations of diverse groups. This coexistence is by no
means without tensions and strife. Yet it becomes possible whenever
these different groups show concern for family, church, and neighborhood organizations. True communities—across ethnic barriers—tend
to emerge in this manner because all ethnic groups strongly identify
with these traditional values that have helped them to persevere individually and as groups. Through such shared values individuals can
understand the lives of others, even total strangers.

I think a strong argument can be made for the continuation of
pluralism, and public policy must take cognizance of pluralistic family
structures. This point is further buttressed by the fact, mentioned above,
that no "scientific" findings allot unequivocal superiority of any one
type of family over another.

American families, in their considerable variety, are anchored in
the wider society through a network of voluntary organizations. As the
family is a mediating structure in its own right, it is also in need of
*other* mediating structures that tie it to more abstract groupings such
as the nation or the state. In the words of the sociologist Jack Douglas:

> The nation of joiners has created a web of overlapping and
> interlocking, yet independent, voluntary organizations for al-
> most every conceivable social purpose, ranging from the pres-
> ervation of redwood trees to the covert overthrow of foreign
> governments, both friendly and unfriendly. Americans have
> been known for their organizational entrepreneurship for al-

---

[18] Daniel P. Moynihan and Nathan Glazer, *Beyond the Melting Pot* (Cambridge,
Mass.: MIT Press, 1964), pp. 1, 7.

most two centuries, and the importance of this entrepreneurial activity must not be underestimated.[19]

In the reshaping of a more adequate perception of the realities of American social life, it is imperative to recognize the continued significance of this network of voluntaristic groups and organizations for the American individual and family. All data I have seen reveal that the vast majority of Americans choose their primary group relations and organizational affiliations along ethnic, church, and neighborhood lines. These preferences are reinforced by the everyday experiences of individual Americans as well as by the growing realization of the failure of other—may we say nonnatural?—groupings and agencies created by a distant state. The plight of the black family is but one example of how governmental policy-making agencies ignore the strength of a particular group that is embedded in voluntaristic structures not recognized by the "official" perception. The writings and presentations of Robert Hill of the National Urban League amply prove this point.

There are, of course, many psychological, economic, and political dimensions and considerations that need to be worked out before the family can be perceived as the major mediating structure between the individual and society. Selma Fraiberg, in *Every Child's Birthright*, presents a position that reflects a long tradition in child psychology. She argues for the vital importance of mothers' taking care of their own children, at least in the early stages of development, as well as for the general significance of family interaction for the emotional development of children. Such arguments must be taken into consideration in the construction of a mediating structures perspective, because they re-open the quest for optimal ways and means to develop healthy individuals, with a capacity for trust and creativity. The policy implications that can be gleaned from these psychological arguments, however, seem to go in a somewhat different direction. Instead of emphasizing the importance of biological parents in infant care, a mediating structures perspective would be much more concerned with society's ability to provide a stable locale for infant rearing as well as for the socialization process beyond the infant years. The significance of biological parents would recede in relation to the significance of a *locale* for stable and individualized socialization. People who are committed and able to take care of the needs of children for a long time—whether they are biological parents (father and mother), single parents (mother or father), grandparents, foster parents, or adoptive parents—and who can provide individualized care for the child should be recognized by

---

[19] Jack Douglas, *American Social Order* (New York: Free Press, 1971), p. 258.

public policy as family. The Fraiberg argument should, in general, make policy makers suspicious of arrangements that work against continuity and stability in child rearing, and should convince them to reject any measures that may weaken existing structures.

As in any other area of social policy, it is advisable to look at the economic dimension of the proposed model for family and child care. From the mediating structures perspective it can be argued convincingly that if public policy were to make the family the major agent and locale of child care, it would provide an economic alternative to increasingly costly social services. Although no windfall could be expected for the besieged governmental coffers, there would nonetheless be a real saving without depriving the children and their families of what they need. In fact, the mediating structures perspective on family and child care provides a rare instance of a public policy in which virtue is also economically rewarding.

I can make only brief reference here to many further implications. Democracy presupposes independent individuals capable of judgment, loyalties, and social commitment. If the socialization processes of society will no longer produce such individuals, democracy is a doomed enterprise. Therefore, in addition to the personal and economic costs of a lopsided understanding of the vital role of the family in child care, there should also be a serious reckoning of the political costs. The evidence available indicates that human beings, in order to develop and flourish, need a setting astonishingly similar to the modern nuclear family in all its pluralistic forms. It is politically important to understand that the modern nuclear family as it has emerged in the West is inexorably tied to a democratic order of life and society. It is no accident that the concepts of democracy, freedom, and individual human rights have been part of the same process that produced the modern family. Although it may be arguable whether any one family form is preferable to another, evidence is convincing that there is no more damaging factor in the development and well-being of an individual than the absence of the intensive and individualized care a nuclear family alone can provide. To disregard this function of the great variety of nuclear families in America, a function vital for both the individual and society, to deny these families the right to care for their children and the choice of services for them, is in the last analysis a denial of freedom.

If there is to be a national family policy, it should not be conceived as a panacea for all problems of society. The policy should recognize the family as the primary institution of child care and at the same time be responsive to different needs. Above all, this policy should guarantee the greatest amount of freedom and choice. The mediating structures perspective is a distinctive approach to public policy for the family and child care inasmuch as it seeks to guarantee the greatest amount of freedom and choice to individuals and groups. I have elsewhere presented the theoretical model of the family as a mediating structure.[20] For convenience, I paraphrase it here.

1. *A national family policy should be based on the understanding that the family and not any other conceivable structure is the most viable locale for child care.* Instead of relying on often self-styled experts of child care and engineers of family welfare, policy should emphasize the role of individual families themselves. After a history of ambivalence and distrust of parents, in particular those who are poor and members of a minority group, parents should again be seen as the best advocates of their children's welfare.

Relying upon parents once more, however, does not imply a return to a restrictive definition of the family. Anyone who is willing to commit himself or herself to the care of a child for a good number of years, and who is willing to take on the responsibility for a child, should be included in the category of parents. In other words, I would urge the acceptance of a great variety of people, with the most varied styles of life, as effective parents, *as long as they meet the above conditions.* Single heads of households, lesbian and homosexual households, households made up of older individuals or couples, and others who do not meet the traditional narrow definitions have to be considered as parents.

2. *Insofar as professional services and agencies have to be involved in the process of child care, they should be ancillary to the family and as far as possible held accountable to parents.* The best way to assure accountability, in my opinion, is through some system of vouchers that are made available to parents and used at their discretion. The intention here is not to oppose the professional as such, but to attempt to clarify the professional's role vis-à-vis the family. There does exist a real need for professional advice and services in the area of child care, and by far the great majority of child-care professionals have the best interest of the child at heart. If, however, the best interest of the child is best served within the family (as widely defined above), then it follows that professional services must be ancillary to the family.

3. *A national family policy should respect the existing pluralism of family life-styles and child care.* This implies that the particular life-style and child-care pattern of any given group—including both the

---

[20] "The Family and Mediating Structures as Agents for Child Care," in Brigitte Berger and Sidney Callahan, eds., *Child Care and Mediating Structures* (Washington, D.C.: American Enterprise Institute, 1979), pp. 12–16.

typical middle class and the poor and ethnic minorities—is neither denigrated nor elevated. It also means that a national family policy should be guided neither by any given middle-class standard or need, nor by what are currently understood to be the needs of targeted groups, such as female-headed, poor ethnic households.

To assure in practice, and not merely in rhetoric, respect for the great variety of American life-styles, for their widely varying perceptions and goals, as well as for the distinctive structures in which they are embedded, and yet to be responsive to the different needs of families and their children, some sort of child-care allowance seems indicated. This mechanism, in my opinion, would resolve most of the issues in the national day-care debate. A child-care allowance would allow individual families the widest possible choice in caring for their small children; it would permit individual options in arranging or making use of the most varied forms of care. Such options should include the possibility that the individual parent (father or mother) would stay home during the crucial perod of infancy and early childhood (or longer), and such arrangements as the use of grandparenting, extended-family members, neighborhood groups, child-care facilities attached to the place of work, part-time, full-time, even hourly arrangements (drop-in centers), as well as existing and future governmental centers of whatever size.

4. *Any national family policy has to free itself from the pejorative myths that have surrounded the black family.* There has been a widespread tendency to view and treat the black family, especially the poor black family, as "disorganized," "broken," and even "pathological." Recent research, such as that of Robert Hill, however, has found that black cooperative and kinship networks in rural areas as well as cities have a vitality, stability, and flexibility previously ignored.[21] These studies suggest that black families have persisted despite poverty primarily through tight kinship bonds and mutual aid. National policy should recognize and support such bonds. The same encouragement of kinship bonds and mutual aid applies to other minorities and groupings as well. Wherever kinship networks do break down, local neighborhood arrangements for the family, such as the House of Umoja in Philadelphia, which emerged within the community on a voluntaristic basis, should be recognized and supported.

5. *The thesis about the primacy of the family should apply to the various categories of "special children," as well.* Over against the trend

---

[21] Robert B. Hill, *Strengths of Black Families* (New York: Emerson Hill Publishers, 1973).

to separate "special children" from their own families, the family should be understood as the most stable structure around able to accommodate the primary needs of special children. When this is not possible, special children should be placed in settings as close to a family situation as possible. Professional staffs and services should be looked upon as supports for families rather than as substitutes for them. This approach may include paying special allowances to families so that family members can afford to stay home to take care of the extraordinary needs of their handicapped children, or can employ help that is accountable to them. One attraction of this approach—but by no means the most important one—is that it would almost certainly reduce costs.

6. *A national family policy must not become an instrument for further weakening the family by emphasizing children's rights more than the rights of their parents.* Family rights should be emphasized in spite of the current preoccupation with child abuse and the tragic cases of true physical abuse (approximately 4 percent of the hundreds of thousands annually reported). According to data presented by Reba Uviller of the American Civil Liberties Union, more than 450,000 children are separated from their parents each year; 150,000 are taken coercively, and about 300,000 are yielded to state custody "voluntarily" by their parents under threat of prosecution for neglect.[22] These children have rarely fared well. Separation from their families means an endless stream of foster homes, confusion, and heartache, frequently resulting in serious disorientation and irreparable psychological damage. A stringent application of existing laws is called for in these tragic cases. But conditions such as parental immaturity, sloppy housekeeping, or "failure to provide for the moral and emotional welfare of a child" are hardly "crimes" that justify breaking up a family.

7. *In the context of the current discussion of income support and income redistribution, a national family policy should be guided by the general principle that reforms intended to diminish poverty defeat their own purpose if they weaken the family.*

---

[22] *New York Times,* April 20, 1977.

# Discussion

QUESTION: In view of the new definition of womanhood, the new vital roles women play today in public life, how can a man respond to the changes that will inevitably result in family life. Wouldn't it be important for men to be *sensitized* to the new kinds of roles women are playing?

PROFESSOR BERGER: The question of the sensitization of men to the newly emerging roles of women is really outside my purview. If you, however, permit me some personal considerations, then I would say that perhaps much of the fashionable talk about the villainous authoritarian American male has been exaggerated. From my personal experiences in a number of very different societies, I find that American male sex roles have been rather egalitarian traditionally, and in more recent history even more so. Judging by the portrayal of everyday American life in the media, and in particular in the more popular television shows, I think an argument can be made that the American male has lost ever more authority and respect. From a once central figure, he seems to have been reduced to a marginal, fumbling, ineffective, if not ridiculous, species. I would even assert that the American male is in just as much an identity crisis as the American female, if not more so. The contradictory demands and barrage of images that are showered on the American male have left him perplexed and have made him an object of ridicule. This, to me, has enormous consequences for the American family. "Sensitization" does not seem the decisive issue in the context of the family. Rather, the key issue for the family is the consequence of this lack of clearly defined social roles for the American male.

QUESTION: Let me then attach a second question to my first, one that concerns itself more directly with day care: Will it not be necessary for the government to provide a number of alternatives in day care so that American women can take advantage of the new roles they can and have to play today? Moreover, as to the children involved, do you really think that part-time day care, say two or three hours a day, along the lines of the Montessori model, for instance, can be harmful for a child? I would think that, on the contrary, it would be good for a child to get out of the neurotic structures that many of our homes have become. In fact, I think that this kind of time away from the home would not only be beneficial for the child but also for the mother.

PROFESSOR BERGER: If we talk about the kind of nursery school a model such as Montessori provides, one that is thought to be of pedagogical value for the child and also incidentally (and very incidentally in Montessori theory at that) provides relief for the mother from the incessant care required for a small child, then we are talking about something very different from day care. Day care has only become a public issue since increasing numbers of women with small children have entered the labor market. In full-time positions now, women no longer can care for their small children. The government enters the picture only because wide sectors of the public perceive that adequate care is not available, and the care that is available is thought to be too costly. The question that public policy must address is to what degree the government is obliged to make such care available, to finance it, and to control it. A second question is whether the government is the best agency to address such fundamental issues.

Now, a claim can be made—and I cannot enter into the debate over this claim—that a small child derives considerable benefits pedagogically as well as emotionally from exposure to peers. But that is not the issue here. Day care has to take all small children into consideration, and not only for two to three hours, but for nine to ten hours. The day-care centers Selma Fraiberg has observed can in no way be compared to the exclusive and highly structured play-groups found in Montessori nursery schools. She was much more struck by the warehousing of children, which she thinks will result in irreparable harm.

No one would disagree that mothers would receive necessary periods of respite from the incessant demands small children make upon them if such nursery schools were available. I am quite sure that if such opportunities existed for all mothers—at no cost to individual families to boot—most women would like to take advantage of them. As Leslie Lenkowski of the Smith-Richardson Foundation—one of the foremost experts on social welfare questions in the country—has so rightly observed: All free services are oversubscribed. The question for national policy, however, is, Why should the government pay for women's leisure? Experiments in California have shown that women,

171

relieved of child-care tasks, tend to go shopping, playing, and visiting. There is nothing wrong with that—but why should other Americans pay for it?

A mediating structures approach to the family is concerned with the question of day care in a quite different manner. Recognizing that different families have different priorities and structure their lives differently, the problem is to respect such differences. Let me emphasize the class aspect of such differences. Middle-class women have always had a variety of choices available to them; working-class women and the poor have not. If they were given a choice that would not punish them economically, studies clearly show they would choose to care for their children themselves. I think it imperative that public policy be concerned not so much with providing day care, but with providing choices. And, again, a recent study by Jim Levine of the Wellesley Center for Women has shown that working-class mothers do not deplore the unavailability of day care for their small children as much as the lack of information about the variety of care presently available.

A final comment on your observation that it is probably good for children to leave the "neurotic structures" of the home: *Who* says they are neurotic, and what *is* neurotic in any case? Is the home worse than the day-care centers Fraiberg describes so hauntingly?

QUESTION: Motherhood does pose certain threats and problems, no matter which social group you look at. The Moynihan report showed, if my memory serves me, that the hazard for children is greatest in the pathological family structure of the black inner city. When I served as an assistant minister in the inner city, I had ample occasion to observe this pathological structure of black families. It was not unusual to see twenty, thirty, forty small black youngsters sitting in front of the television set with mama reclining on the sofa drinking beer. My question to you is whether you and Fraiberg would really be willing to fund the continuation of such pathological structures with welfare money.

PROFESSOR BERGER: Let me first clear up one minor point: Moynihan himself never made a study of black family life. His policy recommendations use the findings of the eminent black psychologist Kenneth Clark. Kenneth Clark, when his studies first gained wide attention in the 1950s, was concerned with finding an explanation for the continuing failure of American blacks to achieve greater participation in the public sphere of American society. He thought at that time he had found a root cause in the "pathological" structure of the black ghetto. Not only did subsequent scholars take issue with Clark's use of the concept "pathological," but they also doubted that the black family structure as such was the chief cause for the malaise of the ghetto. I wonder whether Clark would continue to use this concept today and whether he would still pin the blame on the black family.

I would go along with those scholars who point to the traditional strength of the black family. I am particularly impressed by the capacity of black families to develop ingenious ways (for instance, through voluntary and auxiliary forms) to cope with the particular problems of life in the black ghetto. These voluntaristic auxiliary forms admittedly do not conform to white middle-class expectations, but they are effective in the lives of inner-city blacks. What is so remarkable is that they have emerged from within the structure of ghetto life without the aid of the government, professional organizations, or anyone else. Moreover, I certainly would take issue with any attempt to construct a precise and unambiguous definition of "pathology" and, by extension, any attempt to single out the causes or effects of pathology.

But let me try to react to the general tenor of your comments more explicitly. Since the 1950s, when the black ghetto family was diagnosed as "pathological," many attempts have been made, with the aid of considerable public funding, to break through the "pathological structures"; programs have multiplied, and intervention measures have abounded. Contrary to the interventionist claims, all these attempts have yet to show any positive results: black families in the ghetto have failed to respond to these interventions. There have been changes, to be sure, such as the raising of the subsistence floor, but they have not centered on the so-called pathology of black families. The claim can be made that the original strength of the black family has been undermined. Black inner-city parents today, after all these efforts on their behalf, have become confused and insecure about the effectiveness of their parenting. They come under the tutelage of professionals who are ready to help them at considerable cost to society. In Chicago Jesse Jackson has called this development in the black ghetto the continuing cycle of dependency. He sees in this dependency one of the chief roots of the ghetto problem. I agree with him. I do not think that the foremost problem of inner-city families is rooted in the so-called pathological structure of their family life. On the contrary I perceive the paramount problem to be how to enable the black family to regain confidence in itself, so that it will not relinquish the care of children to outside agencies. Not only have these agenices failed to demonstrate that they are better suited than familes to care for children, but their interference has perhaps been more harmful than the presumed ills they set out to combat.

Your personal observation on the captivity of black inner-city children to the television screen, with the mother reclining and imbibing, calls for a comparison with those facilities observed by Fraiberg where rather similar situations seem to exist. The only difference now seems to be that the adults involved are transitory strangers who are paid for their services from government coffers.

QUESTION: In view of your presentation of the changing conception of womanhood, as well as the increasing conflict between husbands and wives shown in the rising divorce rate, how can individuals be good spouses, good parents, and good citizens all at the same time?

PROFESSOR BERGER: I think we will have to refrain from speculating about what makes for good spouses. Marriage, I confess, is such an extraordinarily difficult matter that it would be presumptuous for me —and perhaps for anyone else—to expound on it. There are all kinds of marital arrangements and accommodations, some more successful than others—and who is to say what is "success" here anyway? In any case, marriage certainly is not of concern to public policy, and to my mind, *should* emphatically not be so.

What is of concern to public policy, however, is the ability or inability of families to take care of their children. Hence your question on what makes for "good" parents is very relevant. Yet, it is precisely my contention that as far as I can see no one has come up with a convincing, clear-cut concept of the good parent, let alone the good family. I am trying to show in our discussions that this quest for the good family has occupied public discourse for quite some time and has created havoc for the family. I am trying to demonstrate that precisely this quest for the good family has made for the substantial loss of function of the family for its children.

The basic thrust of my argument is that now, after decades of search for the good family, no recipes have emerged, and confusion persists about what constitutes effective child care and successful socialization. It would seem to me that we have to turn this question around and ask, after all this experience, Is there any knowledge about what is *harmful* for children? All the evidence we have available to us unambiguously indicates that the single most powerful harm that comes to children is derived from the lack of family or family-like structures and arrangements. It seems to me that what kind of family a child grows up in matters less than that there is a family, any family, to grow up in. Therefore, it is very important that public policy recognize the significance of the family in child care and socialization. Insights

174

of this kind have informed the mediating structures approach to the family.

QUESTION: There emerges a very strong antiprofessional bias from your paper. Is that so because you identify the professionals with the state and, by extension, you see the state to be against the family? Or do you feel that the professionals are "unprofessional" and are really not adequate at their jobs? If they really performed their jobs adequately, perhaps the problem would be lessened?

PROFESSOR BERGER: My position is not antiprofessional as such. Teachers, as well as the members of the "helping professions" such as social workers, counselors, therapists, and the like, most certainly perform necessary functions, and their services will continue to be needed in the future. To what degree their own expertise needs revision is a question all professionals will probably have to face squarely and honestly in the near future.

What I *am* deploring, however, is a broad tendency in our society that fundamentally reverses the supporting function of the helping professions. It is this usurpation of child-care functions by professionals that I am most concerned with, functions that by all the evidence are much better left to the family. I would argue that the child has a much better chance to find continuing devotion, love, and care in the family, any family. To be sure, there are families in which this is not so; there may even be families so constituted as to be pathogenic, but it is downright folly to let these relatively few exceptions blind us to the immense potential of the family. As I see it, through the expansionistic tendency inherent in all organizational structures, more pressure has been put on the family; the failures of the professional interventions on behalf of the family have made the family seem ever more in need of ever more aid and manipulation. What I find most devastating about these professional interventions is how the good intentions of the professionals have led so many parents—and children —to so much confusion and anxiety.

The policy a mediating structures perspective envisages is in no way antiprofessional. But the professional thrust would be redirected, wherever feasible, to give support to the family, as against the present tendency to circumvent or even shut out the family. The policy would not infringe on the independence or authority of the various helping professions; on the contrary, by freeing them of many of the current bureaucratic restraints, it would give them added opportunity to exercise their particular skills.

175

QUESTION: You have used the term "ordinary" persons. I do not know what you mean by this term—except, perhaps, as referring to the working class. But I think I am "ordinary," too, although I come from the middle class. And you come down very hard on the middle-class people for abdicating their child-rearing responsibilities to professionals and for being in favor of day care. But what you say does not reflect my own experiences. I, like many middle-class individuals, care for my children, sometimes with the aid of professionals and sometimes not, and I also see no problem in making use of the day care professionals can supply.

PROFESSOR BERGER: The use of the term "ordinary" may well have confused the issue. You are, of course, right that in a very real sense most of us, if asked, would classify ourselves in this category. What I really wanted to bring out and emphasize was the class aspect in the debate focusing on public policy and the American family.

Public policy has always been shaped by those educated and vocal segments in society—in other words, by the members of the middle, if not upper-middle, classes. By definition then, public policy has been inordinately influenced by the thoughts and interest of one group at the expense of other groups, whose concerns and hopes may or may not be similar to those of the people who shape public policy and who also claim to speak on their behalf. What I am trying to stress is the importance for a pluralistic society of incorporating the traditions, practices, and expectations of those who have so far been left out in the policy-making process. For lack of a better term I call them "ordinary."

The relevance of the class dimension in public policy will perhaps become more obvious when we consider that middle-class families have always had a better *chance* than the working class and the lower class had to resist interference in their family matters. At least they had the knowledge and the verbal means—as well as financial means—to counter the most blatant attempts by professionals and bureaucrats to run their children's lives. I do think that it ought to be a matter of urgent public concern that similar postures become possible for parents who are undereducated and poor. If they lack the material resources for this, public policy should help them get these resources at their disposal, and such help should not come at the discretion of the professionals. Just as importantly, if they lack the words to defend themselves and their children against dependence on the professional-bureaucratic complex, public policy should first give them confidence in themselves again so that they may express their views freely.

A final comment on your point that you see no problem in your making use of professionals and day-care arrangements: It is precisely the significance and the novelty of the mediating structures approach to public policy and the family that no one single understanding of what is best for a particular family is to be elevated above another. The proposal provides the broadest possible range of choices to all families, be they middle-class, working-class, or poor.

QUESTION: Aside from the question of the role of the intellectual in public life, which seems to me, too, to be problematic, the most worrisome aspect of your argument to me is that the family you talk about is so broadly defined. You seem to imply that there are endless varieties of families, so as to take in any group that wants to call itself family. I somehow do not recognize this institution which I  like you—think is very special indeed.

PROFESSOR BERGER: When we talk about social and economic policies, most of us accept without question the repeated use of the term "typical" American family to mean a married man supporting his wife and two children. As Carolyn Shaw Bell is fond of noting, the Census Bureau has revealed that this family type has practically vanished. There are 56 million families in this country and only 3.3 million of them fit the "typical" pattern, a mere 6 percent of the total. If we take inventory of the many different types of families that exist, and have existed in history, we will be struck by the wide variety of arrangements that have been made. We find, coexisting with what we understand today as the "typical" family, families headed by single parents; families in which parents are divorced, remarried, or never married; families headed by grandparents; foster families; lesbian and homosexual families; and so forth.

Aside from personal preferences for a particular structure, which incidentally are more often than not motivated by necessity, who is to say that one kind of family is to be denied the recognition of its child-care capacity by public policy, whereas another kind is not? All the evidence that I have seen makes only one point perfectly clear, namely that any family—regardless how it is constructed—is to be preferred to the absence of a family base for socialization. I realize that by including lesbian and homosexual families as arrangements to be recognized by public policy for being suitable for child rearing, I will raise the level of discomfiture with my proposals for many people. But I must report that there is so far no evidence that would support the claim that lesbians or homosexuals are less adequate parents than those who are inclined otherwise sexually. I personally think it is time to separate the sexual question from the parenting one.

QUESTION: At times your lecture put me at war with myself in a way, and I felt that you were at war with yourself in this respect, as well. As a sociologist, you have to be governed by data, but as an individual you seem to have very definite views about what kind of family you would prefer for yourself and others. I would have liked to see you put the sociologist in you to the side for at least part of your lecture, so as to give an instance of how an ordinary person might make decisions over against the experts.

PROFESSOR BERGER: You, of course, are referring to the old dilemma of all professionals. I certainly do have strong personal views and preferences, but I cannot let these views and preferences shaped by my particular personal history, by the accident of my birth into one group and not another, start to dominate public policy. If I did this, I would simply continue the way policy has always been made, and the novelty of the mediating structures approach would ultimately be discredited.

QUESTION: But my question is, whether you cannot see that you are at war with yourself. Is it really so that you do not make a distinction between any family and the kind of family you personally would advocate? I really would like to hear your personal, and not your "value-free," sociological judgment.

PROFESSOR BERGER: If you put the question that directly, then I have to confess that my personal preferences are for the kind of family where a father and a mother are present and are actively involved in the care of their children; a family with a strong commitment to children, giving priority to their needs over the needs of the parents for individual self-realization and fulfillment. In short, the family I talk about has commonly been called the "bourgeois" family. Although other types of families also love and care for their children, I personally think that the demanding tasks posed by the needs of children in our kind of society will be much more *difficult* to carry out in these other types of families.

If you press me further, I have to confess that it is for this reason alone that I would be skeptical about the homosexual family's ability to care adequately for the needs of children. However, I certainly would not come out *against* homosexual families. I would prefer not to advocate them. If, however, this type of family can indeed be shown to provide the stability and continuity necessary for child care, then public policy should recognize it.

If I were forced—and I would prefer not to be forced—to combine my professional with my personal views, then my position could be formulated as follows: Public policy cannot be prescriptive on the particular structural arrangements for child care as long as the structure is stable and solid enough to care for a child over a considerable period of time. That, to my mind, is the decisive question. It happens that the bourgeois family best meets these criteria.

# Changing the Paradigms: The Cultural Deficiencies of Capitalism

*Michael Novak*

The task assigned me is to summarize the arguments of the last five days —to "pull together" the threads of many separate arguments.[1] In one sense, my twin assignments here, one on the part of the Syracuse University Department of Religion, the other on the part of the American Enterprise Institute for Public Policy Research, have provided the clue I wish to follow. Religion and public policy belong together. Historically, however, they have been pursued in relative isolation. Our task this week has been to try to change the paradigms in which several key issues have conventionally been discussed, whether by scholars of religion or by public policy professionals.

The theology of culture has always been weakest at the point of economics. Theologians have managed, in the last four hundred years, to update many of their ideas about the meaning of Christianity—in liturgy, hermeneutics, historical studies, sexual ethics, medical ethics, and many other areas. Yet the level of discussion in economics has hardly advanced beyond the principles of the seventeenth century. Its ethics of distribution are those of Aristotle; its theory of the just wage, its attitudes toward capital and interest, and its view of production, invention, and enterprise are really more a part of the ancient and medieval world than of contemporary economics.

Similarly, religion is the least developed part of public policy. There are not many areas in which people engaged in public policy are more naive (in some cases have not thought it important to become sophisticated) than in the field of religion. Journalists in Washington had to scurry when it became obvious that Jimmy Carter was drawing on an evangelical population which they hardly knew existed. Fellows who went to Harvard, Chicago, and other schools, writing for the newspapers and magazines, suddenly had to look around for encyclopedia articles on evangelicals. Some of them had never looked into what it means to be a Baptist or what it means to be "born again." They had no compre-

---

[1] It was one of the constraints of this task to be obliged to extemporize from notes. The following text, then, represents an edited transcript rather than an essay.

180

hension that evangelicals are the majority in, the mainstream of, American religion, into which what is called mainline Protestantism is a most influential but small tributary.

There are historical reasons why public policy thinking has been negligent of religion. In the Continental Enlightenment this neglect was deliberate. The reconstruction of society was defined so as to eliminate religion (*"Ecrasez l'infâme!"*). By contrast, in the Anglo-Scottish Enlightenment, the tendency was to regard religion as important for the health of the republic. Still, Adam Smith and others discussed economics in abstraction from religion and described a merely economic man—as if religion and culture were publicly irrelevant. Most economic thinking is still done in that tradition. So is most public policy thinking. Religion (and ethics and culture) is relegated to the private sphere.

One reason for this privatization grew out of the religious wars. People wanted to avoid further divisiveness, to get on with the secular business of producing, in Adam Smith's phrase, "the wealth of nations."

A second reason was that until very recently, our culture still rode upon a high tide of belief in progress, science, and technique. On these matters, the number of doubters and skeptics is growing. The old paradigm about the irrelevance of religion—and moral values and moral considerations—has begun to seem inadequate. The enlightened atheism of the nineteenth and early twentieth centuries is beginning to look old-fashioned.

A third reason for this tradition is that for some time there was a widespread belief in this country that religion, like ethnicity, was a residue which would gradually disappear in the relentless boiling of the melting pot. As the years went on, less and less would be said about religion, some scholars thought. This idea has been badly shaken by the religiously based eruption in Iran and the vitality obvious in Mexico and in Poland on the visits of Pope John Paul II. An embassy official told a friend of mine recently that in India the pope's visit to Poland was considered by some the single most decisive event of the decade, the beginning of the end of the pretense that there is no spiritual energy in the populations of the world. Religion is a fact, with a potency beyond imagining. In particular, Indians were struck by a vulnerability within communism which they had not expected. Even after thirty years of systematic atheism, the pope showed that religion is strong.

In the year I have been at the American Enterprise Institute, religion has come into many discussions. I am not the person who brings it up. There is hardly a place anywhere in the world in which religious vitality is not an important factor.

If the permanence and potency of religion now appear to be a kind of bedrock of reality about which public policy planners must develop a new sophistication, so, on the other side, have religious leaders in the Vatican and at the World Council of Churches given more and more attention to economics and public policy. The proportion of paragraphs in papal encyclicals given to economics is expanding. Papal economic theory, I hasten to argue, is innocent of a great deal of contemporary experience; it seems to ignore the experience of Great Britain and America as too foreign. If you read the encyclicals with an eye to the description of the world we know best, it is a little like reading statements about religious liberty in Vatican documents before the Second Vatican Council (1961–1965) had incorporated the American experience into the Catholic tradition. Nor do the documents of the World Council of Churches since World War II show much economic sophistication. Nonetheless, the weight of religious analysis, particularly in the field of social ethics, is increasingly moving to the economic sphere.

Our collaboration here, attempting to create a language for discussing theology and public policy, with a focus on economic systems, has an obvious importance. We face a territory in which there is an inadequacy of language on both sides. Our task in this conference, then, is to change the paradigms in which the discussion is conducted. What we must attempt to do is to alter the way public policy is looked at, to alter the point of view from which it is approached. This is a task more basic than that of arguing about who is right or wrong within those perspectives. We have been trying to bring about a shift to new paradigms that will include liberal and conservative and other points of view, and that will go beyond the abstraction of economic man or political man. The new paradigms must take into account the dimensions of meaning, of transcendence, and of moral consideration. Such concerns are not merely private. They are social, communal, public. Public policy planning must take note of them. And theologians must come to understand contemporary economics.

I want to recount some of the paradigm shifts we have been groping toward these past few days.

## First Paradigm: From Economics to Cultural Analysis

The first shift is from regarding economic theory, the question of capitalism and socialism, primarily as a matter of economics to regarding it primarily as a matter of culture. I am suggesting that, contrary to the Marxist view, the sphere of ideas, the cultural sector, has an extraordinary importance for democratic capitalism. I draw here upon Daniel Bell's *The Cultural Contradictions of Capitalism*.[2]

Bell makes the important point that there is an asymmetry between socialism and capitalism. Socialism is unitary: it attempts, at least in the Marxist version, to combine in one single vision the economic, the political, and the moral orders. Its hope is that the socialist moral vision will, through the instrumentality initially of the state and eventually of the proletariat, govern the economic sphere. Capitalism, on the other hand, is differentiated into three systems: a political system, an economic system, and a cultural system, each of which has a certain distinctness and autonomy. Bell's originality is most clearly visible in the attention he gives to the cultural sector. The cultural sector consists of the set of ideas, values, symbols, rituals, and practices—changes in which necessarily precipitate changes in the political and economic orders.

Consider, as an example of the way the cultural system works, changes in the public attitude toward work. Senator Henry M. Jackson in his presidential campaign of 1976 said that he stood for jobs, jobs, jobs. He frightened most of his audiences half to death. It turned out that millions of citizens were not nearly so excited about unemployment as the experts were. Many citizens were doing quite well working part time during the year and collecting unemployment for twenty-three weeks in another part of the year. In some cases, husbands have alternated with wives in going on unemployment and working. A change in the work ethic places unprecedented demands on the political system and the economic system.

It is in the cultural sector, says Bell, that capitalism is weakest. Like Joseph A. Schumpeter in *Capitalism, Socialism, and Democracy*,[3] he suggests that democratic capitalism probably will be brought down by its cultural inadequacy. Schumpeter argued, first, that the weakness in capitalism would come from the presence of an idea class, including some of the very brightest people, whose status and economic rewards are not commensurate with their talents. Such persons would be no less bright than their brothers or sisters, who might be corporate executives or doctors or lawyers, but they would be rewarded considerably less; as a result, they would become resentful. Schumpeter argued, second, that the studied lack of ideas—the pragmatism—among corporate executives would prompt them to sell the communists the rope by which they would be hanged. Tom Kahn showed how this is happening today in the transfer of technology to the Soviet Union. This lack of ideas

---

[2] New York: Basic Books, 1976.

[3] Third ed. (New York: Harper & Row, 1950).

among pragmatic men, men not concerned about metaphysics or world views or ideology, men who "get things done," has now been combined with the rising evidence of a hostile and resentful idea class; together, these two factors will eventually bring about the demise of democratic capitalism. In the economic and political spheres, democratic capitalism is plainly superior to its rivals; its fatal flaw lies in the cultural sector.

Bell adds to this another notion: that, given the emergence of this new idea class and the emergence of the power of advertising, an unpredicted but enormous distributive effect of capitalism has transformed America into a consumer society. Everybody foresaw that capitalism would be a great tool for producing wealth, but no one realized that it would be the most effective distributive mechanism the world has ever known.

As a result, the great problem of Communist parties all around the world has become holding onto a proletariat, because when capitalism takes effect, the proletariat begins to disappear. When I was in Italy last spring, I found that this point was the center of discussion among both Communist and Christian Democratic intellectuals: What is the meaning of communism when the working class is no longer a proletariat but has become a middle class, and communist energy begins to shift—as it has in Italy—to the students and others of the new class in society?

Bell's argument is that when this new middle class emerges, because of the unpredicted distributive success of capitalism, it brings with it, in the spheres of advertising and consumption, a new hedonism. This hedonistic attitude undercuts the spiritual qualities on which the vitality of democratic capitalism, in both its political and its economic sectors, depends. When people are besieged day and night by images of escape, of fulfilling their desires *right now*, of automobiles symbolized by beautiful women, and so forth, it undercuts the discipline, the restraint, the saving, the hard work, and the frugality of the bourgeois ethic. Without realizing it, corporations, through their advertising departments, are destroying the very spiritual basis on which their success depends. They cannot get good work out of their workers if the workers don't give a damn. And if the workers are constantly hearing, "You deserve a break today," why should they break their necks? All through the system, workers, managers, and everybody else begin to say, "What the hell?"

Now, Bell suggests, in an interesting way, that this breakdown in the cultural sector of capitalism is precipitated in part *by the corporations themselves*. This is the Schumpeterian irony. The strongest agents of democratic capitalism help to ensure its defeat.

## Second Paradigm: A Shift in Scale

This brings me to the second paradigm of great significance for us. The intellectual, who used to be thought of as a kind of prophetic leaven in the dough, raising the consciousness of society as yeast raises bread, has found his or her function changed by several important factors that may be best summarized simply as a shift in scale. The power of the cultural sector has expanded because of the new technologies of the media. Henry Luce commissioned his inventors to develop a kind of paper that could reproduce photographs with a fidelity not available before, in ink that would dry instantaneously, and on a printing press that could put out a magazine overnight, so that it could be printed and distributed by mail throughout the whole nation in two days. Suddenly, we had a national medium of communication we did not have before, one that was influencing all the journalism in the land. The same kind of change came about with the advent of television. And then there are the national newspapers. The *New York Times* and the *Washington Post* are not read just in New York and Washington; not only their columnists but their actual reports are reprinted in newspapers all over the country.

This industry—which is what it is, an industry—produces not truth but news. There is a rather substantial difference. Not that the media are in the business of producing untruth, but, as their practitioners will tell you, there isn't time to judge. The criterion is what is new. The industry is affected by what people will read for stimulation, and by what will keep them coming back day by day. Thus, important things often go undiscussed until much too late. At that point, ironically, they may make better news, because they appear as crises. There is an insatiable demand for new ideas, new titillations, new attacks on institutions, new attacks on old values, anything that raises the blood temperature by a little bit.

This, I think, is why David Halberstam is able to call his new book *The Powers That Be.*[4] Who are the powers that be? It used to be said that the media were subservient to the advertisers, that hidden advertisers were the powers that be. David Halberstam is arrogant enough to suggest, not only that one national reporter may have the clout of twenty senators, but also that the powers that be, who can make or break corporations, political careers, anybody or anything, are the small handful of national news organizations. And within them, the most powerful actors are not the owners but the reporters. This signifies a really important paradigm shift in the power of the idea sector, the power of those who divine reality by establishing the plausibility structures within which we must think.

---

[4] New York: Alfred A. Knopf, 1979.

Note that, on television, references are made far more often to other television shows than to any other medium. Why? Because we must assume that the television audience is larger than that of any other medium. In a sense, television today may have a broader scope, and a deeper authority, than any other institution. If so, then the "reality" of television may be greater than any other perception of reality available to our society. In the process, the meaning and role not only of the press but of the whole idea class, on whom the press depends, have changed.

The truth about journalists is that they are, necessarily, the most anxious of creatures. A reporter writes daily on subjects about which he or she can by no means be an expert. A reporter may write on SALT, on Zimbabwe/Rhodesia, on the family, and on hundreds of other topics. In such a role, he is constantly afraid he will make an incredible mistake that will destroy his reputation. How does he protect himself against that? Every journalist has sources to whom he or she can go and read a paragraph or get a quotation. The osmosis between the idea sector—not just in the universities, but in the research establishments and elsewhere—and the practicing journalist is exceedingly direct. There is no group for whom journalists have higher esteem, or on whom they have greater dependence, than intellectual experts. Someone like Tom Wicker, invited to speak to General Motors, may be a bit supercilious; invited to speak at Harvard or at Michigan, he might plausibly feel honored. David Halberstam is quite explicit about the new change in status, the new esteem intellectuals have for journalists, and vice versa.

Given this paradigm shift, religious liberalism has returned in full flower, stimulated by the moral impulse of the civil rights movement and the antiwar movement. In a way, we are right back where we were before Reinhold Niebuhr ever wrote. In my own mind's eye, I would like to continue Niebuhr's criticism of such liberalism. If I am right, biblical realism must become especially critical of the power of the educated class—something it never had to worry about quite as much before— because the enlightened conventional wisdom is more powerful than ever before. We now have instruments that tell us incessantly what a well-informed person ought to think, what he ought to say, and what he must avoid saying. I call this "verbal hygiene." Yesterday Brigitte Berger mentioned the word "Negro," because in her reference it was the consensus term at the time, and I was shocked. One does not now say "Negro." And if you say "he" without saying "she," you can feel the rebuke from the audience. Verbal hygiene is the new system of censorship, a very effective censorship.

The power of the idea sector is exceedingly strong. Corporate executives all around the country are made to feel guilty in the face of their children, because the idea has taken root that there is something vaguely evil in the system, in America spelled with a "k," especially in the corporate world. The power to make people feel guilty, not least for matters they don't really think they should feel guilty about, is a very important power. It is a power which lowers people in their own eyes. Thus, the corporate executive today is expected to be humble and nervous when speaking before us and to defer to us—as Dick Madden very kindly did; for we represent the idea sector, the keeper of the system's ideals. In our society, then, power has changed hands. As an intellectual, as a journalist, one can walk into a room full of corporate executives and not defer to them; they will be rather respectful.

As I already noted, there is also today a powerful consensus, originated by or at least helped along by the media, which tells us what a well-informed, sophisticated, enlightened person ought to think. We need to be skeptical about this new form of pressure. For its criteria for sophistication and enlightenment change every four or five years, since the internal necessity of the news industry is to move on, periodically, to something new. Anything held firmly for too long must be regarded as stale. The focus is less on reality and truth than on what is new. For instance, the radical movement of ten years ago was news, but so is the attack upon it some years later. In the phrase "being with it," the "it" refers to the coming crest of the news.

Professor Adams spoke about the separation of powers. If we are to talk about biblical realism, the role of conscience, and the pursuit of truth, then there is imposed on us, I think, an obligation to think much more clearly than we have before about the new power in our society, in some respects stronger than anything in the economic order or in the political order, the power of the idea sector. We have to be more critical, not only about the assertions of the idea sector, but also about the assumptions, passions, and plausibility structures it embodies at any one time. They provide the ocean in which our own capacities to think must now swim.

### Third Paradigm: A New Attitude toward the Bourgeois Ethic

The third paradigm I want to speak about is the shift in our attitude toward the bourgeois ethic. Every time a new class emerges, a new politics, a new ethics, a new morality, a new culture emerge with it. About 1780, when businessmen became the most significant class in the Western world, politics changed; wigs went and lace went; and a new morality came into being. This bourgeois morality was quite different from traditional Christian or Jewish morality, and it was opposed by many divines, as Max Weber notes, as well as by traditional stoics and humanistic philosophers. The old notion had been that the moral imperative was sufficiency. Suddenly Adam Smith and the bourgeoisie were saying, "No, it is not only moral, it is obligatory to go beyond what is sufficient and to produce greater wealth." The ethical demand was no longer sufficiency but productivity. The bourgeois ethic was opposed by every traditional ethic, religious and humanistic. For almost two centuries, artists and moralists, military leaders and priests—all those whose authority rests on prebourgeois conceptions of the heroic—have rivalled one another in putting down the bourgeois ethic.

Today, too, the new class likes to poke fun at "the consumer society" and its "square" (read "bourgeois") virtues. The new class favors the swingers. Recently, however, the celebrated "new morality" of the new class has been doused with skepticism. The new class is not used to vigorous intellectual opposition. Once regarded as mere leaven in the dough, today the intellectual class is the dominant power, the very definer of reality. It was one thing to deride work, saving, rational self-interest, regularity, fidelity, and respectability when the public style was stuffy and there were relatively few critics around to do the necessary needling. It is another thing when the airwaves are filled with "You deserve a break today!" (*Who* deserves a break today? The world owes no one a living. Many human beings, in fact, *don't* get a break.) It was one thing to attack the Puritans when Puritans ruled the psyche. It is another when we are hourly besieged with images of escape, lust, and greed. It is too much when, on top of this, intellectuals then attack the "bourgeois" virtues of fidelity, hard work, loyalty.

It is difficult to find a single essay by a sober intellectual arguing the importance and centrality of fidelity in marriage, a simple notion whose power is readily experienced in daily life. The destructiveness of infidelity is obvious. Yet the intellectual class, eschewing "bourgeois" (or Christian, or Jewish) morality, is loath to defend fidelity and to describe the decadence of infidelity. Patriotism, obedience, and other important values are similarly neglected. The antibourgeois tradition has won. Something unforeseen happened when "the adversary culture," as Lionel Trilling called it, became victorious. Many who earlier had championed the adversary culture, as did Lionel Trilling himself, were reduced to saying, in the end, "This is not what we meant at all. This is not what we had intended."

The attack on the bourgeois ethic came not only from the working class. Although the opening page of Trotsky's autobiography read—as Tom Kahn reminded us—"A happy childhood is a bourgeois illusion"—

the attack on the bourgeoisie is only apparently an attack from below. Actually, it is the upper class, rather than the lower, that hates the bourgeoisie so. Most poor people would love to become middle class. Most are closer to the bourgeois ethic than to the upper class ethic or the ethic of the new class.

Phil Wogaman asked us in his lecture to look at the world from the viewpoint of the black poor rather than from our own middle-class biases. But Wogaman is neither black nor poor, nor are we. Like us, he is a member of the new (antibourgeois) class. What would really have been intellectually startling would have been for Wogaman to ask us to look at the world from a bourgeois perspective. The attack upon the bourgeois virtues, which used to be motivated by the resentments of the aristocratic class, is now conducted by the new (intellectual-journalistic) class. It is not often led by the working class.

The attack on the bourgeois virtues may also be motivated, in part, by ethnicity. When, after 1870, the impoverished Eastern European immigrants, Jewish and Catholic, flooded into the United States, they saw before their eyes a kind of Marxist image. The "ownership of the means of production" was not only in the hands of a different social class but also in the hands of a different ethnic group. Ethnicity and class were joined as one. The "huddled masses," spoken of on the inscription of the Statue of Liberty, had two strikes against them—ethnicity and class. Of these, ethnicity may have been the deeper and stronger, since wealth and education were at first easier to acquire than was acceptance. Themes of ethnicity and class are vivid in the detective novels of Raymond Chandler, Dashiell Hammett, and John D. MacDonald in a later generation.

Many criticisms of capitalism and of the bourgeois ethic have been aesthetic. One of the most telling arguments against capitalism raised by Professor Lekachman, for example, concerned its ugliness. In raising up the working class, capitalism has offended aristocratic tastes. Its ugliness may count against it aesthetically; in terms of democracy and egalitarianism, are aristocratic tastes relevant?

Many of the most telling arguments against capitalism in American history, before the advent of the immigrants from Eastern Europe, have agrarian roots. The historian Charles Beard was neither the first nor the last to attack industrial capitalism from the viewpoint of agrarian aesthetics and values. But do the millions of refugees from agrarian squalor and narrowness judge their urban experience as an advance, or as a decline, from what they had experienced earlier?

The antibourgeois sentiment also has roots in modernism, in ideas about authenticity and alienation. These last two terms have become keynotes in the criticism of the bourgeois ethic. What, for example, is "authentic" Christian action? The word usually means "antibourgeois."

There is, finally, a political dimension: antibourgeois perceptions serve a socialist purpose. The cultural sector has cardinal political influence. Thus, many persons who are not socialists constantly use an antibourgeois and even frankly socialist rhetoric. That in itself constitutes a political victory for socialism, since the power to define issues is half the battle. In most of the world, the issues have been so defined that good associations surround everything socialist and bad associations surround everything capitalist. If you say the word "red" in Latin America, a quite Catholic part of the world, most people will not think first of Pentecost and the Holy Spirit.

Still, a new paradigm has arisen. This is the other side in the battle over symbols. Many persons in the adversary culture are beginning to question their antibourgeois upbringing and prejudices. Such persons are being called, improperly, "neoconservatives." As far as I know, there is only a handful of neoconservatives in America. Most of them have roots in the Social Democratic party; Robert Nisbet and Edward Banfield have always been conservatives, Irving Kristol has become a Republican; all the others are social democrats and labor intellectuals.

One of the key points in the "conversion" of neoconservatives is their relatively sudden reevaluation of the bourgeois ethic. They are beginning to see that none of the institutions they value can survive without the exercise of certain virtues on the part of individuals in every part of society. A republic—as Jefferson said—depends upon the virtue of its citizens. If, for example, there had been less honesty in the period of Watergate, if a few more places had been corrupted, there would have been no rejection of President Nixon. Unless certain attitudes are held by the citizenry, there is no way managers in a garment factory can insist that every coat jacket sewn in their plant will be stitched so as not to come apart the first time it is worn. Managers cannot stand over the shoulder of every worker. There is no way to have excellence in workmanship unless workers believe in excellence. One of my great disappointments as a teacher has been in spending hours correcting term papers, only to find that more than half the students never even come to pick them up. If they don't care, what is the point? A democracy depends upon caring and excellence and responsibility. Similarly, without certain virtues, marriage is not tolerable. No institution can function without a high level of individual virtue. "Systems" do not create the moral context for virtue; virtue creates the moral context for systems.

The ordinary virtues are being undermined in America, both by corporate advertising and by the idea class. This undermining brings our society closer to disintegration. Civil conversation is impossible without virtue, restraint, a love for truth, a respect for evidence, and conscience. Simple virtues are the basic presupposition of democratic capitalism. Yet such simple virtues are not much advocated in our society today. Indeed, even the churches often preach adaptation to an "up-to-date" set of values—currently, sensitivity, assertiveness, the therapeutic consciousness. The consequences of those new values will one day be measured in reality. Shifts in morality have a profound effect on institutions. One day, we will pay a price for present shifts.

Meanwhile, many persons have begun for the first time in their lives to look critically at the antibourgeois rhetoric that was their intellectual inheritance. In my own education, an eye-opening book was *The Woman Who Was Poor*[5] by Leon Bloy, a novel attacking bourgeois Catholicism in France. Bloy's opening line is "This place stinks of God!" He went on to assault the holy-card, church-going piety of the respectable French bourgeoisie. He exalted the "pilgrim of the absolute," the sort of figure, bearded and sandaled and smelly and offensive to bourgeois notions, whom he imagined to be authentically religious. All this is too easy, I now think. Among educated people today, the scandal is not the beatnik or the hippie; the character hard to digest is the honest, hard-working, humble, faithful "square." Yet democracy depends upon the latter.

As with Bloy, so also with Solzhenitsyn. With his prophecy, I am in entire agreement; with his prescriptions for a virtuous society, I find myself repelled by the sort of religious autocracy his regime of virtue might demand. The virtue required for a democratic, republican society is quite different. The genius of the bourgeois ethic is too little sung.

### Fourth Paradigm: Socialism's Moral Edge

A fourth paradigm undergoing change is the moral tendency in favor of socialism. So long as my own writings leaned toward socialism, I won esteem among an important sector of my colleagues that I certainly do not win now. In the moral balance, among intellectuals, socialism has higher standing than capitalism. V. A. Demant recounts in his lectures on capitalism and socialism,[6] following Weber's *The Protestant Ethic and the Spirit of Capitalism*,[7] that one popular nineteenth-century slogan was: "Christianity is the religion of which socialism is the practice."

---

[5] Translated by I. J. Collins (London: Sheed, 1937).

[6] *Religion and the Decline of Capitalism* (New York: Charles Scribner's Sons, 1952).

[7] Trans. Talcott Parsons (New York: Charles Scribner's Sons, 1958).

Imagine someone saying instead: "Christianity is the religion of which capitalism is the practice." So great is the bias that we cannot help being shocked and made uncomfortable by the latter.

Capitalism is deficient in the cultural sector, insofar as it has pictured itself as an economic technique, an abstraction from reality. It has too long left religion, morality, and vision to the archbishops, philosophers, and poets. Adam Smith wrote his moral treatise first, then an economic treatise, and he intended to follow these with a political treatise. He had a more rounded view than is remembered. Yet he did treat economic man in abstraction from politics and morals. Capitalism normally doesn't think of itself as presenting a moral vision; it prefers to think of itself as neutral. It builds better mousetraps; it permits somebody else to worry about moral questions. That is, systemically, a very weak position. Capitalism can work morally only so long as it has implicit moral capital on which to draw, so long as it can assume that people will practice stewardship, honesty, fidelity, and similar restraints upon their behavior. Its cultural system is as important as its economic system. Yet economists who write about capitalism tend to leave politics to the political scientists. Milton Friedman, for example, does not show as much sophistication about the subtleties of democracy as about those of economics. One might say the same about Ludwig von Mises and F. A. von Hayek and others.

Thus, Professor Lekachman, in his criticisms of capitalism, could evoke arguments whose lineage runs back a hundred years. Television did not exist a hundred years ago, but what he said about the moral decadence of television was what earlier socialists were saying about the bourgeois press. His argument against capitalism was preeminently cultural, moral, aesthetic. That is why he could end up by saying that all the original socialist economic programs and political techniques no longer represent the essence of socialism. He is not, he said, a socialist because of socialist economic theory, or because of socialist political theory. "Why am I a socialist?" he asked. And he replied: "For moral reasons."

In his view, four moral principles make a socialist vision morally superior. Part of the moral superiority often attributed to socialism comes from the fact that its thinkers have given much more explicit attention to the moral dimension. Paul Johnson implied this the other day when he said that he was going to do something daring, for which he knew of no precedent: he was going to argue for the moral basis of capitalism. The reason he felt so lonely is that capitalism was invented mostly by and for practical people working in the economic order, who were willing to take for granted the work of archbishops, poets, and philosophers in the moral order. The former did not attempt to give a full moral justification for what they were doing; that was someone else's task. They were interested in producing "the wealth of nations." They were interested in techniques that would work all around the world in various cultures whose moral visions and evaluations and justifications would be diverse.

For a number of reasons, we have no theology of democratic capitalism. With the help of others I have been trying to gather texts on the attitudes of the major theologians toward capitalism. They are almost universally negative. Almost all our major theologians have been socialists. Reinhold Niebuhr made a decisive conversion from socialism at the end of the 1950s—his essay in the Leibrecht *Festschrift* on Tillich[8] is a striking justification for capitalism—but by then his creative work had been slowed by his stroke. Like Niebuhr in his earlier writings, Rauschenbusch, Tillich, Barth, and Moltman have been explicitly socialist.

This lack of a theological justification for democratic capitalism means, in practice, that many Christians in the world of work and the world of the corporations are living in bad faith. They hear, all the time, that the system is at least faintly immoral, as Professor Adams suggested in his comments at the outset. By their own experience and by their own lights, these people are performing a useful service, but the public conscience condemns them. The resulting malaise, the suggestion among theologians that the system is rotten, prevents the development of an adequate theology of work. It is very difficult for a theologian to apply himself to an enterprise that he thinks is faintly—or radically—unworthy.

Even the symbolism of the language we use casts corporate powers as the source of systemic evil in our society—alienation, corruption, profits, greed, and so forth. Tillich was ringingly explicit, calling capitalism and the corporations "demonic forces." This condemnation is not infrequent among theologians. They are, nevertheless, curiously unwilling to offer detailed analyses of economic processes and economic institutions in various historical systems. The prejudice against capitalism, then, is very thick. So, of course, is the prejudice against socialism. Permit me to mention my own surprise at the level of material progress achieved in socialist Czechoslovakia, an example mentioned by Professor Wogaman. In 1974, I visited my family in eastern Slovakia and I was surprised to see how far they had come in three generations. My great-uncle is mayor of a tiny village there. He spent a year studying in Moscow. One youngster in the family attends the nearest

[8] Reinhold Niebuhr, "Biblical Faith and Socialism: A Critical Appraisal," in Walter Leibrecht, ed., *Religion and Culture: Essays in Honor of Paul Tillich* (New York: Harper & Bros., 1959), pp. 44–57.

university. Their standard of living by no means compares with ours, but, on the other hand, they have not been standing still since my grand-parents emigrated ninety years ago. Progress has been made.

It is time, I believe, to start judging the case of socialism versus capitalism empirically. For a century, socialism was an idea that existed solely in books. Now it has been put into practice for at least thirty years in a majority of the countries of the world. Now one can examine it empirically. Does socialism, in fact, produce equality? Does it close the gap between the very rich and the very poor? The empirical evidence I have seen suggests that it does not, that there is less distance between the top 10 percent and the lowest 10 percent in the United States than in the Soviet Union and other socialist countries. In the latter, the privileges inherent in being a party member are far out of the reach of most people —privileges like admission to college and access to better jobs. Thus, economic and social gaps take on a permanence and a rigidity not ex-perienced in capitalist countries.

The general principle here at stake is that we should compare the two systems empirically. We should especially do so, not only in those aspects in which everybody concedes that our system is superior, like efficiency and liberty, but also in those aspects in which the other system purports to be superior, like equality. I would like to see many such empirical surveys. What is equality actually like in socialist lands, even in democratic socialist countries like Sweden and West Germany, let alone in more fully Marxist lands? What is the empirical picture like? Socialism is inevitably being removed from the land of myth and brought into the domain of empirical discussion; this is a major shift in intellec-tual life.

### Fifth Paradigm: The Role of the State

The fifth paradigm shift I want to consider is the move away from the dominant public policy idea of American government since the New Deal. Whatever it was that came before the New Deal, that is not what those sensing this shift want to go back to. The shift in question repre-sents a new vision of the future, not a hankering for the past. The New Deal turned to the state as a moral force for good. In *Liberalism and Social Action*,[9] John Dewey pointed out that this turn to the state repre-sented something new in the history of liberalism. Liberalism had always before represented resistance to the state. What is a liberal liberated from? The state. Liberalism was for centuries an attempt to enlarge the

---

[9] New York: Capricorn Books, 1963.

power of the people against the power of the state. Franklin D. Roosevelt saw in the 1930s that a new moment for liberalism had arrived. The economic problem was so severe that liberalism had to make an alliance with the central state—and not just the individual states like New York or Alabama, but the United States federal government.

The statism that resulted is somewhat different from socialism; there are many American liberals who are statists but not socialists, myself for one. A statist in this sense is one who believes in big government in many areas of life: preeminently in the field of defense, but also in the domestic sphere.

Statism has flaws, however, that have led in recent years to a breakdown in the New Deal. I sensed in this room a certain discomfort with what Phil Wogaman was calling the "prophetic." That sounded very tired, indeed. It sounded like a form of liberal politics now very hard to believe in. Why is it hard to believe in? There is a kind of irresponsibility about "prophecy" that always ends up enhancing the role of the state. State control is expensive; it is inefficient; and it introduces myriad tyrannies into daily life—gas lines, for instance. When the oil companies are no longer responsible for bringing us gasoline, and it now comes to us courtesy of the allocation procedures of the Department of Energy, we will have (as we have this week) gas lines. Then there is the postal service. If the post office went on strike, no one would know for sure for at least thirty days. Then there are the daily petty tyrannies of seat belts and buzzers. I like to wear a seat belt; I don't like Ralph Nader's conscience buzzing in my ear. Tom Kahn mentioned how people felt tyrannized by forced busing, which is a more serious imposition of government on their lives.

In business, there is strong resentment toward government rules and red tape. Chief executive officers will tell you that many of their decisions are no longer business decisions, but legal decisions. They cannot simply decide with their business advisers what they ought to do over the next two or three years; first, they have to talk with their lawyers about what the government will let them do, and what costs the government will impose. Often, they end up making decisions that are bad business decisions but the best that can be done under the circumstances. When legal judgment replaces economic judgment, economic liberty has been abridged. Business cannot proceed without rules and regulations. Government hinders or helps the climate for business. Its regulations have costs as well as benefits.

You and I now face similar constraints with respect to our savings. What is the point of saving for your children's college education when what you put in the bank is going to be worth much less by the time the

195

children are able to use it? Besides, it seems that the less money you save, the more benefits you can get from the government. If you set aside the money, the state will not help you at all; but if you spend it and can show that you are broke, they will give your children scholarships. That, too, is a form of tyranny.

Governmental organizations breed their own unique forms of corruption. In Michael Harrington's *Socialism*,[10] the word "public" connotes moral, good, and selfless, whereas "private" connotes selfish and corrupt. Phil Wogaman spoke of the "biased market." But what about "biased" governmental decisions? The Department of Energy admitted this morning having shortchanged the Washington area on gasoline. Is this not a bias? There is, as a recent article in *The Public Interest*[11] puts it, an asymmetry in our intellectual tradition between its capacity to criticize the private order and its capacity to criticize the public order. That is the asymmetry being addressed in the new paradigm.

Furthermore, we are seeing not just the breakdown of the New Deal, but the breakdown of individualism. Libertarians and individualists find themselves under great pressure in our society. Everywhere there are encounter groups, sensitivity sessions, cults of many kinds. Narcissism and hedonism are flourishing, which isn't what the libertarians meant at all; and in general there is a loss of meaning for individuals. How many times have you met a talented, beautiful, able young person, perhaps of privileged family and good education, who is so unhappy that he or she is unable to be creative? Everything is there but meaning.

Now, the New Deal functioned to give lives meaning; so did the New Frontier. Meaning very often comes from a public idea. A public idea often makes the individual feel important; his or her efforts have significance beyond immediate satisfactions, and that itself gives a longer, deeper satisfaction. To give people an ideal that delights them is a proper task for the cultural sector, but that sector has broken down.

We are unable, then, to go back to individualism alone, for our task is public and social. And we are also unable to be as confident about statism as we were. It is here that the socialist principle hidden behind statism becomes terribly important. What is striking about contemporary socialists—Robert Lekachman, Stuart Hampshire, Anthony Crosland— is that they have become skeptical of the political, programmatic, economic meanings of socialism. Yet they remain socialists because socialism has a moral vision; it promises more equality, a higher public

---

[10] New York: Saturday Review Press, 1972.
[11] Charles Wolf, Jr., "A Theory of Nonmarket Failures," *The Public Interest*, no. 55 (Spring 1979), pp. 114–33. I consider this a watershed article.

aspiration, a rejection of mere individualism, and so forth. Such a vision is an important part of our cultural inheritance, but it represents a shift, a new kind of socialism. Michael Harrington asserts that people who think socialism means a bigger state are wrong.[12] If so, a lot of people have been wrong for a long time. Harrington says that what socialism means is more vital communitarian democratic communities on a smaller scale. He sounds more and more like G. K. Chesterton and Eric Gill, the theoreticians of distributivism, rather than like Marx. He is not alone among socialists in arguing a new, nonstatist vision of socialism.

Similarly, the capitalist principle has changed. First of all, "capitalism" is an example of negative labeling. It was Marx who gave the system that name, not Adam Smith; it is a misleading name, a name intended to mislead. "Capitalism" points to owners and money. But no democratic capitalist system has only owners and money. There are things money cannot buy, such as good workmanship and republican virtue. I believe our system needs another name, and I would like to suggest an inelegant description: "incentivism." Incentives in the system work for the investor; they also work for the worker. From all the rural areas of Europe in the eighteenth and nineteenth centuries, the incentives of better food, better clothing, better housing, and better opportunity drew immigrants to industrial centers.

But there is another meaning to "capital," too. Capital comes from *caput* (L., head) and, just so, democratic capitalism depends upon intelligence, invention, imagination. Better than having money is having a productive idea. The primary form of capital is inventiveness. Democratic capitalism encourages this priceless quality with such incentives as it can. Its moral attraction lies in the freedom it gives the imagination; the power a market system gives individuals over their own economic priorities; and the power its democratic institutions distribute to individuals for choosing their own beliefs, symbols, and actions.

### Sixth Paradigm: Religious Attitudes

The sixth paradigm that is shifting has to do with the church. One of the great discoveries of this conference—and it is time, I think, to begin facing it—is the irreducibility of liberal Protestant, Jewish, and Catholic perceptions. There are fundamental differences in the frames of reference of these three traditions, which are becoming more and more evident as we talk about religion.

The liberal Protestant vision of religion and public policy—ex-

---

[12] *Twilight of Capitalism* (New York: Simon & Schuster, 1977), pp. 50–53.

pressed in loving and intelligent style in the lectures by Professors Wogaman and Adams—tends to strive for reasonableness and tolerance, and to be as minimalist as possible regarding differentiation. Liberal Protestants seem to like to stand on common ground. Their tendency is to believe that progress is not likely to be made on those points about which there are serious differences of opinion. Progress depends on cooperation, on broadening the denominator. This attitude is not necessarily shared by those of other faiths. Those Protestants here who are not liberal Protestants have expressed the same sense of discomfort in some of our discussions that some Catholics and Jews have felt. This issue is subtle and difficult to pin down. It first makes itself felt when the liberal Protestant appeals to reasonableness and a kind of universality, just where others attach greater value to particularity, to stubbornness. Sometimes one does not want to be reasonable; one wants to stand and argue about differences and to take the consequences.

Similarly, where the liberal Protestant tradition is pushing for tolerance and a recognition of commonality, other traditions may sometimes delight in finding the edges of difference. It is like having a broken tooth, whose edges your tongue cannot resist probing. Several persons in various discussions this week have expressed dissatisfaction with efforts to find a common ground, a lowest common denominator. They prefer to state differences clearly and to try to work around them. They take pleasure in the broken points, not the smooth points.

Third, many who are not liberal Protestants emphasize circles of loyalty, clearly defined, which are held intensely. Instead of trying to be minimalist, they feel a strong urge to find and to state those things they want to be loyal to, even if it means breaking off the dialogue a little.

When we talk about the role of conscience in our society, and the spiritual crisis in our society, it is important to be aware of these diverse religious orientations. They represent different approaches not only to religion but also to public policy, and each has its own weaknesses.

### Seventh Paradigm: Mediating Structures

Finally, in dealing with mediating structures, we have been shifting to a paradigm that is neither individualistic nor statist; yet it is one in which we hope to find a certain efficacy and concreteness. Mediating structures have been so neglected by intellectuals that we approach them in great ignorance. We don't know the terrain, haven't mastered the detail. When Mr. Madden told us something about the way his corporation works— for instance, how before this conference he submitted his paper to his fellow managers, and they approached it as a communal paper—that was an enlightening vignette. I hadn't quite expected that; I thought corporations were more autocratic. It occurred to me that there must be different types of corporations: Potlatch probably is not run the way General Motors is run, and GM probably is not run the way Hewlett-Packard is run, and so on.

Once we enter this terrain, we will have to develop a theology of corporations. One idea that suggests itself is the Latin phrase *corpus Christi*, "body of Christ." The human body has been the traditional metaphor for the Christian community—and, as the Second Vatican Council said, this Christian body includes everybody (so that, as the joke went, even Satan is a "separated brother")—but the corporation might be an even more illuminating metaphor. A corporation contains multiple models of human community; it is not an individual, but it is not just a community, either. It doesn't operate the way a sensitivity session operates. It includes unions and other subgroups just as the Christian community does. In any case, theologians have much to learn about the history, legal structure, types, functions, limits, and problems of corporations.

The other mediating structure I want to touch on is the family. Much has been said in this conference—in the examples Brigitte Berger used, for instance—about the war against the souls of husbands, wives, and children that is being conducted every day in our society. We are besieged by ideas, ideals, and solicitations that on reflection we find morally repulsive. My parents don't quite understand why my wife and I don't want our children to watch certain television shows, which to my parents seem entirely innocent. I have nothing against Mork and Mindy, or Sonny and Cher, but I wouldn't want my children to marry one of them. I don't want them to live like that. I don't want them to think like that. And I don't want to be solicited myself by their image of what a fully mature, liberated man ought to do. *Playboy* is an interesting example, as someone pointed out this week, of the worst in capitalism, its hedonism, married to the worst in socialism, its faddish left-wing ideas. This combination is at the heart of the war that is being waged against our souls, which it seems to me is corrosive of the inner workings of the family, of the attitudes of children toward their parents, and of spouses toward each other.

Tom Kahn suggested that many marriages are breaking up nowadays because of economic pressures. But in many other foundering marriages the economic situation of the family is sound, their members have enjoyed every privilege of education, culture, and political potency. Theirs is not a political or economic alienation. It is a destruction from within by false values and unrealistic ideas of how one should live, insinuated into the minds of children and spouses by the potent cultural sector.

In summary, I have been trying to suggest the ways in which we at this conference have been shifting paradigms. It has been impossible for me to summarize everything, or to draw every possible thread together. But I have already used far too much time, simply trying to think through what we have been up to. We have not so much been engaged in re-solving arguments, as in attempting to look at a number of phenomena from a new perspective. We are far from exhausting the tasks we have undertaken.

# Discussion

QUESTION: I would like to add something to your sixth paradigm shift, on the notion of liberal religion. One feature of the Jews' experience in Europe was their inability to perceive that the threat posed to their group survival by conservative racial anti-Semitism was no greater than that posed by enlightened liberalism. Anti-Semitism threatened to kill them, but liberalism was just as willing to obliterate their identity and to atomize them.

When Europe agreed to de-Christianize itself, the Jews foolishly agreed to de-Judaize themselves, following the path of liberalism toward the lowest common denominator.

My question has to do with something we have been talking about all week, and that is the idea of intellectuals as reality shapers. I want to suggest what seems to me to be a contradiction in some of the things you have said and in some of the things Professor Berger said last night. First, I think we ought to clarify at some point who the nonintellectuals are that we are talking about—whether we want to call them ordinary people, or whatever. Given that, the contradiction I see is as follows. It seems to me that underlying the notion that mediating structures will somehow solve some of the problems we have described is the belief that ordinary people, in their voluntary associations, in their families, and in their neighborhoods, possess a kind of wisdom about life that provides value and meaning and so on. If that is not true, then strengthening the mediating structures is absolutely fruitless. On the other hand, you have depicted the intellectuals as those who mislead people by using symbols to create a false reality. That presupposes a different view of ordinary people, that they are unable to recognize a bad idea, a wrong idea, or a fraudulent interpretation when they hear one. It seems to me that it is tough to maintain both of those ideas at the same time.

DR. NOVAK: That problem is a fascinating, difficult one. My own wrestling with it leads me along these lines. First, about 13 percent of the American population has had four years of college; I think that is one useful index for measuring what I have called the new class. That means 87 percent of American adults have not graduated from college. Now, in the busing controversy in Boston, few educated whites wanted to speak out against busing. Most of those who did speak out were without a college education, and they spoke badly. Most of the black leaders who spoke in favor of busing, on the other hand, were college-educated and marvelously articulate. If one looked not at race but at articulation, the one side was far superior to the other. I don't think the former had the better side of the argument, but it sure sounded better.

There used to be some things on "All in the Family" that were interesting in this respect. If you remember, Archie Bunker's next-door neighbor for a long time was a black. That didn't cause scandal throughout America. Most white people who live next door to blacks are working class. But when you go into a union hall on a political campaign, having read or heard in the media about the racial resentment of white workers, you are stunned when you see the integration of so much working class life. That doesn't mean one worker doesn't call another "nigger" or "honky," but it does mean that when a guy needs a cup of sugar from next door, he goes over and asks for it. He gets an insult, but he gets the sugar.

In brief, articulateness matters; but it is not the same as wisdom. Nowadays, the media fill the air with "public opinion." It is sometimes almost a manufactured product. There is almost no room for the public to form its own opinions outside its pressures. Yet sometimes people do resist the tide.

QUESTION: For whom, then, is this new class creating reality? You expect to find racial hostility, but the people about whom this is being said don't know anything about it.

DR. NOVAK: It feeds back on them, because they see the way they are treated in the media. If this is the way the rest of the world thinks—and that is what they see on television—then they begin to discount the validity of their own experience.

QUESTION: You appear to agree with Professor Lekachman that consumerism in some form is a necessary feature of any healthy capitalist system. That implies that either consumerism is a necessary moral corruption, or it is not a corruption. It seems to me you can argue that it is not a corruption by pointing to the vigor and vitality of religion, the extent of evangelical religion, and its permanence in this country. If that is true, then people appear to have more good sense about consumerism than you seem to credit them with.

Dr. Novak: Consumerism is a negative label which, I might add, is contrary to my experience. I don't think of myself as a consumer; nor are my neighbors. I know of a family with five children. That family has two incomes, but they are not wealthy. They go without all sorts of things. All of those kids will have to work their way through college. Each kid has different talents, so they need to buy different equipment for each of them. That costs money. When one kid gets interested in fish, you need an aquarium; then there are music lessons, tennis lessons, whatever. But I don't think of that as consumerism. That family doesn't go out looking for things to consume.

Ironically, it is the new class that is the most precious target of the advertisers. Most advertising is directed at the top 10 percent of the population, the people with the most discretionary income and the most expensive tastes, readers of *Consumer Reports*. It is exactly the people who don't think of themselves as consumers who are the best consumers. They buy the Volvos. They buy the best wines. They buy the best of everything.

In the streets of the mill town where my father was brought up, people are still working eighty-hour weeks. And they are out fixing their cars on Sunday, because they don't buy new cars. On the other hand, they do have a television set and a dishwasher, they may have a camper, they may have an expensive rifle. They choose their few luxuries. That is exactly the point of a free economic system, that people who used to be peasants now share some of the possibilities of those who are better off.

Question: But then this television advertising isn't as pernicious as you paint it. Your moral outrage at it seems misplaced.

Dr. Novak: Yes, I did give one side of the argument. I have written a book on the media, unpublished, with a chapter in defense of commercials. It is commercials that keep the networks free from government. Furthermore, the quality of the commercials as symbolic narratives is at times superior to anything else on television for sheer visual beauty. The point of that book is that you have to teach yourself to be an active television viewer, to look at television the way you look at paintings, just as you have to teach yourself to be an active reader. And commercials often show more exact vignettes of American life than programs do. Television programs, in trying to reach the lowest common denominator, usually represent no community known to you, whereas commercials at times exactly represent people you know.

QUESTION: I appreciate and agree with a great deal of what you have said, but I still have a reservation about your notion of democratic capitalism. I admire both democracy and capitalism, at least so far as to agree with Churchill that democracy is the worst form of government except for all the others ever tried. Capitalism is, I think, superior as an economic system, but it has an insufficient moral vision. If you examine the development of both democracy and capitalism, you find that they both require a steady critique from a larger moral and cultural perspective. Jesus drove the money-changers out of the temple for good reason. People like Erasmus, Alexander Pope, Thomas Carlyle, Tolstoy, Solzhenitsyn, and many others have rightly applied some very harsh words to the manifestations of humanity's baser tendencies implicit in both democracy and capitalism. The basis of capitalism is striving for one's own self-interest, and the root notion of democracy is doing what the majority wants. Neither idea is morally or culturally sufficient.

What we need, then, is not an exaltation of democracy and capitalism, in and of themselves, but an awareness that their value is instrumental. They both need an addition. For example, I, too, don't particularly care to have my children watching Mork and Mindy or taking Sonny and Cher as their models, but my reservation there—like yours, I suspect—doesn't have much to do with either democracy or capitalism. The values that make us feel that way come from a source beyond.

Even the virtues associated with capitalism—thrift, hard work, savings—have been proved by German and Japanese militarists not to be particularly profound morally—disastrous, in fact—by themselves.

The virtues you have extolled and I would extol—fidelity, kindness, benevolence, humaneness—simply are not implicit in capitalism or democracy. Both of those concepts need an additional informing culture or tradition in order to be what you and I want them to be.

DR. NOVAK: I agree with that, and my fuller response would go something like this. I was calling for a renewed sense of vocation. Living in this world, we have responsibilities in politics and economics. Of all political and economic orders, the least sinful, or the most creative and the most open to possibility, are democracy and capitalism. Still, our spiritual life depends on transcending economic and political virtues. Thus there is a danger of politicizing Christianity and reducing it to political activism. Consider the millions of Christians whose spiritual fidelity has been accompanied by political impotence. In concentration camps, where there was no way they were going to change the system, they still found scope for conscience, because the whole enterprise of survival depended on keeping faith, refusing to believe the lies, even the lies of their own enforced humiliation, refusing to allow themselves to feel as subhuman as they were being treated by the guards. Religion and humanism can reach their highest beauty and fullest flower in such constrained political circumstances. They transcend political and economic categories. But they do not escape economic and political responsibilities.

QUESTION: I would like to suggest two or three reservations I have about some of the points you made, and perhaps you would comment on them.

Regarding your argument that the idea class, the intellectuals, help to shape the paradigm, it strikes me that an alternative approach is to say that the intellectuals are shaped by the paradigm. The paradigms shift not because of the power of the intellectuals but because of a whole complex of social, economic, and political events. One could argue that the leftist intellectuals of the 1930s became the champions of the consensual society and the celebrators of American capitalism in the 1950s, having come to see that their youthful socialist predilections made no sense in the era after World War II. Then, when we moved toward the radical sensibility of the late 1960s, after Vietnam, forces such as the civil rights movement, the sexual revolution, and women's liberation shaped what the intellectuals wrote about. We may be moving now into another period.

Second, I don't believe the intellectual class is that powerful. I think it is going to be increasingly less powerful. Perhaps the world of editors and authors in New York and Washington constitutes a class apart, but certainly the academic intellectuals are entering a period of decline. They are not being validated by their best students, who are not going into graduate school. The money isn't there. The mobility isn't there. The status increasingly will not be there. It is clear now that there was no greening of America, no flourishing of countercultures among us.

Here, it seems to me, may be the key to the attack against bourgeois culture: it is an attack not by the intellectuals but by the bourgeois culture itself, or at least by its agents in the Dodge rebellion. And that, in a sense, is a product of American affluence. I don't want my kids to watch Mork and Mindy, either. Everybody is saying that. I have relatives who are executives in the television business, and they and their friends don't want their children to watch what they produce, either. No one seems to want to watch it, but they produce it because a lot of people do watch it. What it celebrates is not socialism, not individualism.

What it does celebrate may not be capitalism, but it *is* the affluent culture, which is certainly not an adversary culture.

Third, I agree with your final point, that liberalism is in decline, as is the individualism of the 1960s. Capitalism may be in decline, too, as a set of ideas that capture the imagination, but that does not mean we are moving to a statist or a socialist vision. Socialism has never had heavier weather. After what has happened in southeast Asia, Great Britain, and totalitarian Eastern Europe, American socialists don't know where to go. What we are facing now is a crisis of confidence for intellectuals on all sides, and that will not necessarily lead in a socialist direction.

DR. NOVAK: Jeane Kirkpatrick, who specializes in political thought and is a colleague at the American Enterprise Institute, has given me strong reinforcement on that first point. I originally tended to analyze things from the perspective of social forces moving intellectual ideas. Even my analysis of the new class was based primarily on its economic and political position. She pointed out that the interesting feature of the new class is that it is an *idea* class, that there are people in it who are led by their ideas to choose things that, in an economic sense, may be against their own interests. For example, freedom is a major long-range interest of intellectuals. There are signs in the universities today of greater resistance to government involvement, even though that carries an economic penalty. Therefore, I have begun giving more attention to the power of *ideas* relative to social and economic forces, though the latter are always present.

Your second point, that the new class is losing power, may very well be true in the academic sector, but there are still growing numbers of experts in and around Washington coming out of both the corporate sector and the governmental sector. I would say that the center of power in the new class is moving into these two sectors. The new class is taking over the corporations through their advertising departments and their public affairs departments. These experts are people-movers, people-motivators. And they are often adversaries of democratic capitalism, even though they work for corporations. There will always be a fundamental dissonance between excellence of intellect and the marketplace. The value inherent in a really brilliant piece of creative work is of a kind the market cannot measure. The tension is endemic.

Finally, you said that liberalism is in decline, and capitalism, too. But I think you were a little bit wrong about the way this serves socialism. While socialism as an idea is certainly dead in the Soviet Union, and socialist theoreticians in the West are arguing about why socialism has failed, society's momentum is still toward a more powerful state. Look at the death of the nuclear power industry. Nuclear power production has been rendered impractical for private enterprise now; that possibility has almost been destroyed. Explicitly socialist organizations, which did the organizing work for the last six or seven years, finally reached a great public audience. Public sentiment toward the nationalizing of the oil companies is still strong. But more deeply than that, in the world at large, I see a shrinking democratic-capitalist world and an expanding Marxist-socialist world. This has less to do with ideology than with an imperial power of considerable boldness and confidence. The Russian characteristic known best to neighboring peoples is a willingness to push and push and push and push. They are not daring, they don't risk their own troops very much, but they take every opportunity. So I think that socialism is more in the ascendant than you suggest, even in the version which is represented by Soviet power. The *idea* of socialism seems emptier, but the reality grows stronger.

QUESTION: I find that your reading of Schumpeter is not quite on the mark. Schumpeter argued that capitalism will give way to socialism not because of capitalism's failures, but because of its successes. And he does not ground this transformation in the domain of ideas, but rather in the dynamics of economic evolution. His first reason for the decline of capitalism was that it was founded on the actions of daring, courageous entrepreneurs; but with the evolution of capitalism, greater productivity would necessitate concentrated economic power and increasingly large corporations, so that decisions would no longer be made by the entrepreneur, but by the committee. Consequently, the individual would be stifled and his talents smothered in the increasingly bureaucratic structure of the corporation he created. The second reason was also an economic reason, namely, that capitalism, in order to cleanse itself of its inefficient elements, has cycles in which the weaker firms go under, leading to increasing concentration, a plea for greater rationality in the economic system, and, finally, government intervention to soften these cyclical fluctuations.

I bring this up because I believe Schumpeter's mode of analysis for the direction of capitalism and the direction of ideas is very important. That is, he attempts to see ideas not as living in a domain independent of the rest of social reality, but rather as being generated through the dynamics of that reality.

DR. NOVAK: I accept 70 percent of your correction of my comments on Schumpeter. I was not wrong in reporting his attitude about the idea class and the idealessness of the corporations, but I did omit the points you have wisely made. I did that because, since Schumpeter wrote, it has become apparent that ideas are a much more powerful basis of the economic order than anybody realized. Corporations die because the ideas behind them are obsolete. That may yet happen to the oil companies; it already has happened to all sorts of industries. A company can be killed in two years by some discovery on the part of its competition, which it does not duplicate. That is why I think there is a shift of paradigm. The importance of ideas as sources of wealth is extraordinary. Now, some corporations are organized to defeat the tendency Schumpeter mentioned by splitting into small, autonomous units to keep alive the entrepreneurial daring you mentioned. Some people learn from Schumpeter a way to defeat his pessimism. And regarding the cycles of concentration, the more I look into this the more I am struck by the way the market does correct things. Didn't Mr. Madden say he was surprised by the study that showed how, in markets where concentration isn't useful, it doesn't happen?

QUESTION: Could I add one more point? Part of Schumpeter's argument was that, once corporations became hierarchical and smothered the individual, this would have an impact on popular consciousness; that is, people would say, "If it is now done by a team, then why should the profits go to private individuals rather than to society?" That would be the idea shift that would lead from capitalism to socialism.

DR. NOVAK: There are some tendencies that way, but experience also has led people to draw back—above all, the experience of the loss of incentives.

QUESTION: I would like to pursue a little further the idea you were developing about meaninglessness and the need for a search for public meaning. It seems to me that there is a public meaning and a private meaning, and what we do in a theological inquiry probably would be viewed by our officially neutral public sector as related to private conviction. How do you think, in a pluralistic but secular society, public meaning and private meaning might support each other? Many people nowadays seem to reject the notion of a public meaning, which fifty years ago was not the case. At Notre Dame University, "God, Country, and Notre Dame" is still over the cathedral door. Yet I don't think that many Catholics today feel that it is God, country, and Notre Dame—you have to take your choice.

DR. NOVAK: Well, public meanings, like private meanings, go in cycles. One can feel a rhythm in one's own life; you are happy with yourself for a while, and then all of a sudden you get sour about what you are doing. If that didn't happen, there wouldn't be growth. Public meaning in the United States in the age for which we are nostalgic was actually quite deficient. We were a more diverse people than was represented in those paradigms. There are books on "the American character" which do not represent all the types of character our people actually brought here— my Uncle Emil's, for example. To look at it another way: this country was born in racism, but because Jefferson and the others had an idea of doing something much more noble, we give them credit now for their high ideals, sometimes overlooking the sin they wrote into the structure of the nation.

We have come to the end of one cycle of public meaning, since the civil rights struggle, the antiwar movement, and the like. Now we are suffering from self-doubt, loss of purpose, loss of will; and we also have a very weak national leader who is unable to articulate a public sense of well-being for us or for the world. When the OPEC nations said today that they were raising oil prices, one reporter commented that this was a blow to the prestige and power of the United States, since they could with impunity raise by 30 percent the tribute we are to pay on oil. "Not one penny for tribute!" we would have said in an earlier era. Now we say, "Oh, fellas, we didn't mean to insult you. Please don't raise it so much next time." There is an obvious loss of purpose, and an inability to use our power, a willingness to put money into gasoline that we will not put into an army and arms.

You can recreate this sense of public and political purpose, but you have to be very careful; it can be the malicious purpose of a Hitler. On the other hand, if enough private consciences become awakened and enough people begin to say, "I can't take this anymore, I have to take a stand," then that changes the public policy debate.

At present, our public speech is more secular than our private lives. The assumption in most public discussions is that everybody is an atheist. You would never guess from the public speech of many of us that we are quite serious about religion. Now, the only way to halt this misleading behavior is by being willing to be different, to speak in our own voice. Not all of us share the same moral world view, but if we always defer to one another's sensibilities, nobody will ever make a moral statement. The only way you can have moral statements is if each one says—understanding that, in a civil society, no one will always prevail—"This is what I believe." I think this is appropriate in a pluralistic society.

QUESTION: I am concerned about what you seem to be saying here. The mediating structure approach, for that matter, although it is attractive in many respects, is somewhat analogous to the notion of the church—or any institution—as mediator between individual conscience and divine sources of understanding. That idea was seriously called into question by the Reformation, and it led to incredible devastation for a time in European history as one source of a conflict that was irreconcilable except by military means. Subsequently, an appeal was made to something that was thought to be able to reconcile those differences—reason, and the Enlightenment. This was necessary partly because it seemed there was no way for people of religious conviction to resolve their differences on the basis you are advocating, that is, by standing firm in their moral convictions, their theological understandings, and so on.

DR. NOVAK: On a given issue, sometimes opposing views simply are irreconcilable. For example, abortion. Will it or will it not be legal? One side is going to win and one side is going to lose. I regret very much that partisans on both sides have demanded too much, that they didn't settle earlier for a compromise. The Supreme Court also went too far in its first decision. I wish it had stopped a little short of where it did. I think then we would have had a much different kind of climate. That is one example. But there are many other examples in which it is politically possible to recognize the legitimate rights and different needs of both sides and to have a pluralistic program—to do one thing for one region of the country, and another for another region.

QUESTION: I wonder if the impact of the new class, as a shaper of reality, isn't felt most strongly by that class itself. Out in the boondocks, so to speak, there is a certain stubbornness or resilience; people have developed a resistance to the signals of television, so that while they hear what the opinion-setters say, they still keep going about their business. Radical chic never established a very firm beachhead in Danville, Kentucky. We don't feel invaded by professionals intervening in our family life, for example. To some extent, we may be fooling ourselves in thinking that we live our own lives; but I do think our perceptions are different from those in, say, New York or Washington.

DR. NOVAK: I agree that this battle looks very different in Kentucky from the way it looks in Washington, and that the role of the intellectual in the two communities is different. The paradigm of the intellectual as the leaven in the dough is more likely still to be valid in Danville and similar places. On the other hand, I would warn you, as I have been warned, that the idea class, in the name of enlightening the local community, can often be the carrier of debilitating viruses. When Pope John XXIII called the Second Vatican Council, he said he wanted "to open the windows" of the church to let fresh air in. There was one mistake in that: he assumed that the air outside the church was fresh. There is a terrible danger that, unwittingly, the intellectual will carry into the local community, in the name of enlightening it, ideas that would destroy it. The importance of ideas within a system of democratic capitalism is extraordinary because such a society is free. As will follows intellect, so do ideas, freely circulated, have consequences. The idea class—the cultural sector—must generate its own antibodies, its own self-criticism, if democratic capitalism is to be nourished by ideals that revivify it and do not destroy it.

# Bibliography

## Mediating Structures in the Democratic Context

Berger, Peter L., and Richard John Neuhaus. *To Empower People: The Role of Mediating Structures in Public Policy.* Washington, D.C.: American Enterprise Institute, 1977.

Johnson, Paul. *Enemies of Society.* New York: Atheneum, 1977.

Lekachman, Robert. *Economists at Bay.* New York: McGraw-Hill, 1977.

Lippmann, Walter. *The Public Philosophy.* Boston: Little, Brown & Co., 1955.

Loebl, Eugen, and Stephen Roman. *The Responsible Society.* New York: Regina Ryan Books/Two Continents, 1977.

Niebuhr, Reinhold, and Paul E. Sigmund. *The Democratic Experience.* New York: Praeger, 1969.

Novak, Michael. *The Rise of the Unmeltable Ethnics.* New York: Macmillan Co., 1971.

————. *The American Vision: An Essay on the Future of Democratic Capitalism.* Washington, D.C.: American Enterprise Institute, 1978.

Robertson, D. B., ed. *Voluntary Associations: A Study of Groups in a Free Society.* Richmond, Va.: John Knox Press, 1966.

Schumpeter, Joseph. *Capitalism, Socialism, and Democracy.* 3rd ed. New York: Harper & Row, 1950.

## Church

Adams, James Luther. *On Being Human Religiously.* Boston: Beacon Press, 1976.

Maritain, Jacques. *Integral Humanism.* Notre Dame, Ind.: University of Notre Dame Press, 1973.

Norman, Edward. *Christianity and the World Order.* New York: Oxford University Press, 1979.

Ogden, Schubert. *Faith and Freedom.* Nashville, Tenn.: Abingdon, 1979.

Vree, Dale. *On Synthesizing Marxism and Christianity*. New York: Wiley-Interscience, 1976.

Wogaman, J. Philip. *The Great Economic Debate*. Philadelphia, Penn.: Westminster Press, 1977.

## Corporation

Anshen, Melvin, ed. *Managing the Socially Responsible Corporation*. New York: Macmillan Co., 1974.

Kristol, Irving. *Two Cheers for Capitalism*. New York: Basic Books, 1978.

Lindblom, Charles E. *Politics and Markets: The World's Political-Economic Systems*. New York: Basic Books, 1977.

Mueller, Robert K. *Metadevelopment: Beyond the Bottom Line*. Lexington, Mass.: D. C. Heath, 1977.

Sethi, S. Prakash. *Up Against the Corporate Wall: Modern Corporations and Social Issues of the Seventies*. Englewood Cliffs, N.J.: Prentice-Hall, 1977.

Smith, Michael G. *Corporations and Society: Social Anthropology of Collective Action*. Chicago: Aldine, 1975.

## Labor Union

Aronowitz, Stanley. *False Promises: The Shaping of American Working-Class Consciousness*. New York: McGraw-Hill, 1973.

Brades, Stuart D. *American Welfare Capitalism, 1880–1940*. Chicago: University of Chicago Press, 1976.

Chamberlin, Edward H., et al. *Labor Unions and Public Policy*. Washington, D.C.: American Enterprise Institute, 1958.

Cobb, Jonathan, and Richard Sennett. *The Hidden Injuries of Class*. New York: Random House, 1973.

Novak, Michael. *The Guns of Lattimer*. New York: Basic Books, 1978.

Roberts, B. C. *Trade Unions in a Free Society*. London: Institute of Economic Affairs, 1962.

Rodgers, Daniel. *The Work Ethic in Industrial America*. Chicago: University of Chicago Press, 1978.

Sowell, Thomas. *Race and Economics*. New York: Longman, 1975.

## Family

Bane, Mary Jo. *Here to Stay: The American Family in the Twentieth Century*. New York: Basic Books, 1976.

Berger, Brigitte. *Societies in Change.* New York: Basic Books, 1971.

Berger, Peter; Brigitte Berger; and Hansfried Kellner. *The Homeless Mind.* New York: Random House, 1973.

Lasch, Christopher. *Haven in a Heartless World: The Family Besieged.* New York: Basic Books, 1979.

Stephens, William N. *The Family in Cross-Cultural Perspective.* New York: Holt, Rinehart & Winston, 1963.

Vogel, Ezra F., and Norman W. Bell, eds. *A Modern Introduction to the Family.* Revised ed. New York: Free Press, 1968.

Zaretsky, Eli. *Capitalism, The Family, and Personal Life.* New York: Harper & Row, 1976.

# Contributors

JAMES LUTHER ADAMS is professor emeritus of Christian ethics at Harvard Divinity School. He has also taught at Meadville Theological Seminary, at Chicago Divinity School, and at Andover Newton Theological School. He is a past president of the American Society of Christian Ethics, of the Society for the Scientific Study of Religion, and of the American Theological Society. He has been honored with numerous awards and lectureships. His many books include *Taking Time Seriously, The Theology of Paul Tillich, Religion and Culture,* and *On Being Human Religiously.*

BRIGITTE BERGER is professor of sociology at Wellesley College and an acknowledged authority on the family. Her articles have appeared in *Commentary* and elsewhere. She is the author of *Societies in Change* and a coauthor of *Sociology: A Biographical Approach* and *The Homeless Mind.*

PAUL JOHNSON holds the Dewitt Wallace Chair of Communications at the American Enterprise Institute. He is a British journalist who edited the London political weekly *New Statesman* (1964 to 1970). For the last ten years he has been engaged in historical studies, and his books include a history of the English people, *The Offshore Islanders; Elizabeth I: A Study in Power and Intellect; Enemies of Society;* and *A History of Christianity.* He is now preparing a major history to be entitled *Modern Times: The World from the Twenties to the Eighties.*

TOM KAHN is assistant to the president, AFL-CIO, in Washington, D.C. He was educated at Brooklyn College and Howard University. He has served as executive director of the League for Industrial Democracy, and as chief speechwriter for Senator Henry M. Jackson. He has taught at the Urban Affairs Center, New School for Social Research.

215

ROBERT LEKACHMAN is distinguished professor of economics at Lehman College (CUNY). He has also taught at Barnard College and at The State University of New York at Stony Brook. He is a columnist for *Dissent*. His books include *A History of Economic Ideas, The Age of Keynes, Inflation: The Permanent Problem of Boom and Bust,* and *Economists at Bay.*

RICHARD B. MADDEN is president and chief executive officer of Potlatch Corporation, a San Francisco-based forest products firm. He is on the executive committee of the board of trustees of the American Enterprise Institute. He was educated at Princeton, University of Michigan, and New York University. He has served in several capacities with Mobil Oil Corporation.

MICHAEL NOVAK is resident scholar in religion and public policy at the American Enterprise Institute and adjunct professor of religion at Syracuse University. He has also taught at Harvard, Stanford, and The State University of New York at Old Westbury. He has published widely in *Commentary, Commonweal, Harper's,* and *The New Republic,* among others. His books include *Belief and Unbelief, The Rise of the Unmeltable Ethnics, Choosing Our King, The Joy of Sports,* and *The Guns of Lattimer.* His *The American Vision: An Essay on the Future of Democratic Capitalism* is another American Enterprise Institute publication in this series.

J. PHILIP WOGAMAN is dean and professor of Christian social ethics at Wesley Theological Seminary, Washington, D.C. He is a past president of the American Society of Christian Ethics. His books include *A Christian Method of Moral Judgment* and *The Great Economic Debate: An Ethical Analysis.*

Published by the American Enterprise Institute

## Capitalism and Socialism: A Theological Inquiry

*Michael Novak, ed.*

Addressing the problems posed for the world religions by rival economic systems, some thirty-five theologians, professors of the humanities, and graduate students gathered for a week to sharpen their understanding of the religious values at stake under capitalism and socialism. This volume presents the texts of ten lectures together with highlights from the discussion and bibliography. Contributors include *Irving Kristol, Seymour Martin Lipset, Peter Berger, Muhammad Abdul-Rauf, Ben J. Wattenberg, and Penn Kemble.*

*1979 / Symposium / 193 pp. / 2153-0 Cloth    $12.25 / 2154-9 Paper    $6.25*

## To Empower People:
## The Role of Mediating Structures
## in Public Policy

*Peter L. Berger and Richard John Neuhaus*

The authors propose a lively alternative to the conservative fears and liberal disillusionment about public policies designed to meet human needs.

Berger and Neuhaus focus on the "mediating structures" of family, neighborhood, church, voluntary associations, and ethnic and racial subcultures—the institutions closest to the control and aspirations of most Americans. Public policy not only should refrain from weakening or undercutting these structures, they suggest, but also should use them to advance legitimate social goals, in the areas of education, child care, law enforcement, housing, social justice, and health care. *To Empower People* introduces the guiding principles of a three-year AEI project on mediating structures, directed by the authors.

Peter L. Berger is professor of sociology at Rutgers University and author of *Pyramids of Sacrifice: Political Ethics and Social Changes* (1975). Richard John Neuhaus is senior editor of *Worldview* magazine and author of *Time toward Home: The American Experiment as Revelation* (1975).

*"In a concrete and suggestive fashion, they move between the areas of political theory and public policy."* NEW OXFORD REVIEW

*1977 / Political and Social Processes Study / 45 pp. / 3236-2    $3.25*

*Prices subject to change without notice.*

## SELECTED AEI PUBLICATIONS